Tropic of Chaos

ALSO BY CHRISTIAN PARENTI

Lockdown America

The Soft Cage

The Freedom

TROPIC OF CHAOS

Climate Change and the
New Geography of Violence

CHRISTIAN PARENTI

NATION
BOOKS
New York

Published by Nation Books,
A Member of the Perseus Books Group
116 East 16 Street, 8th floor
New York, NY 10003

Nation Books is a co-publishing venture of the Nation Institute and
the Perseus Books Group.

Books published by Nation Books are available at special discounts
for bulk purchases in the United States by corporations, institutions, and other
organizations. For more information, please contact the Special Markets
Department at the Perseus Books Group, 2300 Chestnut Street, Suite 200,
Philadelphia, PA 19103, or call (800) 810-4145, ext. 5000, or e-mail
special.markets@perseusbooks.com.

Designed by Brent Wilcox

Library of Congress Cataloging-in-Publication Data
Parenti, Christian.
    Tropic of chaos : climate change and the new geography of violence /
Christian Parenti.
        p.   cm.
    Includes bibliographical references and index.
    ISBN 978-1-56858-600-7 (hardcover : alk. paper)—ISBN 978-1-56858-662-5
(e-book)   1. Climatic changes—Political aspects.   2. Geopolitics—
Environmental aspects.   3. Violence—Environmental aspects.   4. Political
violence—Environmental aspects.   I. Title.
QC903.P37 2011
304.2'5—dc22

                                                                2011010638

10 9 8 7 6 5 4 3 2 1

*For Juliet and her whole generation,
with apologies*

The pressure of the hungry and desperate billions has not yet become so great that world leaders see Kurtz's solution as the only humane, the only possible, but fundamentally sound one. But that day is not far off. I see it coming. That is why I read history.

—SVEN LINDQVIST, *Exterminate All the Brutes*

CONTENTS

PART IV

LATIN AMERICA

I

LAST CALL FOR
ILLUSIONS

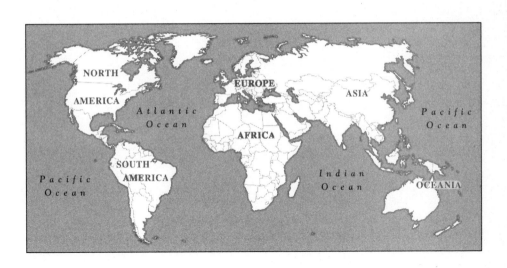

CHAPTER 1

Who Killed Ekaru Loruman?

What are the roots that clutch, what branches grow
Out of this stony rubbish? Son of man,
You cannot say, or guess, for you know only
A heap of broken images, where the sun beats,
And the dead tree gives no shelter, the cricket no relief,
And the dry stone no sound of water.

—T. S. ELIOT, *The Waste Land*

EKARU LORUMAN lay beneath a flat-topped acacia tree, its latticework of branches casting a soft mesh of shade upon his body. He wore a silver earring and khaki shorts and lay on his side with his arm twisted awkwardly beneath him. The left side of Ekaru's forehead was gone, blown away by the exit of a bullet. His blood formed a greasy, black slick on the desert floor. His sandals, shawl, and gun had been stolen.

Ekaru had been a pastoralist from the Turkana tribe, who live in northwest Kenya, on the arid savannas of the Rift Valley. He had been killed the day before when a neighboring tribe, the Pokot, launched a massive cattle raid. Ekaru's corpse lay here on the ground, exposed to the elements with goats and sheep browsing nearby, because the Turkana do not bury people killed in raids. They believe doing so is bad luck, that it will only invite more attacks. So they leave their dead to decompose where they fall. But these supernatural precautions will not hold the enemy at bay, for profound social and climatological forces drive them forth.

The group of Turkana I was visiting had been pushed south by severe drought and were now grazing their herds at the edge of their traditional range, very close to their enemies, the Pokot. In the pastoralist corridor of East Africa, a basic pattern is clear: during times of drought, water and grazing become scarce, the herds fall ill, and many cattle die. To replenish stocks, young men raid their neighbors. The onset of anthropogenic climate change means Kenya is seeing rising temperatures and more frequent drought. Yet, overall it is actually receiving greater amounts of precipitation. The problem is, the rain now arrives erratically, in sudden violent bursts, all at once rather than gradually over a season. This means eroding floods, followed by drought.[1] The clockwork rains, upon which Kenyan agriculture and society depends, are increasingly out of sync.

Climate War Forensics

Why did Ekaru Loruman die? What forces compelled his murder? Ekaru, who had been about thirty-five years old—age among the Turkana is usually just estimated—had three wives, eight children, and about fifty head of cattle. He had been an important and powerful man in his community: a warrior in his prime, old enough to have plenty of experience and wisdom but still young and strong enough to run and fight for days on little food or water. And now he was dead.

We could say tradition killed Ekaru, the age-old tradition of "stock theft," cattle raiding among the Nilotic tribes of East Africa. Or we could say he was murdered by a specific man, a Pokot from the Karasuk. Or that Ekaru was killed by the drought. When the drought gets bad, the raiding picks up.

Or perhaps Ekaru was killed by forces yet larger, forces transcending the specifics of this regional drought, this raid, this geography, and the Nilotic cattle cultures. To my mind, while walking through the desert among the Turkana warriors scanning the Karasuk hills for the Pokot war party, it seemed clear that Ekaru's death was caused by the most colossal set of events in human history: the catastrophic convergence of poverty, violence, and climate change. This book is an attempt to understand the death of Ekaru Loruman, and so many others like him, through the lens of this catastrophic convergence.

The Facts

The scientific consensus about the status of the climate takes institutional form in the Intergovernmental Panel on Climate Change (IPCC). The IPCC does not conduct independent research but is, instead, a government- and UN-supported international clearinghouse. It collects and summarizes all published scientific literature on climatology and related issues in biology, hydrology, oceanography, forests, glaciology, and other disciplines so that governments may respond to climate issues based on fully vetted research.

The IPCC has been attacked by climate-change denialists as alarmist and wrong because of several minor errors in its 2007 Fourth Assessment Report. Addressing these did not, however, change the report's overall conclusions. In fact, because the IPCC operates on the basis of consensus, its conclusions are quite conservative, and its reports lag years behind the latest scientific developments. The IPCC represents the lowest common denominator of fully accepted conclusions from the scientific mainstream.

The IPCC has concluded that civilization's dependence on burning fossil fuels has boosted atmospheric concentrations of carbon dioxide (CO_2) from around 280 parts per million (ppm) before the Industrial Revolution to 390 ppm today. Analyses of ancient ice cores show 390 ppm to be the highest atmospheric concentration of CO_2 during the last 10,000 years.[2]

Atmospheric CO_2 functions like the glass in a greenhouse, allowing the sun's heat in but preventing much of it from radiating back out to space. We need atmospheric CO_2—without it, Earth would be an ice-cold, lifeless rock. However, over the last 150 years we have been loading the sky with far too much CO_2, and the planet is heating up.

As the Pew Center on Global Climate Change explains, "The Earth's average surface temperature has increased by 1.4°F (0.8°C) since the early years of the 20th century. The 11 warmest years on record (since 1850) have all occurred in the past 13 years. The five warmest years to date are 2005, 1998, 2002, 2003, 2007."[3]

Less than 1°C warmer over a hundred years may not sound like much, but scientists believe it is enough to begin disrupting the climate system's equilibrium. The negative-feedback loops that keep Earth's climate stable are increasingly giving way to destabilizing positive-feedback loops, in which departures from the norm build on themselves instead of diminishing over time. The Greenland and Antarctic ice sheets—which reflect large amounts of solar radiation back into space and regulate the flow of ocean currents—are melting at rates much faster than climate scientists had predicted even a few years ago. The loss of reflective ice means more solar radiation is absorbed, and the world heats faster. Polar ice is melting rapidly, disgorging billions of gallons of fresh water, which alters the chemistry and currents of the oceans and, adding volume, threatens to raise sea levels by up to a meter over this century.[4]

The Social Challenge

Climate change is happening faster than initially predicted, and its impacts are already upon us in the form of more extreme weather events, desertification, ocean acidification, melting glaciers, and incrementally rising sea levels. The scientists who construct the computer models that analyze climate data believe that even if we stop dumping greenhouse gases into the atmosphere, CO_2 levels are already so high that we are locked into a significant increase in global temperatures. Disruptive climate change is a certainty even if we make the economic shift away from fossil fuels.

Incipient climate change is already starting to express itself in the realm of politics. Extreme weather events and off-kilter weather patterns are causing more humanitarian crises and fueling civil wars. The United Nations has estimated that all but one of its emergency appeals for humanitarian aid in 2007 were climate related. Already climate change adversely affects 300 million people per year, killing 300,000 of them. By 2030—as floods, droughts, forest fires, and new diseases grow worse—as many as 500,000 people per year could be killed by climate change, and the economic cost of these disruptions could reach $600 billion annually.[5]

Rising sea levels will be one of the greatest stresses. In 2007, the IPCC projected that sea levels could rise by an average of 7 to 23 inches during this century. These numbers were soon amended, and scientists now believe sea levels will rise by an average of 5 feet over the next 90 years.[6] Such sea-level rises will lead to massive dislocations. One recent study from Columbia University's Center for International Earth Science Information Network projects that 700 million climate refugees will be on the move by 2050.[7]

Perhaps the modern era's first climate refugees were the five hundred thousand Bangladeshis left homeless when half of Bhola Island flooded in 2005. In Bangladesh 22 million people will be forced from their homes by 2050 because of climate change. India is already building a militarized border fence along its 2,500-mile frontier with Bangladesh, and the student activists of India's Hindu Right are pushing vigorously for the mass deportation of (Muslim) Bangladeshi immigrants.[8]

Meanwhile, twenty-two Pacific Island nations, home to 7 million people, are planning for relocation as rising seas threaten them with national annihilation. What will happen when China's cities begin to flood? When the eastern seaboard of the United States starts to flood, how will people and institutions respond?

The Catastrophic Convergence

Climate change arrives in a world primed for crisis. The current and impending dislocations of climate change intersect with the already-existing crises of poverty and violence. I call this collision of political, economic, and environmental disasters *the catastrophic convergence*. By catastrophic convergence, I do not merely mean that several disasters happen simultaneously, one problem atop another. Rather, I argue that problems compound and amplify each other, one expressing itself through another.

Societies, like people, deal with new challenges in ways that are conditioned by the traumas of their past. Thus, damaged societies, like damaged people, often respond to new crises in ways that are irrational, shortsighted, and self-destructive. In the case of climate change, the prior traumas that set the stage for bad adaptation, the destructive social response, are Cold War–era militarism and the economic pathologies of neoliberal capitalism. Over the last forty years, both these forces have distorted the state's relationship to society—removing and undermining the state's collectivist, regulatory, and redistributive functions, while overdeveloping its repressive and military capacities. This, I argue, inhibits society's ability to avoid violent dislocations as climate change kicks in.

In this book I examine the prehistories of the climate disaster in order to explain how the world came to be such a mess and, thus, so prone to respond to climate change in ways that exacerbate the social fallout of the new extreme weather. In much of the world, it seems that the only solidarity forthcoming in response to climate change is an exclusionary tribalism, and the only state policy available is police repression. This is not "natural" and inevitable but rather the result of a history—particularly the history of the Global North's use and abuse of the Global South—that has destroyed the institutions and social practices that would allow a different, more productive response.

The Cold War sowed instability throughout the Third World; its myriad proxy wars left a legacy of armed groups, cheap weapons, smuggling networks, and corrupted officialdoms in developing countries. Neoliberal economic policies—radical privatization and economic deregulation enforced by the International Monetary Fund and World Bank—have pushed many economies in the Third World—or, if you prefer, the Global South—into permanent crisis and extreme inequality. In these societies, the state has often been reduced to a hollow shell, devoid of the institutional capacity it needs to guide economic development or address social crises.

Sometimes these forces have worked together simultaneously; at other times they have been quite distinct. For example, Somalia was destroyed by Cold War military interventions. It became a classic proxy battleground.

Though it underwent some limited economic liberalization, its use as a pawn on the chessboard of global political struggle caused its collapse. The same holds true for Afghanistan, which was, and still is, a failed state. It never underwent structural adjustment but was a proxy battleground. On the other hand, Mexico, the north of which is now experiencing a profound violent crisis, was not a frontline state during the Cold War, but it was subject to radical economic liberalization.

Climate change now joins these crises, acting as an accelerant. The Pentagon calls it a "threat multiplier." All across the planet, extreme weather and water scarcity now inflame and escalate existing social conflicts. Columbia University's Earth Institute and the International Crisis Group, combining databases on civil wars and water availability, found that "when rainfall is significantly below normal, the risk of a low-level conflict escalating to a full-scale civil war approximately doubles the following year."[9] The project cites the example of Nepal, where the Maoist insurgency was most severe after droughts and almost nonexistent in areas with normal rainfall. In some cases, when the rains were late or light, or came all at once, or at the wrong time, "semiretired" armed groups often reemerged to start fighting again.

Between the Tropic of Capricorn and the Tropic of Cancer lies what I call the *Tropic of Chaos,* a belt of economically and politically battered postcolonial states girding the planet's mid-latitudes. In this band, around the tropics, climate change is beginning to hit hard. The societies in this belt are also heavily dependent on agriculture and fishing, thus very vulnerable to shifts in weather patterns. This region was also on the front lines of the Cold War and of neoliberal economic restructuring. As a result, in this belt we find clustered most of the failed and semifailed states of the developing world.

According to a Swedish government study, "There are 46 countries—home to 2.7 billion people—in which the effects of climate change interacting with economic, social, and political problems will create a high risk of violent conflict."[10] The study's list covers that same terrain—those mid-latitudes that are now being most affected by the onset of anthropogenic climate change.

Western military planners, if not political leaders, recognize the dangers in the convergence of political disorder and climate change. Instead of worrying about conventional wars over food and water, they see an emerging geography of climatologically driven civil war, refugee flows, pogroms, and social breakdown. In response, they envision a project of open-ended counterinsurgency on a global scale.[11]

Mitigation and Adaptation

The watchwords of the climate discussion are *mitigation* and *adaptation*—that is, we must mitigate the causes of climate change while adapting to its effects. Mitigation means drastically cutting our production of CO_2 and other greenhouse gases, like methane and chlorofluorocarbons, that prevent the sun's heat from radiating back out to space. Mitigation means moving toward clean energy sources, such as wind, solar, geothermal, and tidal kinetic power. It means closing coal-fired power plants, weaning our economy off oil, building a smart electrical grid, and making massive investments in carbon-capture and -sequestration technologies.

Adaptation, on the other hand, means preparing to live with the effects of climatic changes, some of which are already underway and some of which are inevitable—in the pipeline. Adaptation is both a technical and a political challenge.

Technical adaptation means transforming our relationship to nature as nature transforms: learning to live with the damage we have wrought by building seawalls around vulnerable coastal cities, giving land back to mangroves and everglades so they can act to break tidal surges during giant storms, opening wildlife migration corridors so species can move north as the climate warms, and developing sustainable forms of agriculture that can function on an industrial scale even as weather patterns gyrate wildly.

Political adaptation, on the other hand, means transforming humanity's relationship to itself, transforming social relations among people. Successful political adaptation to climate change will mean developing new ways of containing, avoiding, and deescalating the violence that climate change fuels. That will require economic redistribution and development. It will also require a new diplomacy of peace building.

However, another type of political adaptation is already under way, one that might be called the *politics of the armed lifeboat*: responding to climate change by arming, excluding, forgetting, repressing, policing, and killing. One can imagine a green authoritarianism emerging in rich countries, while the climate crisis pushes the Third World into chaos. Already, as climate change fuels violence in the form of crime, repression, civil unrest, war, and even state collapse in the Global South, the North is responding with a new authoritarianism. The Pentagon and its European allies are actively planning a militarized adaptation, which emphasizes the long-term, open-ended containment of failed or failing states—counterinsurgency forever.

This sort of "climate fascism," a politics based on exclusion, segregation, and repression, is horrific and bound to fail. There must be another path. The struggling states of the Global South cannot collapse without eventually taking wealthy economies down with them. If climate change is allowed to destroy whole economies and nations, no amount of walls, guns, barbed wire, armed aerial drones, or permanently deployed mercenaries will be able to save one half of the planet from the other.

The Argument

The chapters that follow tour the Tropic of Chaos, that violent and impoverished swath of terrain around the mid-latitudes of the planet. And in exploring places, I explore history and use a historical analysis. If at first glance you expected a book about the future, in fact you are holding a book of history. From understanding the past, we can better analyze both the present and the dangerous future ahead. I begin by laying out how the security forces of the Global North are moving toward an embrace of militarized adaptation. I then look at the history of counterinsurgency both as one of the historical streams leading into the catastrophic convergence and as a central feature of militarized adaptation.

Next I return to the question of who killed Ekaru Loruman in a series of chapters on the history and politics of climate change in East Africa.

The story then moves to Central Asia to explore the climatic elements of the Afghanistan war and the Pakistan-India conflict. While in the region, we take a side trip to Kyrgyzstan, because it is an extreme case of climatically driven social breakdown. Moving east, we visit Andhra Pradesh to explore the links between neoliberalism, climate change, and the spread of Maoist guerillas in eastern India. Jumping across the Pacific, we resume the story in Brazil, where I link climate change in the *Nordeste* to extreme violence in Rio de Janeiro's favelas. In that section, Cold War–era repression and neoliberalism are seen working in concert. Then we move north to the border between Mexico and the United States, delving more deeply into the legacy of neoliberal capitalism, which—far more than Cold War violence—is the main root of instability in Mexico. We return to the United States and look at how border militarization and xenophobia are increasingly shaped by the meltdown in northern Mexico.

Finally, I consider what is to be done. I argue that the best way to address the effects of climate change is to tackle the political and economic crises that have rendered us so vulnerable to climate-induced chaos in the first place. But ultimately, mitigation remains the most important strategy. The physical impacts of climate change—rising sea levels, desertification, freak storms, and flooding—are certainly frightening, but so are the emerging social and political aspects of adaptation, which too often take destructive and repressive forms. We must change that.

Ultimately, the most important thing is mitigation: we must decarbonize our economy.

CHAPTER 2

Military Soothsayers

Dealing with such fractured or failing states is, in many ways, the main security challenge of our time.

—ROBERT GATES, *secretary of defense, 2010*

THE PENTAGON IS planning for a world remade by climate change. You could even say that the Pentagon is planning for Armageddon. In the summer of 2008, Dr. Thomas Fingar, deputy director of national intelligence for analysis, gave the US Congress a classified briefing on the military implications of climate change: "Food insecurity, for reasons both of shortages and affordability, will be a growing concern in Africa as well as other parts of the world. Without food aid, the region will likely face higher levels of instability—particularly violent ethnic clashes over land ownership."

"Closer to home," continued Fingar, "the United States will need to anticipate and plan for growing immigration pressures. . . . Extreme weather events and growing evidence of inundation will motivate many to move sooner rather than later. . . . As climate changes spur more humanitarian emergencies, the international community's capacity to respond will be increasingly strained."[1]

Military planning, conceived of as a response to events, also shapes them. Planning too diligently for war can preclude peace. America's overdeveloped military capacity, its military-industrial complex, has created powerful interests that depend on, therefore promote, war. Now the old military-industrial complex—companies like General Electric, Lockheed, and Raytheon, with their fabulously expensive weapons systems—has been joined by a swarm of smaller security firms offering hybrid services. Blackwater, DynCorp, and Global come to mind, but private prison companies like Corrections Corporation of America, Management and Training Corporation, and The Geo Group are also involved. This new security-industrial complex offers an array of services at home and abroad: surveillance; intelligence; border security; detention; facility and base construction; antiterrorism consulting; military and police logistics, analysis, planning, and training; and, of course, personal security.

Their operations are found wherever the United States projects power: in Afghanistan, running supply convoys, serving food, and providing translators; in Columbia, spraying coca fields and training the military; in the Philippines, training the police; in Mexico guarding businessmen; and all along the US-Mexico border, processing immigrant detainees. This new economy of repression helps promulgate a xenophobic and bellicose ideology. For example, private prison companies lobbied hard for passage of Arizona's tough anti-immigration law in 2010.[2]

As a politics of climate change begins to develop, this matrix of parasitic interests has begun to shape adaptation as the militarized management of civilization's violent disintegration.

The Apocalypse on Paper

A slew of government reports has discussed the social and military problems posed by climate change. In 2008, Congress mandated that the upcoming 2010 Quadrennial Defense Review—the policy document laying out the guiding principles of US military strategy and doctrine—consider the national-security impacts of climate change. The first of these investigations to make news, a 2004 Pentagon-commissioned study called "An Abrupt Climate Change Scenario and Its Implications for United States National Security," was authored by Peter Schwartz, a CIA consultant and former head of planning at Royal Dutch/Shell, and Doug Randall of the

California-based Global Business Network.[3] The report was made at the behest of octogenarian military theorist cum imperial soothsayer Andrew Marshall. Known to his followers as Yoda, after the wrinkled, dwarflike puppet of *Star Wars* fame, Marshall got his start at the RAND Corporation in 1949 as a specialist on nuclear Armageddon and its alleged survivability. He moved from RAND to the Pentagon during Richard Nixon's presidency and served every president since.[4] (It is interesting to note the presence of atomic-era Cold Warrior physicists among both the climate-change denialists and the military adaptationists. In his book *How to Cool the Planet*, Jeff Goodell remarks on the same set's infatuation with the high-tech solutions promised by geoengineering, in particular Lawrence Livermore Laboratory's Lowell Wood, a tie-dye wearing disciple of Edward Teller.[5])

Schwartz and Randall's report correctly treats global warming as a potentially nonlinear process.[6] And they forecast a new Dark Ages:

> Nations with the resources to do so may build virtual fortresses around their countries, preserving resources for themselves. . . . As famine, disease, and weather-related disasters strike due to the abrupt climate change, many countries' needs will exceed their carrying capacity. This will create a sense of desperation, which is likely to lead to offensive aggression in order to reclaim balance. . . . Europe will be struggling internally, large numbers of refugees washing up on its shores and Asia in serious crisis over food and water. Disruption and conflict will be endemic features of life. Once again, warfare would define human life.[7]

In 2007 there came more reports on climate and security. One, from the Pentagon-connected think tank CNA Corporation, convened an advisory board of high-ranking former military officers to examine the issues— among them General Gordon Sullivan, former chief of staff, US Army; Admiral Donald Pilling, former vice chief of naval operations; Admiral Joseph Prueher, former commander in chief of the US Pacific Command; and General Anthony Zinni, retired US Marine Corps and former commander in chief of US Central Command. That report envisioned permanent counterinsurgency on a global scale. Here is one salient excerpt:

> Climate change acts as a threat multiplier for instability in some of the most volatile regions of the world. Many governments in Asia, Africa, and the Middle East are already on edge in terms of their ability to provide basic needs: food, water, shelter and stability. Projected climate change will exacerbate the problems in these regions and add to the problems of effective governance. Unlike most conventional security threats that involve a single entity acting in specific ways at different points in time, climate change has the potential to result in multiple chronic conditions, occurring globally within the same time frame. Economic and environmental conditions in these already fragile areas will further erode as food production declines, diseases increase, clean water becomes increasingly scarce, and populations migrate in search of resources. Weakened and failing governments, with an already thin margin for survival, foster the conditions for internal conflict, extremism, and movement toward increased authoritarianism and radical ideologies. The U.S. may be drawn more frequently into these situations to help to provide relief, rescue, and logistics, or to stabilize conditions before conflicts arise.[8]

Another section notes:

> Many developing countries do not have the government and social infrastructures in place to cope with the types of stressors that could be brought on by global climate change. When a government can no longer deliver services to its people, ensure domestic order, and protect the nation's borders from invasion, conditions are ripe for turmoil, extremism and terrorism to fill the vacuum . . . the greatest concern will be movement of asylum seekers and refugees who due to ecological devastation become settlers.[9]

In closing the report notes, "Abrupt climate changes could make future adaptation extremely difficult, even for the most developed countries."[10]

Another report from 2007, the most scientifically literate of the lot, titled *The Age of Consequences: The Foreign Policy National Security Implications of Global Climate Change*, was produced by the Center for Strategic and International Studies and the Center for a New American Security. Its prominent authors included Kurt Campbell, former deputy assistant secretary of defense; Leon Fuerth, former national security advisor to Vice President Al Gore; John Podesta, former chief of staff for President Bill Clinton; and James Woolsey, former director of the Central Intelligence Agency.

Age of Consequences laid out three plausible scenarios for climate change, each pertaining to different global average-temperature changes. The authors relied on the Fourth Assessment Report of the Intergovernmental Panel on Climate Change but noted, "Recent observations indicate that projections from climate models have been too conservative; the effects of climate change are unfolding faster and more dramatically than expected."[11] The report conceives of future problems not in terms of interstate resource wars but as state collapse caused by "disease, uncontrolled migration, and crop failure, that . . . overwhelm the traditional instruments of national security (the military in particular) and other elements of state power and authority."[12] Green ex-spook James Woolsey authored the report's final section laying out the worst-case scenario. He writes:

In a world that sees two meter sea level rise, with continued flooding ahead, it will take extraordinary effort for the United States, or indeed any country, to look beyond its own salvation. All of the ways in which human beings have dealt with natural disasters in the past . . . could come together in one conflagration: rage at government's inability to deal with the abrupt and unpredictable crises; religious fervor, perhaps even a dramatic rise in millennial end-of-days cults; hostility and violence toward migrants and minority groups, at a time of demographic change and increased global migration; and intra- and interstate conflict over resources, particularly food and fresh water. Altruism and generosity would likely be blunted.[13]

The Allies

Other developed states have conducted similar studies, most of them classified. The Australian Defense Forces (ADF) produced a report on climate conflict in 2007, a summary of which was leaked two years later: "Environmental stress, caused by both climate change and a range of other factors, will act as a threat multiplier in fragile states around the world, increasing the chances of state failure. This is likely to increase demands for the ADF to be deployed on additional stabilisation, post-conflict reconstruction and disaster relief operations in the future."[14]

The European powers are also planning for the security threats of a world transformed by climate change. The European Council released a climate-security report in 2008, noting that "a temperature rise of up to 2°C above pre-industrial levels will be difficult to avoid. . . . Investment in mitigation to avoid such scenarios, as well as ways to adapt to the unavoidable should go hand in hand with addressing the international security threats created by climate change; both should be viewed as part of preventive security policy."

In familiar language the report noted, "climate change threatens to overburden states and regions which are already fragile and conflict prone," which leads to "political and security risks that directly affect European interests."[15] It also notes the likelihood of conflict over resources due to reduction of arable land and water shortages; economic damage to coastal cities and critical infrastructure, particularly Third World megacities; environmentally induced migration; religious and political radicalization; and tension over energy supply.[16]

Geography of Climate Chaos

War has an uneven geography that follows the history of imperialism and the uneven development of capitalism on a global scale. National security intellectuals, in and out of government, have started to imagine a militarized geography of social breakdown on a global scale; they have coalesced around the idea of war and permanent counterinsurgency as planetary crisis management. Containing and policing failed states is at the center of the project.

Among the security-intellectual set we find Thomas Barnett, a self-described military philosopher, whose research focuses on the international geography of political violence. He offers a new map of world conflict:

> Show me where globalization is thick with network connectivity, financial transactions, liberal media flows, and collective security, and I will show you regions featuring stable governments, rising standards of living, and more deaths by suicide than murder. These parts of the world I call the Functioning Core, or Core. . . . But show me where globalization is thinning or just plain absent, and I will show you regions plagued by politically repressive regimes, widespread poverty and disease, routine mass murder, and—most important—the chronic conflicts that incubate the next generation of global terrorists. These parts of the world I call the Non-Integrating Gap, or Gap. . . . So where do we schedule the U.S. military's next round of away games? The pattern that has emerged since the end of the cold war suggests a simple answer: in the Gap.[17]

In reality, this new map is just the old map—the geography of empire. Barnett even sounds a bit like economic historian Immanuel Wallerstein, using the "periphery" and "core."[18] Or consider how John Stuart Mill famously described colonial geography at the dawn of mercantilist capitalism: "Our West Indian colonies cannot be regarded as countries with a productive capital of their own. . . . [Instead, they] are places where England finds it convenient to carry on the production of sugar, coffee and a few other tropical commodities."[19]

Capitalism has always functioned as an international system. The origins of this mighty global economy arose from connections that stretched across the globe and involved the spice trade of the Dutch East Indies, the Atlantic slave trade, and the flow from Russia and Poland of grain, honey, and timber. And it may well be along these same lines that the world capitalist economy begins to unravel. Barnett's Gap is not so much excluded (or, as he says, "nonintegrated") as it is historically exploited and politically subjugated. Thus, its states are too often weak and corrupt. Now, add climate change, and this geography—which had been making some progress in terms of the United Nations' human-development index of well-being measured primarily in terms of income, life expectancy, and education—will sink into greater misery and violent chaos.[20]

Hard State versus Failed State

Political adaptation presents stark choices. There is a real risk that strong states with developed economies will succumb to a politics of xenophobia, racism, police repression, surveillance, and militarism and thus transform themselves into fortress societies while the rest of the world slips into collapse. By that course, developed economies would turn into neofascist islands of relative stability in a sea of chaos. But a world in climatological collapse—marked by hunger, disease, criminality, fanaticism, and violent social breakdown—will overwhelm the armed lifeboat. Eventually, all will sink into the same morass.

However, another path is possible. Progressive political adaptation—coupled with aggressive and immediate mitigation—can involve moving toward greater cooperation and economic redistribution within states and between North and South. I will touch on these ideas at the end of this book. Unfortunately, the early stages of political adaptation do not inspire much confidence. The politics of the armed lifeboat seem to be winning.

CHAPTER 3

War for a Small Planet: Adaptation As Counterinsurgency

> The United States possesses overwhelming conventional military superiority. This capability has pushed its enemies to fight US forces unconventionally, mixing modern technology with ancient techniques of insurgency and terrorism. . . . Defeating such enemies presents a huge challenge to the Army and Marine Corps.
>
> —FM 3-24, *US Military Counterinsurgency Field Manual,* December 2006

IT WAS A SPLENDID little war in a pathetic little country—a classic case of old meets new, banana republic meets failed state. No one was sure why, but the two main ethnic groups were at war; refugees needed humanitarian assistance, and panicked crowds had to be controlled. The NGOs and a gaggle of pestering journalists were not helping. To restore order, the US Marine Corps had landed.

"Get back!" shouted a young marine trying to contain civilians who surged toward some sort of a feeding or detention station.

"What's going on?" I asked.

"These civilians need humanitarian assistance, and we have to screen them, check out that none of them are armed," the marine said. A helicopter swept low overhead. From a high-rise building nearby came the muffled pop of gunfire.

When the young marines emerged from securing the high rise, they were clad in strange new fatigues, made up of a sooty, bluish-gray "T-pattern" of overlapping squares, rectangles, and lines—like some sort of pixilated abstract cityscape. The gray hues invoked Nazi tunics; the patterns, a confusing and dangerous street grid in a polluted Third World megacity. The broken-down little country where this was happening might have been called the Breakaway Province of Lower Nowhere or the Democratic Republic of Chaos, but it was actually Oakland, California. The year was 1999, and I was watching the future as imagined by the United States Marine Corps: a war game called Urban Warrior taking place on the grounds of a decommissioned naval hospital.

The Marines were expected to move seamlessly from managing refugees, to keeping the peace between warring factions, to attacking renegade militias. In 1999 they called that combination of tasks the "three-block war." At other times they termed it "military operations other than war." Now it is known by the old name, "counterinsurgency" (COIN), which one US Army Special Forces colonel once described as "total war at the grassroots level."[1] Call it what you please—small wars, limited war, low-intensity conflict—this type of fighting is moving to the center of the US military agenda just as that agenda begins to address climate change.

The catastrophic convergence of poverty, violence, and climate change is helping fuel the renewed focus on irregular warfare. Implicit in the climate-related writing of the security intellectuals is a central role for counterinsurgency. Throughout their reports are lines such as "Weakened and failing governments, with an already thin margin for survival, foster the conditions for internal conflict, extremism, and movement toward increased authoritarianism and radical ideologies. The U.S. may be drawn more frequently into these situations to help to provide relief, rescue, and logistics, or to stabilize conditions before conflicts arise."[2] The military's new *Tactics in Counterinsurgency Field Manual* (FM 3-24.2) describes "the realities of today's operational environment" as "modified by a population explosion, urbanization, globalization, technology, the spread of religious fundamentalism, resource demand, climate change and natural disasters and proliferation of weapons of mass destruction."[3]

Asymmetry from Above

At the heart of the matter is a strange fact: the US military arsenal is overdeveloped. The United States can annihilate any conventional foe and destroy the planet several times over; it spends more on arms than the fourteen next-largest militaries. But the apocalyptic power of the US atomic arsenal is politically effective only if it is not actually used. It only functions as a threat.

To be effective in a world of failed states, rebellions, coups, civil wars, tribal clashes, pogroms, banditry, narcoviolence, piracy, terrorism, and desperate surges of refugees, US military violence must be applied with restraint—*tremendous* restraint, given its potential—and with precision. The empire cannot hunt fleas with a sledgehammer. America's application of real violence requires smaller weapons, greater agility, and subtler tactics capable of achieving nonconventional political victories, such as the pacification of restive populations, the defeat of irregular forces, the containment and exclusion of refugee flows, and the suppression of hungry urban mobs. Thus, COIN is in fashion.

Unfortunately, the current romance with COIN is part of the problem, not the solution. Its methods are, by definition, socially corrosive and destructive. As a doctrine, counterinsurgency is the theory of internal warfare; it is the strategy of suppressing rebellions and revolution. Its object is *civilian society* as a whole and the social fabric of everyday life. Whereas traditional aerial bombing (which is notoriously ineffective) targets bridges, factories, and command centers, COIN targets—*pace* Foucault—the "capillary" level of social relations. It ruptures and tears (but rarely remakes) the intimate social relations among people, their ability to cooperate, and the lived texture of solidarity—in other words, the bonds that comprise society's sinews.[4]

Conventional warfare seeks to control territory and destroy the opposing military, but counterinsurgency seeks to control society. It is thus "population centric." In an insurgency, the military force—the state or the occupying power—already has (at least nominal) control of the battle space, but it lacks control of the population. Guerrillas, irregular forces, and even small, unpopular terrorist groups all rely on the populace, or parts of it, for recruits, food, shelter, medical care, intelligence, and, if nothing else, simple cover. Mao Tse-tung summed it up: "The guerrilla must move amongst the people as a fish swims in the sea." Thus, the anti-insurgent's task is to isolate and destroy the guerrillas by gaining control of the population through violence as well as psychological and ideological means.

Under these conditions, strategy and tactics now pivot on individual psychology, religion, age structures, rituals, traditions, family bonds, economic activities, and sense of place—in short, all the formal and informal institutions of everyday life. Society is the target, and as such it is damaged. Counterinsurgency is especially destructive because it attacks the social fabric. Like the revolutions it seeks to suppress, counterinsurgency intentionally attacks and attempts to remake the social relations of a place. In the process, it helps set off self-fueling processes of social disintegration.

The Receipt

In Vietnam it was called "winning hearts and minds," or in the cheeky military argot of the time, "WHAMing the peasantry." Today, as in the past, such militarized "social work" can involve real economic development and progressive political reforms designed to ameliorate the legitimate grievances of the people—that is, to win their actual support and make the revolutionary promises of the insurgents less appealing. Or it can mean genocidal, society-destroying total war at the grass roots, as in "draining the sea to catch the fish." In Guatemala during the 1980s, that approach allowed government forces to put to the torch more than four hundred Indian villages. They were simply wiped out, their inhabitants killed, raped, detained, scattered.

Whether hard or soft, counterinsurgency always attempts to remake social relations. In the process, it often rends without rebuilding, causing a breakdown of social norms and values; it tatters the bonds of solidarity and voluntary social regulation. Typically, anomie, normlessness, trauma, and lawlessness are its legacy.[5]

Contrast the effects of counterinsurgency with those of aerial bombardment during conventional war. Though more murderous and economically destructive, aerial bombardment tends not to damage society and social relations. If anything, it has been found to increase solidarity among its victims. Britain during World War II is the quintessential example: Nazi bombardment was met with evacuation, rationing, conscription, and an unprecedented leveling of class differences. Britain united under the bombs and fought even harder. As Minister of Labor Ernest Bevin would explain, when "a nation is involved in a great crisis . . . [it] is bound to become collectivist."[6] Similar effects arose in wartime Germany and Japan, as well as in North Vietnam under US carpet bombing; one would expect a similar culture of united opposition in the tribal areas of Pakistan now subject to drone attacks.[7]

Thus, counterinsurgency has been central in setting up the catastrophic convergence of poverty, violence, and climate change. Irregular, proxy conflicts—insurgency and counterinsurgency in the Third World—defined the American and Soviet methods during the Cold War. Those methods primed many areas of the world for serious instability. The United Nations documented around 150 armed conflicts in the Third World between 1945 and 1990. In these so-called small wars of the Third World, 20 million people died, 60 million were injured, and 15 million had been deracinated as refugees by 1991. Derek Summerfield, a psychiatrist and academic who specializes in the mental-health effects of modern war, described the situation as follows:

> Five percent of all casualties in the First World War were civilians; the figure for the Second World War was 50 percent, and that for the Vietnam War was over 80 percent. In current armed conflicts over 90 percent of all casualties are civilians, usually from poor rural families. This is the result of deliberate and systematic violence deployed to terrorize whole populations. . . . Population, not territory, is the target, and through terror the aim is to penetrate into homes, families, and the entire fabric of grassroots social relations, producing demoralization and paralysis. To this end terror is sown not just randomly, but also through targeted

assaults on health workers, teachers and co-operative leaders, those whose work symbolizes shared values and aspirations. Torture, mutilation, and summary execution in front of family members have become routine.[8]

In others words, COIN, or small-wars theory, means social mutilation. If militarized adaptation means more low-intensity conflict, and if Pentagon soothsayers see irregular warfare, rather than conventional conflicts, as central to the world remade by climate change, then we must review the history of these methods in theory and practice.

Small Wars Past

Reviewing the history of America's small wars, three distinct phases emerge. From the late eighteenth to the early twentieth century, asymmetrical wars formed part of the European imperial conquest of the Global South and the colonial policing that followed. In this phase, traditional societies fought for the continuation of their traditional lifeways. For them, asymmetrical warfare was essentially defensive action against invaders. The Zulu warriors in what is now South Africa, the Plains Indians of the American West, and the Pashtun tribal columns that attacked the British in the nineteenth century all waged their guerilla wars to defend old social orders, not to promote new ones.

Then, from the 1920s through the 1990s, small wars became increasingly (but not always) characterized by ideologically motivated insurgencies. Yes, poor peasants fought because they had grievances—too much exploitation—but the ideological and political aspects of the wars were crucial in articulating those grievances. The colonial and former colonial powers essentially fought defensive counterinsurgencies against these communist or nationalist liberation struggles that had modernizing aspirations and leaders driven by new ideas, people like Augusto Sandino, Mao Tsetung, Fidel Castro, and Ho Chi Minh. All of these movements had well-developed, if sometimes flawed, theories about society.

With the end of the Cold War, asymmetrical conflict and counterinsurgency has become less ideological and certainly less intellectual. Now insurgent movements are increasingly motivated by simple loot, survival, or irredentist and conservative, backward-looking ideas that almost always, upon examination, reflect simplistic moral philosophies rather than social theories.[9] Or they have no ideas at all. The Taliban are an example, as are the various guerrilla armies of West and Central Africa, like the truly insane and now-defunct Revolutionary United Front that maimed, raped, and looted across Sierra Leone for eleven years starting in 1991; or the Lord's Resistance Army, a still-active, genocidal cult-militia of child soldiers that rampages through parts of Uganda; or the postideological gangster remnants of the Revolutionary Armed Forces of Colombia, or FARC.

One military intellectual, writing in the Army War College's journal *Parameters*, recognized this third, post-ideological phase as part of a historical transformation away from growing stability toward increasing chaos: "Since the Treaty of Westphalia in 1648, this process has been one of increasing law and order that led to prosperity for many Western nation-states, their public institutions, and their peoples. The cycle now may be shifting away from stability toward chaos, suggesting that the nation-state may be entering a period in which its usefulness as a concept for organizing societies will be severely challenged. . . . We may expect increasing chaos during the shift from what has been called the 'modern' era to its successor."[10]

The "successor" age—if climate-change mitigation and progressive adaptation are not embraced—will be that described by James Woolsey: civilization in decline, opened-ended counterinsurgency, a rising tide of violence.

Colonial Origins

Native Americans were early on subjected to a project of simple brutality at the hands of settlers, but later the US government fashioned a project of assimilation and pacification that was pseudoscientific and pseudohumanitarian in its discourse. The "civilization" program imposed upon the Cherokee served as an early example of this. "They must either change their mode of life, or they must die!" railed one anti-Cherokee US senator.[11] The Cherokee chose the former.

Something like modern counterinsurgency characterized wars against the Plains Indians during the 1860s and 1870s. The American army beat the Sioux in part by imitating them: small, light, mobile cavalry units replaced large infantry formations, cutting the army's dependence on long, vulnerable supply trains. The mounted detachments worked closely with Indian scouts and mercenaries, typically from the Crow and Arikaras nations. At times, these small, mobile army units were bested or, in the case of General George A. Custer, annihilated.

The imitation of Indian methods was of course bolstered by the American military's superior firepower, transportation, and communications—that is, by America's industrial might. A crucial terrain of the warfare was economic. Native American hunting was restricted as the buffalo were exterminated, in part for their fur, in part to deny sustenance to the renegade bands that refused reservation life. Final victory over the Sioux came when Nelson Miles, out to avenge Custer, used the arrival of winter, which limited the Indians' mobility and access to food, to force the Sioux onto reservations. Once confined there, the Indians were subjected to all the methods of modern statecraft: identification, regimentation, surveillance, religious indoctrination, wage labor, money, ledgers, fines, military courts, and jails. The reservations were "total institutions" as defined by sociologist Erving Goffman. And as such, they destroyed, or remade, Indian culture and subjectivity.

In New Mexico, as General George Crook pioneered the use of small counterguerrilla patrols to harass Geronimo's Apache warriors, he also set up a system of mountaintop mirrors that communicated in a type of semaphore; this expanded his informational control over a wide area of intensely rugged terrain.[12] Railroads, telegraphs, barbed wire, propaganda, ideological indoctrination, photography, legal legerdemain, fast-action repeating rifles, and Hotchkiss light field artillery all gave those brutal campaigns of subjugation a modern profile. Call it the prehistory of the Predator drone.

Thus, in the Indian wars, as in modern antiguerrilla campaigns, the military targeted civilians: attacking villages, burning crops, taking women and children hostage, and concentrating the refugee populations at military forts so as to better watch over them. Divide-and-conquer tribalism was also fomented to facilitate in-fighting and the creation of local Indian auxiliaries. Recall, Sitting Bull was killed by his own former warriors turned reservation police.[13]

A Doctrine Emerges

The plains wars produced no written doctrine or theory of pacification, but British officers, facing similar tasks at the end of the nineteenth century in the African, Indian, and Southeast Asian domains of the Crown, did write about their methods. As John A. Nagl lays out in his classic *Learning to Eat Soup with a Knife: Counterinsurgency Lessons from Malaya and Vietnam*, the British officers, far away from their government, were often unable to receive instruction. Thus, they had to apply themselves to the study and development of new tactics.

The first classic in this genre was *The Defensive Duffers Drift* by Major General Sir Ernest Swinton. A strange little volume, *Duffers Drift* describes Swinton's experience as a young captain leading a British company in the Boer War. The book is arranged as a five-part dreamscape of interconnected and repeating nightmares. In each, the Boers trick and attack Swinton in new and more devious ways. Each nightmare is followed by a list of lessons, which grow more ruthless with each repetition of the cycle.[14] Realizing that he is fighting not only guerrillas but a whole people, Swinton concludes, "There are no *flanks*, no *rear*, or, to put it otherwise, it is *front all round*."[15] From this he concludes, never trust the locals; detain them, burn their farms, and starve them out, the women and children included. Attack their social fabric, for that is what the guerillas depend on.

Later works include Charles Caldwell's *Small Wars: Their Principles and Practice* and Charles Gwyn's *Imperial Policing*. Both helped establish core features of counterinsurgency doctrine—minimal use of force, civilian and military coordination, development of proxy forces—but they lack the trippy, laudanum-laced quality of *Duffers Drift*.

Banana Wars

For American forces, small-war tactics matured considerably with the rise of the so-called banana wars. Between the late 1890s and the late 1930s, US military forces intervened in Chile, Haiti, Hawaii, Nicaragua, China, Panama, the Philippines, Cuba, Puerto Rico, Dominican Republic, and many other places. All of these conflicts were more or less irregular and asymmetrical and entailed controlling the civilian population rather than annihilating a conventional force.

The order of the day was measured violence, small-unit tactics, mobility, cultural and psychological warfare, and the modern methods of administration, regulation, and surveillance. Detainees, often civilians, were concentrated in camps; checkpoints and official identification documents controlled civilian movement. At times these campaigns involved destroying the enemy's means of sustenance; burning whole villages was routine practice. Hungry civilians then became dependent on the food handouts, or "modern" economic-development programs, of the occupiers, and the areas of the guerrilla operations were effectively depopulated.[16]

Central to victory was the creation and training of local auxiliary forces. When the Marines pulled out, they wanted to count on the local constabulary, *guardia civil*, or gendarmerie to repress any reformist politicians, trade unionists, nationalists, or socialists who might seek to upset the existing order by taxing foreign business and redistributing wealth.[17]

This use of ethnic minorities to divide and conquer has been dubbed "ethnoliberation opportunism" by anthropologist Philippe Bourgeois. It occurs again and again in small wars—examples include the CIA's use of mountain tribes in Laos during the Vietnam War; the arming of mujahideen mercenaries against the Soviets during the Afghan jihad of the 1980s; and now the development of Shia death squads and the Sunni based *Safwa* militia in Iraq.[18] Cultivating these proxies almost always means cultivating criminals and fanatics. Their names from the Cold War include Brooklyn Rivera in Nicaragua, Joseph Savimbi in Angola, and Gulbuddin Hekmatyar in Afghanistan. These useful sociopaths are never easy to control and when they have served their purpose as proxies, they are let go to wander violently across the landscapes of their own societies.

The Manual

From the US Marine Corps' banana wars in the Caribbean and Latin America came a book, the *Small Wars Manual*, published in 1940. By that point, the Marines had some experience to draw on. As the manual's first edition noted, "The Marine Corps has landed troops 180 times in 37 countries from 1800 to 1934. Every year during the past 36 years since the Spanish-American War, the Marine Corps has been engaged in active operations in the field."[19] Small wars were constant and ongoing.

The Marines' small-war methods tended to combine carrot and stick, terror and reconciliation. Violence was applied to dislodge the authority of the rebels or the offending government. The Marines burned crops and homes, took prisoners, and terrorized the common people. Smedley Butler said that his troops burned down most of northern Haiti. Official reports used subtler language to describe the same: "Troops in the field have declared and carried on what is commonly known as 'open season,' where care is not taken to determine whether or not the natives encountered are bandits or 'good citizens' and warehouses have been ruthlessly burned merely because they were unoccupied and native property otherwise destroyed."[20] Once populations had submitted, however, they were permitted to return to their normal lives and economic activities.[21]

The Nation described it more bluntly: "U.S. Marines landed in Haiti, seized the gold in the National Bank, took over the customs-houses, closed the legislative assembly, and refused payment of salaries to Haitian officials who refused to do the white man's will."[22] Butler, a veteran of many small wars, put it even more directly: "I spent most of my time being a high-class muscle man for big business, for Wall Street and the bankers. In short I was a racketeer for capitalism." Butler said he had "helped in the raping of a half dozen Central American republics for the benefit of Wall Street."[23]

Cold War Proxies

In 1952 the US military created the Special Forces. With this development, counterinsurgency became further institutionalized and more clearly
associated with a political doctrine of defending capitalism. A few years
later, Ernesto Che Guevara published *Guerrilla Warfare*, which is similar to
the *Small Wars Manual* in that it is full of practical, even commonsense
advice: "Movement by night is another important characteristic of the
guerrilla band, enabling it to advance its position for an attack and, where
the danger of betrayal exists, to mobilize in new territory."[24] But *Guerrilla
Warfare* also emphasizes the role of ideas and politics. For Guevara ideology is both means and end. According to him, only a self-consciously political insurgency can win: "The guerrilla fighter needs full help from the
people of the area. This is an indispensable condition. This is clearly shown
by considering the case of bandit gangs that operate in the region. They
have all the characteristics of a guerrilla army, hegemony, respect for the
leader, valor, knowledge of the ground and often very good understanding
of the tactics to be employed. The only thing missing is the support of the
people; and inevitably these gangs are captured and exterminated by public forces."[25] For Guevara, the military superiority of the guerrilla band is
born of its relationship to political ideals: "We must come to the inevitable
conclusion that the guerrilla fighter is a social reformer, that he takes up
arms responding to the angry protests of the people against their oppression and that he fights in order to change the social system that keeps all
his unarmed brothers in ignominy and misery."[26]

Thus enters the struggle for hearts and minds. Indeed, it was President
John F. Kennedy who first had Che's book translated into English.
Kennedy was intimately interested in counterinsurgency: at his behest the
Special Forces first donned their eponymous green berets. It was a strange
and unwitting tribute to Che, whose iconic image has him wearing a beret.

Before long the Special Forces were operating in Laos and Vietnam.
The war in Indochina was marked by colossal violence—carpet bombing
by B-52s; napalm; large, conventional-style engagements between the
North Vietnamese army and American forces. But it also involved intense

counterinsurgency, at the heart of which was the Strategic Hamlet Program, which entailed the destruction, then reconstitution, of pro-Vietcong civilian communities.

No country saw a more devastating counterinsurgency than Guatemala. Beginning in 1981, the military government of General Rios Mont combined a genocidal, scorched-earth campaign against civilians with a classic "secure-and-hold" development strategy called *frijoles y fusiles*, or "beans and bullets." After destroying Indian villages and massacring many of their inhabitants, the military concentrated the surviving civilians in "model villages." They forced male survivors to participate in civil patrols, lightly armed vigilante forces that served as the eyes and ears of the military—and often as their human shields. An estimated one hundred thousand civilians were murdered during the Guatemalan Civil War, the vast majority by government forces.

I had an opportunity to see this war firsthand, in 1988, when I hiked across the Ixill Triangle in the highlands war zone. The trails were littered with government and guerrilla propaganda—small handbills exhorting the people to join one side or the other. The area was still at war, but the guerrillas were in retreat. Everywhere we saw the methods of counterinsurgency: trails cleared of trees on all sides, air patrols, civilian militia checkpoints, burnt villages, and new ones under strict government control. In one model village, a company of Guatemalan soldiers was dug in around a helicopter landing pad on the highest point of the ridge. Later, in 1991, I traveled with, and reported on, the Resistencia Nacional, part of the Farabundo Martí National Liberation Front, or FMLN. The hills of Cabañas, El Salvador, bore similar physical and social scars.

Today, the Guatemalan highlands and the small towns of El Salvador remain violent, but instead of guerrilla operations and counterinsurgency, the plague is crime. The global average homicide rate is less than eight per one hundred thousand, but the UN Office on Drugs and Crime reports that in Central America the murder rate between 2003 and 2008 averaged sixty-one per one hundred thousand in Honduras; fifty-two per one hundred thousand in El Salvador; and forty-nine per one hundred thousand in Guatemala.[27] One Latin American scholar writing in 2006 found that "crime rates have risen globally by an average of 50 per cent over the past

25 years, and the phenomenon is widely considered to contribute significantly to human suffering all over the world. This is particularly the case in Latin America, where violence has reached unprecedented levels due to rising crime and delinquency."[28]

All three of those countries were sites of intense counterinsurgency from the late 1970s to the early 1990s, and the legacy of that is anomie: a weakened society, a social fabric frayed, resulting in a gun culture with large populations of unemployed men habituated to violence, discipline, secrecy, pack loyalty, brutality; trained in the arts of smuggling, extortion, robbery, and assassination. In other words, an invisible army of criminals occupies society. The political class is steeped in violence, and much of it sees society as a battlefield; enemies must be destroyed, social problems eliminated by force. Walls and armed guards dominate the landscape. The police are hooked on habits of torture, disappearance, and drug running.[29]

Meanwhile, relative deprivation defines the psychological terrain: these societies are more unequal than ever, and the revolutionaries and progressive social movements, in raising class-consciousness, have enlightened the masses about the inherent unfairness of the situation.[30] The spectacle of modern media, in advertizing riches and fame, makes the common people aware of what they lack. All of this feeds criminogenic relative depravation.

Post–Cold War

Famously, the American defeat in Vietnam turned the US military away from the study of counterinsurgency, though the methods of irregular warfare remained part of the instruction for US proxy forces in El Salvador, the Philippines, Columbia and elsewhere. Counterinsurgency doctrine made a return after US Army Rangers got into trouble in Mogadishu, Somalia, in 1993, during a botched raid on the compound of Somali warlord Mohamed Farrah Aidid. After a Blackhawk helicopter was shot down in the city, a seat-of-the pants rescue mission eventually shot its way into, then back out of, the city but not without considerable loss of life—particularly for the Somali militiamen, eight to thirteen hundred of whom were killed— and a spectacular humiliation for the US Army.[31]

After that, the Pentagon began to think more seriously about how to fight irregulars in cities and failed states. Soon the RAND Corporation put out a study called "the urbanization of insurgency," and a December 1997 National Defense Panel review "castigated the Army as unprepared for protracted combat in the near impassable, maze-like streets of poverty-stricken Third World cities. As a result, the four armed services, coordinated by the Joint Staff Urban Working Group, launched crash programs to master street-fighting under realistic third-world conditions."[32]

In Iraq, I saw the new doctrine playing out in the streets of Baghdad, Fallujah, Summara, and Baquba. During one firefight, as I hid behind a parked car, my mind drifted back to the war game in Oakland. The shootout in Baghdad encapsulated the whole war—confusing and labor intensive, overly and dysfunctionally technological, and awkwardly urban. The US troops had more firepower than they could use, and they didn't even know exactly where or who the enemy was. Civilians hid in every corner as bullets hissed past.

Greg Grandin's *Empire's Workshop: Latin America, the United States, and the Rise of the New Imperialism* makes clear the links between counterinsurgency in Iraq and its antecedents in Central America. Grandin quotes an American counterinsurgency expert who describes the ferocity of US-funded and -trained forces in Central America as "going primitive." As Grandin explains, "With the United States failing to defeat the [Iraq] rebels on its own, the Pentagon came to debate the 'Salvadorian option,' that is the use of local paramilitary forces otherwise known as death squads, to do the kind of dirty work that it was either unwilling or unable to do. It turned to men like James Steele, who in the 1980s led the Special Forces mission in El Salvador and worked with Oliver North to run weapons and supplies to the Nicaraguan Contras."[33]

The Shia death squads of the government of Prime Minister Nouri al-Maliki are the result. Peter Maas of the *New York Times Magazine* tagged along with Steele and described the situation:

Looking through the doors, I saw about 100 detainees squatting on the floor, hands bound behind their backs; most were blindfolded. To my right, outside the doors, a leather-jacketed security official was slapping and kicking a detainee who was sitting on the ground. . . . A few minutes after the interview started, a man began screaming in the main hall, drowning out the Saudi's voice. "Allah!" he shouted. "Allah! Allah!" It was not an ecstatic cry; it was chilling, like the screams of a madman, or of someone being driven mad. "Allah!" he yelled again and again. The shouts were too loud to ignore. Steele left the room to find out what was happening. By the time he returned, the shouts had ceased. But soon, through the window behind me, I could hear the sounds of someone vomiting, coming from an area where other detainees were being held, at the side of the building.[34]

Maas concluded his article with a lapidary summation: "In El Salvador, Honduras, Peru, Turkey, Algeria and other crucibles of insurgency and counterinsurgency, the battles went on and on. They were, without exception, dirty wars."

That is the essence of militarized adaptation to climate chaos: dirty war forever. In the following chapters, the social wreckage of counterinsurgency past will be evident in the form of crime, smuggling, civilian militias, death squads, regions glutted with light arms, and routine use of detention and torture. Because counterinsurgency is war that, by design, attacks the social fabric, it has sowed chaos and set the stage for the catastrophic convergence. Leaving corruption, ignorance, crime, and anomie in their wake, small, dirty wars have created societies totally incapable of dealing with climate change. And now, armed adaptation is set to double down on a bad bet by applying more counterinsurgency to the global matrix of crisis.

II

AFRICA

CHAPTER 4

Geopolitics of a Cattle Raid

There is shadow under this red rock,
(Come in under the shadow of this red rock),
And I will show you something different from either
Your shadow at morning striding behind you
Or your shadow at evening rising to meet you;
I will show you fear in a handful of dust.

    —T. S. ELIOT, *The Waste Land*

IF THE IMPERIAL CORE of the world system is preparing to adapt to climate change by resort to military methods, then what does incipient climate-driven collapse in the Global South look like? How are the poor adapting? How is the catastrophic convergence lived on the ground? What are its textures and histories? For answers, I traveled to East Africa, and there, one hot morning, I found myself looking down at that dead man, Ekaru Loruman, who was, in many ways, killed by climate change.

As mentioned in chapter 1, this group of Turkana had been pushed south by severe drought and were grazing their herds very close to their enemies, the Pokot. With water and grazing scarce, the herds were ill. To replenish stocks, young men raided their neighbors.[1] And this increased violence is very clearly linked to climate change. Surface temperatures are rising, and the clockwork rains of the Intertropical Convergence Zone

(ITCZ), are out of sync. At the same time, the waters flowing from the glaciers on Mount Kenya are also in trouble: a century ago, the peak held eighteen glaciers; today, only eleven remain, and four of those are greatly reduced.[2] The same is true next door in Tanzania where the Intergovernmental Panel on Climate Change (IPCC) reports that "during the 20th century, the areal extent of Mt. Kilimanjaro's ice fields decreased by about 80 percent."[3]

As one Kenyan veterinarian who works with the Maasai, pastoralists explained to the *Guardian*'s John Vidal, "In the past we used to have regular 10-year climatic cycles which were always followed by a major drought. In the 1970s we started having droughts every seven years; in the 1980s they came about every five years and in the 1990s we were getting droughts and dry spells almost every two or three years. Since 2000 we have had three major droughts and several dry spells. Now they are coming almost every year, right across the country."[4]

The extreme weather is pushing northern Kenya toward desertification, and that means pastoralists must compete for grazing and water. The situation is so bad in some areas that people are now killing each other for water—shooting it out for control of wells and pasture. This is perhaps the most direct example of how climate change plays out as violence.

The Raid

The Turkana are here—in a place called Kotaruk southwest of the village, or "sublocation," of Naipa—to be close to a borehole, a well drilled years ago by an NGO. Not far away rise the Karasuk Hills—sharp, barren mountains that thrust up abruptly from the flat desert. When the tribesmen have diesel to run the pump, this narrow well sucks up a trickle of ancient groundwater. In these dry times, which seem to go on and on, well water alone keeps the cattle alive. Without cattle, the Turkana would disappear. They would die or migrate to cities, and their culture would exist only in the memories of deracinated urban slum dwellers.

For now, the well functions, drawing life to the surface. But the well also causes problems. Either due to the ill-informed logic of some forty-year-old aid project or due to simple geological and hydrological necessity, the borehole was drilled dangerously close to Pokot territory—basically on the boundary where the two tribes meet. Here, the mountains drop into a steep valley that opens onto the plains. You can actually see the place if you check Google Maps. It is about halfway up the western edge of the Turkana plains where the muddy and fast-moving Turkwel River comes closes to the mountains. Look closely, and you can see where a steep valley cuts up into the Karasuk Hills. The Pokot use that pass for their raiding.

The enmity between the Pokot and Turkana goes back a long way. The Pokot border the Turkana on the south and, like the Turkana, are of Nilotic lineage. But the Pokot speak a different language and belong to the large, loosely defined group of tribes called the Kalenjin—a cultural formation of relatively recent invention and dubious internal coherence. It is a post–World War II political invention, a banding together of minor tribes seeking to counterbalance the power of the socially and economically dominant Kikuyu.[5]

Small in number, historically weak, and under pressure from all sides, the Pokot were thus forced up into their rocky, infertile mountain redoubt. But their weakness and vulnerability has made them tough, ruthless, and bold. All their neighbors fear and respect the Pokot because, for at least the last generation or so, they have survived by bringing war to their enemies, raiding and killing far afield, adopting paramilitary tactics, and using the Kenyan-Ugandan border as a sanctuary, crossing back and forth as they wish. In the process of striking back at those who had so long hounded and pressured them, the Pokot began to transform traditional, ritualized, cattle raiding into a modern hybrid of irregular warfare and organized crime.

Now, Pokot war parties raid cattle and ambush vehicles on one side of the border only to slip away and sell their loot on the other side. They make long driving attacks deep into northern Kenya and beat a hasty retreat into the rugged hills of Uganda. They buy weapons and bullets in Uganda to use in Kenya, and cut deals with Ugandan military officers and Kenyan politicians to sell their stolen cattle. The Pokot are unequivocally tough and have a reputation as ruthless. The heaviest losses of the Kenyan military since independence have been sustained during ill-fated campaigns to suppress the Pokot.

Inflamed Anew

For months the Pokot had been raiding hard into sublocation Naipa. Ekaru's people had been hit only one week before. In that attack, an adult and two children were killed. During other recent raids, the Pokot stole a few children, to keep and raise as their own, and took adults who were dismembered and thrown in the path of the stolen cattle herds to be trampled. As a chief at sublocation Naipa explained, this was a cross between a traditional protective curse and modern terrorism.

Pressed up against the edge of Pokot territory, the Turkana group who Ekaru had lived with were feeling grim. Many families had sent their women and children to huddle in a small town and await relief donations while skeleton crews of young men went to guard the herds. These young men, the *moran*, or warriors, ranged in age from about seventeen to forty-five and displayed an array of personal styles: homemade sandals fashioned from discarded tires, tartan skirts, plastic beadwork, and an assortment of T-shirts and paramilitary field jackets ranging from khaki, to camouflage, to marching-band grey, to the faded black, pocket-laden garments of some Nairobi-based private security firm. A few of the *moran* wore small, alpine-style brimmed hats; others bore rows of decorative facial scars. All carried arms: Kalashnikovs with painted and carved wooden stocks or German-made G-3s, powerful rifles with a long range, good for fighting and hunting in the massive open spaces of the Turkana.

The sublocation bore witness to past violence. Just off the dirt track stood the burned-out walls of what had been a school and a dispensary, destroyed in an earlier stage of the war between the Turkana and the Pokot. Through a translator, the *moran* explained what had happened the previous day.

The raid began at mid-morning and lasted six hours. About ninety of the Pokot attacked from two sides, plunging deep into the flat savanna between the hills and the Turkwel River. They moved east and then swept back west toward the hills like an armed human net, driving thousands of animals before them in an attempt to push the cattle through the pass and up into the Karasuk.

If they could get to the pass and up into the hills, they could hold off, or even decimate, any pursuing Turkana warriors. In the hills at the mouth of the canyon, the Pokot had prescouted gun emplacements from which to ambush anyone who gave chase. About two months earlier, just such a Pokot raid, followed by an ambush, had left twenty-six pursuing Turkana dead and fourteen injured.[6]

If the cattle made it into the hills, the raiders would break the stock into smaller herds and scatter deep into the district of West Pokot, and then maybe across the border into Uganda. Or they could sell the beef cattle to brokers with links to abattoirs in Nairobi and keep the sheep and goats for themselves.

As the Pokot moved in, the shooting started. Other Turkana men heard the crack of the AK-47s on single shot and then the high-pitched war cries of the Pokot. Alert to the threat, battered and on edge from a summer of unrelenting violence, aware that they could be reduced to penury in a day if the raid was successful, the *moran* rushed toward the sound of the guns.

As they attacked, the Pokot danced, weaving and bobbing with their guns, ululating and calling out the names of their prize cattle before squeezing off single shots or bursts of three. With only limited ammunition, the Turkana answered the Pokot, snapping off well-aimed single shots, calling out their pledges of valor, their deadly vows, and the descriptions of their prize bulls: *This is for the gray bull with a white face.* If a warrior kills a man, he can then split the drooping ears of his prize bull so the world will know what he has achieved.

The battle ranged over about six kilometers and lasted for several hours of running, hiding, firing, and chasing the cattle. The Pokot were pushing the cattle and "the shorts"—the sheep and goats—west toward the gap in the Karasuk. Stretched out across several kilometers, the Pokot had warriors at the head of the herd, guarding the sides, and in back guarding the rear.

The Turkana, outnumbered and outgunned, ran desperately to get ahead of the raiders, to outflank them, cut them off, block their retreat into the mountains, and scatter the animals before they entered the narrow valley pass. This time it worked. Many of the sheep and goats panicked, but instead of running, they bunched up, each animal trying to hide inside the flock, all of them pressing into a dense, immobilized mass. Other animals got tangled up in the brush.

The Pokot raiders were stuck on the savanna, trying to get the frightened little beasts to move west. But the sheep and goats were too scared and confused; not understanding the human drama around them, they just tried to hide. Brown and white and golden, the little shorts jammed in closer and closer together, the dust rising among them while the Pokot warriors—their own fear mounting as the delay grew more dangerous— kicked, pushed, and yelled at the animals to move. From the brush, Turkana warriors occasionally snapped off harassing rounds. But most of the Turkana men raced past the flocks, running west toward the hills in an attempt to outflank the raiders. They had to beat the Pokot to the mouth of the pass, block their escape, and scatter the herds back onto the savanna.

When the Pokot finally unjammed the stolen flocks and arrived at the pass, the Turkana were there waiting. The two forces collided, the Turkana firing into the Pokot as they came forward. The blocked and furious Pokot rustlers, determined to get the beasts into the pass, fired back.

The raiders were mostly young men led by a group of older, rougher, seasoned veterans. For both sides, everything was at stake. They were fighting for all that is important in life: honor, status, wealth, love, survival, all of it embodied by cattle, which in turn become money and all that money can buy.

Here, nothing happens without cattle. To marry, a young man must provide a bride price in the form of cattle. And if the cattle are few, or scrawny, or there are no special prize bulls among the lot, the young woman will be insulted. To store wealth, one builds up a herd. Animals are currency: if a child needs medicine or an education, you sell or trade cattle. Tobacco, soap, jewelry, clothes, and weapons are all purchased with cattle or the cash from their sale.

The soothsayers, or *emuron*, dream of cattle, smear cattle with mud in their rituals, read the entrails of goats, and receive payment for their services in cattle. A man with many cattle is respected; a man with few cattle is not. A good wife takes care of the herds, fending off disease, nursing ill animals, keeping track of stays. Sons become men and honor their fathers by taking the herds far afield to find pasture and water and returning with all animals safe and accounted for. So the battle—brought on in part by drought, which had reduced the herds and is very linked to climate change—was a fight for everything of value.

As the rounds from the Turkana's guns zipped past all these needs, fears, and passions mixed with a furious will to survive, the Pokot raged forward and straight into the line of Turkana sharpshooters, beyond whom lay the fastness and safety of the Karasuk Hills. For the Turkana it was the same: everything dear to them depended on these cattle now being stolen right in front of them by sworn enemies, thieves, killers who mutilate the dead.

The heavy, tumbling bullets of the Turkana's guns cut down six Pokot raiders. One or two died quickly; one bled out slowly; a few were wounded and no doubt executed point-blank, like Ekaru had been. Three Turkana, including Ekaru, also died. But most of the cattle were scattered and sent back onto the arid scrubland along the Turkwel River. The raid had been another near miss, a calamity avoided in a land where drought and harsh new weather patterns are pushing the old ways of life to the edge of annihilation.

As the Pokot retreated into the hills, they shouted threats of a prompt and lethal return. Some shorts were missing, though as one angry herder let slip, other Turkana had probably stolen these during the chaos of battle. The next day, the *moran* were still wired from the fighting and ready for the next raid. The Pokot war party remained close.

"The Pokot said, 'We did not get enough. Watch out. We'll be back,'" explained one of the men. "Look, we have no bullets. Each bullet costs fifty shillings. Each of us has only one or two bullets left," explained another. The men were now showing me their nearly empty clips. "We need bullets."

For a moment, looking down at Ekaru's corpse, I almost wished I'd brought them some. All I have to offer is a kilo of raw tobacco, which the Turkana mix with salt and chew, roll up into newsprint cigarettes, or smoke in little brass pipes.

Rain Cloud and Kalashnikov

The raid that killed Ekaru Loruman took place in the heart of "the pastoralist corridor," a region of mountains, savannas, marshes, and deserts straddling the borderlands of Kenya, Uganda, Sudan, Ethiopia, and Somalia. Plagued by regular drought and flash flooding, this landscape belongs to well-armed nomadic and seminomadic tribes that live in a delicate balance with each other and their environment. Largely ignored by colonial authorities and modern African states alike, people in this region live much as they always have: cattle are the economic and cultural center of life. The land is generally too dry to farm but can be grazed. The basic socioeconomic unit here is a man, his wives, their children, and their cattle.

The pastoralist corridor, however, is now suffering increasingly extreme weather, marked by drought and sudden flooding, and that puts it on the front lines of the catastrophic convergence where poverty, violence, and climate change combine and collide. Here, the process has resulted in partial state failure and paramilitary violence.[7] This grinding disorder is the expression of a "conflict system," a self-reinforcing political economy of violence that links pastoralists, illegal militias, crime groups, politicians, states, militaries, markets, the aid industry, and climate.[8]

Most major climate models, aggregated by the IPCC, predict this region of Africa will face intensified desertification with the onset of accelerated global warming. The Sahara to the northwest may be greening, but the weather belts to the south appear to be drying. In recent decades, the drought cycle has intensified, even as overall precipitation levels have risen, because a warmer atmosphere holds more water vapor and energy. Now the rain comes all at once, in intense deluges. At the same time, incipient state failure expresses itself as lawlessness, underdevelopment, corruption, and lack of basic services. All of this is epitomized by northern Kenya's proliferating gun culture.

Over the last several decades, drought and flash flooding have become more common in northern Kenya. Most scientists believe this reflects climate change taking hold. The larger and longer-term implications of this new pattern are frightening. Consider the 2006 findings of the UK government's Meteorological Office (or Met Office). Based on vast amounts of data and observation, and produced by a 150-year-long institutional tradition of climatology, the Met Office modeling has found that under current trends, *fully one-third of the planet's land mass will be desert by 2100, while up to half the land surface will suffer drought.* The study also predicts that, during the same period, the proportion of land in "extreme drought" will increase from the current 3 percent to 30 percent.[9]

In 2006, Christian Aid commissioned livestock specialist Dr. David Kimenye to study how Kenyan herders are coping with an increasingly desiccated environment. Kimenye talked to pastoralists in five areas across the Mandera District, in northeastern Kenya (due east of the Turkana) and home to 1.5 million people. He found the following:

- Incidence of drought has increased fourfold in the Mandera region in the past twenty-five years.
- Adverse climatic conditions have already forced one-third of herders living there—around half a million people—to abandon their pastoral way of life.
- During the last drought, so many cattle, camels, and goats were lost that 60 percent of the families who remain as pastoralists need outside assistance to recover. Their surviving herds are too small to support them.[10]

Since 1997, parts of the Kenyan economy have fallen into a prolonged torpor due to inadequate and erratic rainfall. In fact, growth rates in the heavily agricultural economy of Kenya track rainfall almost exactly: normal rains mean normal or robust growth. Bad rains bring economic trouble.[11] A typical US Agency for International Development situation report, dated December 2007, reads, "Northern pastoral areas of Kenya have experienced a below-normal short-rains season. In addition, while control operations are underway, locust swarms in northern Kenya also threaten pastoralists' access to pasture and browse during the upcoming dry season. The impact of the failed March-May cropping season continues to affect the region. Dry weather continues to hamper crop production along the Kenyan coast. Much of the season has already passed and rainfall totals are well below normal."[12]

Kenya by Road

To better understand how climate change and regional political history are shaping local cattle and water wars, I rented a four-wheel-drive vehicle and headed north from Nairobi into the pastoralist corridor. Joining me for the seven-hundred-kilometer trek was a young journalist named Casper Waithaka. A Kikuyu from outside Nairobi, Casper did not speak Turkana, but he did speak Swahili, the lingua franca, and had lived in the Turkana for six months when he was jump-starting his career.

"No one wanted to go there, and there were always *lots* of good stories: rapes, murders, thieving. Lots of good stories. Just take your pick," said Casper, rolling his *r*'s for dramatic effect. He agreed to show me the way to Lodwar, one of the Turkana's main towns. The trip—two days of treacherous, white-knuckle, pothole slalom on small mountain roads dominated by oncoming trucks and buses—offered a rolling lesson in Kenya's physical, social, and economic geography.

Forty minutes outside Nairobi, we ascended the Elgeyo Escarpment, the western wall of the Great Rift Valley. The Rift is not really a valley so much as a region—a thirty-nine-hundred-mile-long, hundreds-of-miles-wide basin created by the separation, or rift, of two tectonic plates. Bounded by mountain ranges and parallel fault lines, the Kenyan part of the basin contains smaller mountains, plateaus, valleys, lakes, rivers, and, up north, desert. Much of the Rift drains south into Lake Victoria.[13] Descending the escarpment, we continued into the cool, moist plateau of the western highlands. The tarmac gave way to stretches of ragged, washed-out, rutted dirt roads.

On the northwest edge of the highlands, we stayed the night at Kitale, a Luhya-dominated farming town surrounded by smoke-shrouded internally displaced person (IDP) camps full of Kikuyu victims of the recent postelectoral pogroms. The Kikuyu are the politically and economically dominant tribe in Kenya, and after the disputed election of December 2008, other tribes rampaged against them. The scars of that convulsion—the blue tarpaulin hovels of the IDP camps, the burnt-out farms and storefronts—belie the Kenyan landscape's peaceful appearance.

The following day, we ascended into the misty Cherangani Hills, Pokot territory, the eastern shoulder of the ice-capped Mount Elgon on the Kenya-Uganda border. There began our final descent into the semidesert of the Turkana, the lowlands of the Rift Valley, and the drive straight north for three hundred more kilometers, on kidney-pulverizing dirt tracks, deeper and deeper into the quiet savanna and the epicenter of the cattle wars.

Turkana

"This is an operational area," said a young officer leaning into my window, scanning the inside of the jeep, then slowly thumbing through my passport. This was the last checkpoint before the badlands.

"You don't have any security. Maybe you should take an escort."

Dozens of travelers have been killed on this road in recent years. Each week the Nairobi papers carry lurid stories of trucks and buses attacked and robbed. Murdered passengers have included priests, politicians, even women and children. As a result it is now typical to travel the worst stretches with armed security. The public buses all carry two well-armed cops. The officers of the Kenyan National Police offer this service in exchange for a $5 or $10 fee. Underpaid and poorly supplied, they need the money badly. Two cops in the backseat may or may not fend off highwaymen, but if you do not accept the assistance, a cop might call ahead to tip off the very same bandits.

"I think it is good to take the security," said Casper.

So I accepted, or rather did not refuse, the offer, and a young policeman named Eric climbed into the backseat. Twenty minutes up the road,

Eric loudly chambered a round into his G3 and pointed the barrel out the window.

Eric had the gloomy affect of occupying soldiers anywhere. He viewed the local population and the desert with a mix of contempt and admiration. "The desert is ugly. Where I am from, you can grow anything," he said.

And what about the people here?

"They have no respect for life. They will kill you just as easily as they would kill a goat. And they are all sharpshooters." He explained that three officers from his post, including a commander, had died in recent months fighting Turkana cattle raiders. "We called in helicopters and reinforcements."

Why is it so violent here?

"Drought," said Eric. "Tradition, lack of education, and drought. And Uganda can't control its border."

His explanation made sense: without rain, the browse and grass decline; the herds grow weak and die. To replenish their stocks, the young men go raiding. All around stood dead acacia trees, gray skeletons. At intervals along the road we passed tall, hard-faced Turkana women selling long, thin burlap bags of charcoal. Stalked by famine, they now burn the drought-stricken trees into charcoal.

We dropped Eric off in the scorching roadside town of Lokichar. Our next escort was a police reservist, an older Turkana with a weather- and alcohol-battered face. He carried an AK-47 and two full clips of ammunition, and he wanted a ride out into the bush so he could check on his cattle.

He said he was assigned to guard buses going to the Sudanese boarder. Not long ago, he had been on a bus that was ambushed. Thieves had stepped into the road and shot out the tires and into the windshield. The passengers all hit the floor, while the police reservist and his comrade fired back at the highwaymen, straight through the smashed up windshield. "We killed one and drove away the other two," said the old reservist. "The dead one was Sudanese. You could tell by the markings on his face."

Then, in the middle of nowhere, the old man asked us to stop. "I get out here." And with that, he tramped off into the bush.

The Nomad Town

Eventually, we reach Lodwar, the heart of the Turkana. The town sits at the junction of the A-1 and the Turkwel River. Small and compact, Lodwar has a strange vitality. The town is nothing much, but it is the big city and bright lights for this area. Its main road and the one-lane steel span bridge across the muddy Turkwel River are clogged with herders and their thick flocks of goats and sheep. Improbably rugged trucks and diesel buses, packed with people and piled high with luggage, stop over in Lodwar on their way in and out of South Sudan. The town is dense with hardware stores selling buckets, knives, axes, shovels, rope, aluminum pots, brightly striped plastic water jugs, and bolts of cloth; grubby little restaurants; and foul-smelling open-air bars where patrons hide from the sun behind roughhewn latticework. A few thick old trees loom over the unpaved streets. At night the slowly passing cars stir up dust that floats in the glow of the headlights, giving Lodwar a gloomy, ghostly, narcotic ambience.

In Lodwar I meet Lucas Ariong, head of the small peace-building NGO Riam Riam. Tall and thin, Lucas has handsome, almost delicate features, but his face is splashed with scars, as if a bottle was once smashed on it.

"These are resource conflicts," said Lucas, referring to the cattle wars. "And now the climate is changing. The rains are late; the land is turning to desert. People are burning the acacia trees for charcoal, killing each other for control of waterholes."

Lucas's concern about the raiding cycles is personal: his father was killed in a raid when Lucas was young. Many of his friends have died in raids. And Lucas owns "about 50 cows" and many more shorts, all kept under the watchful eyes of armed men, his sons, and hired hands.

To explain the crisis, Lucas brings out a sheaf of UN-commissioned maps that show the locations of pasture, water holes, salt licks, rivers, roads, arable land, small towns, schools, clinics, and the appallingly low ratio of teachers and medics to population. The maps also indicate the raiding corridors and tribal boundaries, which sometimes overlap with water and pasture resources and thus define the front lines of the Turkana's little climate-driven resource wars.

Lucas pointed out the sites of several recent conflicts: up in the northwest, the Ugandan military had just crossed over into Kenya and bombed a Turkana cattle camp, probably in hot pursuit of Turkana rustlers who had been preying on Ugandan Kalenjins. In the summer of 2007, cross-border raids even compelled the governments of Uganda and Kenya to negotiate cattle swaps. To the south, the Pokot have been stealing cattle and ambushing vehicles. From the north and northeast, guns are smuggled in from South Sudan and Somalia; ammunition is readily available due east in Uganda. The conflict system took on visual form.

What should the state do?

"More wells. We needed boreholes," said Lucas. "The issue is drought."

The Land of Raiding

The annals of northern Kenya's drought-fueled violence—its little climate war—grow by the day. Here are reports culled from just one month in late summer 2008:

> *August 5:* Seventy-four people are dead in a weekend of attacks on three villages in Lokori Division, Turkana South District. More than twenty-two hundred cattle are stolen.
>
> *August 12:* Pokot raiders gun down more than thirty Turkana herdsmen at Lokori Division, in Turkana South District. Scores of others are believed wounded; seven hundred head of cattle are stolen.
>
> *August 20:* Turkana raiders attack herders at Galasa water point, stealing more than twenty thousand animals. Security forces give chase; eight local police reservists and raiders are killed.
>
> *August 22:* The Ugandan military kill ten and wound four Turkana pastoralists who cross the border in search of water and pasture. Ugandan soldiers steal four hundred animals.
>
> *August 24–30:* A raiding party of more than one thousand Sudanese Toposa tribesmen crosses into Kenya; over the next week, they attack

two villages, kill eight people, abduct three children, and steal an estimated five thousand animals in Lokichoggio, northwestern Turkana.

September 2: Two police reservists are killed repelling other Toposa raiders who have crossed in from southern Sudan.

September 4: Pokot raiders kill two people in Kotaruk and steal more than six hundred animals.[14]

In mid-2007, the Small Arms Survey, a project of the Graduate Institute of International Studies in Geneva, conducted research among households along the Sudan-Kenya border. The survey sought to measure the social impacts of small-arms proliferation. It found epidemic gunplay with "both actual and perceived levels of insecurity . . . significantly worse on the Kenyan side of the border than they were in South Sudan, which is recovering from a 21-year civil war." Sixty percent of respondents had witnessed a cattle raid, and more than 60 percent said that disarmament would decrease security.[15]

If this isn't war, it is something close.

CHAPTER 5

Monsoons and Tipping Points

Now I am become death the destroyer of worlds.

—*Vishnu in the Bhagavad Gita, as quoted by Robert J. Oppenheimer*

EAST AFRICA, KENYA in particular, has complicated weather. To learn how it works, I visited the headquarters of the Meteorological Department. The place is deceptively calm—here, they are concerned with the clouds. But in agriculturally dependent Kenya, clouds rule the lives of people, sometimes with devastating consequence. At the end of a long hall in a forecasting room flanked by rows of humming old PCs, I met Chief Meteorologist James Muhindi. Like Muhindi's flared blazer and hint of sideburns, the machines seem a decade or so out-of-date. With more that thirty years on the job, Muhindi knows the quirky details of Kenyan weather like he knows his family. "We have so many microclimates," he said with a mix of exasperation and national pride. "Climate plays a key role in socioeconomic activity—our economy is very weather dependent. Most Kenyan farmers rely on the two rainy seasons, one in the spring, the other in autumn."

Over 70 percent of Kenya's working population is employed in agriculture or closely related sectors. The primary products are tea, coffee, corn, wheat, sugarcane, fruit, vegetables, dairy products, beef, pork, poultry, and eggs, and the big cash export, cut flowers. Most of this agriculture is rain fed rather than irrigated, and as Muhindi put it in the *Rainfall Atlas for Kenya*, "Failure of rains and occurrence of drought during any growing season often lead to severe food shortages and loss of animals if there is lack of strategic planning."[1] Though there is an acute shortage of long-term economic and social planning in Kenya, the country does have a fairly good famine-response system, linking government, business, and the international aid industry.

Delivering emergency food can take up to six months. If famine is not anticipated well in advance, even a rapid and robust response will come too late, and thousands may die. The Meteorological Office's most important mission is to detect early warning signs so that the famine-response system—including local administrators, the aid agencies, and transport companies—can prepare. Even subtle indications of late rains or sudden floods can trigger food-security early-warning and mitigation procedures. The gears of the mighty international aid industry will begin to turn—as fast as they can, but still rather slowly.

Life, Death, and Clouds

When Kenya's climate follows a normal pattern, most of the country has two rainy seasons, or bimodal rainfall. The first season running from March to May is known as the "Long Rains"; then, from October to December come the "Short Rains."

The planet's climate system is extremely complex and interconnected, but if a single force could be said to rule East Africa's weather patterns, it would be the Intertropical Convergence Zone (ITCZ). In simple terms the ITCZ is a belt of high humidity, low pressure, and calm winds that girds the equatorial latitudes of the planet. It is produced by the collision of the northeast and southeast trade winds—masses of warm, moist tropical air—both of which move toward the equator. When they collide, the horizontal airflows give way to vertical rising air.[2] The wet, warm air rises to form a belt of clouds that varies from about twenty to two hundred miles in width: it tends to move more over the landmass of Africa and narrow in the Americas and across the Pacific. These clouds produce rain.[3]

The point of maximum condensation and precipitation within the ITCZ—the zone's core cloud belt—follows the path of the overhead sun.

When directly overhead, the sun produces the maximum amount of heat on the ground below. That means more warm air rising, carrying more evaporated water and thus producing more condensation and precipitation.

That core belt of clouds oscillates north and south across the equator, following the sun's annual transit from the Tropic of Cancer—which lies at 23.5 degrees north and is the northernmost latitude at which the sun appears directly overhead—down across the equator, to the Tropic of Capricorn—lying at 23.5 degrees south, which is, conversely, the southernmost latitude at which the sun appears directly overhead. As the sun moves, it pulls the ITCZ's center of precipitation with it.[4] On the ground in Kenya, this oscillation produces the two rainy seasons. But as average global surface temperatures rise, the ITCZ is falling out of rhythm.

"Key to it all," explained Muhindi, hunched in front of one of the bulky old PCs, "is the Pacific. The Pacific is the mother of all oceans, and the other oceans, the children, obey her signals. When the Pacific warms and there is an El Niño effect off Peru, the monsoon and trade winds in the Indian Ocean increase, and there is strong wind, more rain, and flooding here in East Africa. With La Niña, the ocean off Peru cools, the winds weaken, and less water reaches East Africa, and we tend to have drought."

Though Kenya is suffering more droughts in recent decades, it is actually receiving greater amounts of precipitation. But the rainfall is arriving in sudden bursts, massive shocks in which the rain falls hard and all at once rather than gradually over a season. This brings flooding that strips away topsoil, followed by drought. "We see it here from the weather station reports," explained Muhindi. "Extreme weather events are more frequent, like the severe 1997–1998 floods and the 1999–2000 drought."[5] In short, the clockwork rains upon which Kenyan society depends are out of sync.

A bevy of local factors also shape Kenyan weather, among them deforestation. Logging of forests in the Congo Basin and across East Africa minimizes water storage, evaporation, condensation, and regionally generated precipitation. Higher local temperatures mean less snow on Mounts Kilimanjaro, Kenya, and Elgon, thus more sudden runoff, more flooding, and then lower dry-season river levels. "The best we can do to adapt to climate change is maintain our forest cover," concluded Muhindi.

Feedback Loops and Tipping Points

I was in Kenya in 2008, and when the Short Rains of that year finally arrived, they hit with tremendous force: flash floods left 300,000 people in need of relief aid. Landslides and floods displaced hundreds. Flooded pit latrines fouled many shallow wells, and typhoid was soon killing people. That year packed a one-two punch: drought chased down with violent flooding. By January 2009, 10 million people needed food aid to fend off starvation.[6] According to the Kenya Meteorological Department, "above-average temperatures in the Indian Ocean" had caused the heavy rains.[7]

Were the Kenyan calamities of that year definitively linked to climate change? No. The climate system is too complicated to blame any one weather event on anthropogenic climate change. But the trend lines all head in the same direction: as atmospheric carbon dioxide (CO_2) rises, average temperatures increase and weather patterns become less stable.

Many civilizations have lived in the shadow of their own end-time narratives, and it is tempting to describe climate change as just such a vision, only played out in a secularized aesthetic. But climate change is real, and our understanding of how it is happening is based on very serious and reliable science. And the unraveling of the current climate system seems to be happening faster than scientists had predicted.

It is worth reviewing the facts once more. Researchers from a variety of disciplines—meteorologists, oceanographers, paleontologists, biologists, and so forth—are together arriving at fairly firm conclusions about how our climate works, what its history has been, and where it is probably headed due to our massive emissions of greenhouse gases. They note that Earth's climate is warming, and this will have consequences soon—for most of us, *within our lifetimes.*

The outline of the scientific consensus runs as follows: For the last 650,000 years atmospheric levels of CO_2—the primary heat-trapping gas in Earth's environment—have hovered between 180 and 300 parts per million (ppm). At no point in the preindustrial era did CO_2 concentrations go above 300 ppm. By 1959 they had reached 316 ppm and are now at 390 ppm. At current rates, CO_2 levels will double by mid-century.

Climate scientists believe that any increase in average global temperatures beyond 2°C (35.6°F) above preindustrial levels will lead to dangerous climate change, causing large-scale desertification, crop failure, inundation of coastal cities, widespread extinctions, proliferating disease, and possible social collapse. They fear that beyond the 2°C threshold, climate change could become self-reinforcing due to positive-feedback loops.

Scientists now understand that ecosystems, and Earth's climate as a whole, do not always operate according to a smooth linear logic. Instead, natural systems are prone to rapid and sudden shifts. The population of a species can decline slowly or collapse rapidly, almost at once. Witness the near total disappearance of bat colonies in the northeastern United States due to the white nose fungus or the sudden decline of honeybee populations in recent years. Both problems can hopefully be reversed, but they illustrate how quickly natural systems can break down.

Throughout the climate system there exist dangerous positive-feedback loops and tipping points. A positive-feedback loop is a dynamic in which effects compound, accelerate, or amplify the original cause. Tipping points in the climate system reflect the fact that causes can build up while effects lag. Then, when the effects kick in, they do so all at once, causing the relatively sudden shift from one climate regime to another. The worst-case scenario, though not the most unlikely, would see positive-feedback loops accelerate climate change to a tipping point beyond which the process would be self-propelling and impossible to reverse, no matter what we do.[8]

Two Degrees Celsius

Around 125,000 years ago, average global temperature was only about 1°C higher than it is today, but the sea level was fully four to six meters higher. Any heating beyond 2°C will likely cause catastrophic changes, transformations too sudden and radical for civilization to cope with. The 2°C threshold runs throughout the most recent reports from the Intergovernmental Panel on Climate Change (IPCC), and it is the official stabilization target of numerous governments and the European Union.[9]

The question then becomes, What is the corresponding limit on atmospheric concentrations of CO_2? For years it was assumed to be around 450 ppm. To meet this goal, the IPCC recommends that developed countries reduce their greenhouse gas emissions to about 40 to 90 percent below 1990 levels by 2050. This would require global targets of at least 10 percent reductions in emissions per decade—starting now. Those sorts of emissions reductions have only been associated with economic depressions. Russia's near total economic collapse in the early 1990s saw a 5 percent per annum decline in CO_2 emissions.[10]

Calculations by the United Kingdom's Tyndall Centre for Climate Change Research demonstrate that, without radical mitigation efforts, we are almost inevitably on course to reach atmospheric CO_2 levels of 450 ppm. Even with drastic emissions reductions over the next 20 years, cumulative atmospheric CO_2 could easily surpass 450 ppm.[11] If that's not grim enough, James Hansen of NASA's Goddard Institute for Space Studies at Columbia University now believes the tipping point at which climate change becomes a runaway, self-fueling process is closer to 350 ppm. We are already at 390 ppm.[12] In terms of adaptation, that would mean we must prepare to deal with a 4°C increase in average global temperatures and the massive social dislocations that will bring.

Bone-Eating Storks

Across northern Kenya there are various responses to drought and flooding—some more violent than others. In the Turkana, people live amidst the gun culture and raiding cycle. But further east, near the desert outpost of Garissa, despite devastated herds and brutal drought, violence is relatively uncommon.[13] To find out more about that equation, I drove the 375 kilometers out to Garissa with an American photojournalist, Dan McCabe, and a Kenyan friend of his named Tim. We reached Garissa as the sun was setting. The town begins at a checkpoint and a narrow bridge over the wide, shallow waters of the river Tana. Its waters rise hundreds of miles away, among the snows, rains, and mist of Mount Kenya. By the time it drains to Garissa, it is the desert's main lifeline.

Guarding the bridge were huge, blue and white, buzzard-like creatures called marabou storks; massive flocks of them perched everywhere. They look like pelicans, have ten-foot wingspans, and do not sing or squawk. The only sound they make comes from the occasional clacking of their huge beaks.

Marabous are "colony breeders," and they like to live near people. The storks scavenge carrion from the drought-felled cattle and are known to carry bones high into the sky, then drop them onto rocks to break them open and scrape out the marrow. In town, perched on the bare, desiccated acacia trees, the birds seemed to be the mascots of drought. As if to highlight the theme of scarcity even further, it was Ramadan, the month of fasting and nicotine withdrawal; in Garissa most people are ethnic Somali Muslims. Not only was it hard to find beer, but there was no food or coffee available by day.

The next morning we pushed out past the town into the desert. The road soon turned soft and sandy. Again, the flattop acacia trees were all dead and bleached, like standing driftwood, and cast an eerie blue sheen, the empty sky reflecting off the pale wood. Shepherd boys waved us down with their empty plastic jugs hoping we were from an NGO with water.

About fifty kilometers north of Garissa, on the road toward the lawless border with Somalia, we reached Shambary, a Somali village—or, really, a nomadic pastoralist camp that was turning into a village as the herds died and were replaced by aid. The village consisted of little more than a collection of stick-and-burlap huts clustered around a big tree and two small adobe buildings: a one-room schoolhouse and a clinic, both empty for lack of staff. Not far away was the water pan, a football-field-sized pit of dust that was supposed to catch rainwater. The only things keeping these people alive were the occasional relief handouts and a barely functioning borehole well. In the pounding heat, one felt as if the sun itself hated Shambary.

The headman said the rains had not come for two years. His herd had dropped from fifty cows to three. Twenty men had, as he put it, "gone mad and just walked away," abandoning their families. Some of the other men listening to the interview laughed nervously when he said this.

Interestingly, there had been no violence here. When I asked about this, people attributed the relative peace to Islam. A combination of other factors is, I believe, more important: Proximity to a mostly paved road linking Nairobi and the port of Mombasa allowed aid to reach them and offered avenues of escape for men seeking waged work. Proximity to the Tana River and its thin border of flood plain allowed some to farm. Also, the village had organized a water committee to manage the borehole and hash out who got water, when, and in what amounts, and to raise money to buy diesel for the pump. Perhaps this collective organization helped prevent violence by keeping the community united rather than allowing young men to peel off in small groups to raid.

But the most powerful factor limiting violence, I suspect, is simply the physical barrier of the desert. The dying savanna around Shambary is vast and so dry that transiting stolen cattle across it would be very difficult. Trapped by the pounding heat and sandy wastes, rival clans are essentially quarantined to their boreholes, the banks of the Tana, and the roadside "aid camps" that have formed around food-relief distribution points. These pastoralists were peaceful because they were essentially dropouts, in the process of giving up the cattle-centered nomadic life—raiding and everything else.

Evidence that peace is a by-product of ecological and economic collapse (rather than the pacific teachings of Islam) is found seven hundred kilometers further north, in the small city of Mandera on the Somalia-Kenya border. There, Kenyan Somali pastoralists, also Muslims, are engaged in all-out cattle raiding and a bloody little resource war. Every day brings new reports of clans fighting pitched battles and burning down each other's villages: the Garre clan against the Murulle. Both are attempting to control the overstretched Lulis Dam. The violence has been intense since 2005, punctuated only by occasional punitive military operations and failed peace talks. Over one thousand families have fled the area.[14]

Sifting for Causality

A central question in understanding climate change and conflict is whether violence is a response primarily to scarcity or to opportunity. Do the

Turkana raid because they *lack* cattle or because their neighbors *have* cattle to steal?

Two anthropologists who studied Marsabit District in north-central Kenya found that drought and scarcity were actually associated with a decline in raiding. The authors, Adanoo Roba and Karen Witsenburg, found "no evidence that violence is increasing in relative terms, nor that ethnic violence is related to environmental scarcity."[15] Instead of scarcity causing conflict among Samburu pastoralists, it led to greater cooperation, as communities came together both physically, congregating at the boreholes for water, and politically, in the organizations demanded by formal water management. Roba and Witsenburg emphasize history, human agency, complexity, and specificity and are careful not to generalize beyond the district where they did their research. That said, the village of Shambary would support their thesis.

Not even Thomas Homer-Dixon, the scholar most associated with the argument that scarcity drives violence, argues a simple one-to-one causal relationship. Instead he attempts to tease out the attenuated links between climate, economic scarcity, state policy, and violent social conflict. Here is a good encapsulation of his thinking: "Falling agricultural production, migration to urban areas, and economic contraction in regions severely affected by scarcity often produce hardship, and this hardship increases demands on the state. At the same time, scarcity can interfere with state revenue streams by reducing economic productivity and therefore taxes; it can also increase the power and activity of 'rent-seekers,' who become more able to deny tax revenues on their increased wealth and to influence state policy in their favour. Environmental scarcity therefore increases society's demands on the state while decreasing [the state's] ability to meet those demands."[16] Thus, in Homer-Dixon's formulation, environmental crisis is *displaced* through time and space: rural resource crises are often expressed as urban ethnic, religious, or political struggles over state revenues and services.

Looking more specifically at pastoralist violence in Kenya, Kennedy Agade Mkutu focuses in his fine book *Guns and Governance* on the role of small-arms availability in driving conflict; at the same time, he places environmental factors front and center. Mkutu argues that "when drought and famine and disease reduce the herds, the people must get more through raiding."[17]

Historians of Kenya find the same. David Anderson, one of the most famous scholars of colonial East Africa, noted an increase in cattle theft during droughts. The pattern of violence seemed to be driven by a combination of need and opportunity. During drought, in decades past as well as today, herds became more concentrated around the few available water holes. With that, the opportunity to steal the neighbors' stock increased. "Opportunist theft from other Africans required no planning or organization beyond the ability of members of a family or a group of herders to seize cattle belonging to others carelessly herded near their own stock. Such thefts were most common in the vicinity of watering places, salt licks, and dry-season grazing areas shared with other herders. Drought tended to afford greater opportunities for this type of theft, when pastoralist resources were scarce and livestock belonging to different peoples more likely to be temporarily congested together."[18]

Gangsters

"Traditional" Rift Valley cattle raiding does not exist in a vacuum. From as early as the 1920s, raiding has had links to the cash economy, the economic life of towns and cities, national markets and even international trade. Very often the facilitating groups are organized-crime networks or political bosses. "By the 1930s," writes Anderson, "theft was being committed not just as a means of wealth accumulation for the individuals involved, but as part of a wider system of trade to supply livestock to parts of East Africa where demand was high."[19] So it is to this day.

In the high, misty mountain town of Kapenguria, the capital of West Pokot, I met Edward Koech, a journalist for the Kenyan daily, the *Nation*. We lunched on thick greasy meat stew and blocks of soft *ugali*, the heavy corn mash that is the East African staple. The restaurant was full of quiet, hard-looking Pokots. After lunch, we decamped to my small 4x4 and parked on a side road to talk.

Though of the Nandi tribe, Koech has deep links to the Pokot power structure and knows the political economy of West Pokot. He confirmed that powerful businessmen and politicians fund cattle raids, commissioning seasoned warriors to organize and train groups of young men from the countryside, who then set out on extended two- and three-week missions into the Turkana or Uganda. The captured livestock are resold in Kampala and Nairobi.

Koech said that the last five years had been very dry in Pokot territory. (Remember, Kenya has notoriously localized weather patterns that can vary almost from district to district.) Compared to normal times, West Pokot is lately either dry or getting pounded with heavy rains and flooding. This erratic weather makes farming, already difficult on these thin soils, even more challenging. And so, for West Pokot, raiding is good business.

The police, NGO personnel, and Turkana pastoralists themselves all told me that when they tracked stolen herds into the Karasuk Hills it was not uncommon to find the animals' trails ending at informal corrals away from which led the tire tracks of big transport trucks. The implication was that some Pokot raiders delivered the herds, prearranged, to professional resellers. Anecdotal evidence also suggests that Ugandan military officers keep prize Turkana bulls, confiscating them as a tax from Pokot rustlers who have crossed illegally into Uganda.

Thus, trade circuits and social networks link the myriad local conflicts across the pastoralist corridor to organized-crime structures, political bosses, regional military groups, and legitimate markets. The influence of urban-based sub-rosa economics upon raiding reveals not merely a one-way displacement (*pace* Homer-Dixon), from the countryside to the city, but a continual back-and-forth exchange of crises, from the rural economy to the urban, then back to the rural. Within this conflict system, climate change is beginning to act as a radical accelerant, like gasoline on a smoldering fire.

CHAPTER 6

The Rise and Fall of East African States

> I would annex the planets if I could; I often think of that.
> It makes me sad to see them so clear and yet so far.
>
> —CECIL RHODES, *last will and testament, 1902*

THE EAST AFRICAN conflict system is a specific and evolving political economy of violence that links pastoralists, militias, organized crime, political elites, markets, and changing climatological patterns. Its historical evolution illustrates elements of the catastrophic convergence—the collision of poverty, violence, and climate change—which is to say, the imbrications of neoliberal economic restructuring and Cold War militarism with the effects of global warming. The recent disruptions of the Intertropical Convergence Zone, for example, play out on a stage set by human history. Thus there can be no proper understanding of the social effects of climate change without some knowledge of the concrete history of the places where these climatological changes are happening. And no plans for adaptation or mitigation can be successfully developed or implemented without such history.

Returning to the whodunit question posed by the dead man, Ekaru Loruman, we might ask, Why is the Turkana region of Kenya awash in firearms? The short answer is this: Uganda, South Sudan, and Somalia all have been, or still are, failed states. All hemorrhaged small arms into Kenya.

Next question: Why and how did these states form, transform, and collapse? This history shapes the current conditions of East African societies and thus informs their ability to adapt to climate change.

Creating Kenya

The British annexation of East Africa began in the early 1890s. The Berlin Conference of 1885 set off the European "Scramble for Africa." As part of this, Queen Victoria's government chartered the Imperial East Africa Company under Scottish shipping magnate Sir William Mackinnon, who then controlled more tonnage than anyone in the world. The company's task was to open what is now Kenya and Uganda to exploitation and possible settlement.[1] Beginning in 1888, the East Africa Company attempted to take hold of parts of what is now Uganda but quickly antagonized the local Kikuyu tribes along the way. When Sir Gerald Portal passed through the area, he blamed the company for provoking violence "by refusing to pay for things." He wrote that "by raiding, looting, swashbuckling and shooting natives, the Company have turned the whole country against the white man."[2]

The company failed and faced financial collapse. Colonization only began in earnest in 1895, when the British Foreign Office (and then the Colonial Office in 1905) took charge. London's main interest was strategic: controlling the Nile headwaters and thus, theoretically, supporting British interests downriver in Sudan and Egypt. Toward this end, a railroad was built from costal Mombasa into Kisumu on Lake Victoria. Completed in 1901, the railway quickly opened the country to white settlement, commercial exploitation, and political pacification. A contemporary article explained, "The Uganda railway, in addition to the political effects of its construction, must have, and indeed already has had, a marked effect on the habits and mode of life of the natives. It has brought them into immediate contact with civilization, and opened up possibilities of trade. It has calmed inter-tribal animosities, and checked the feudatory raids of the aggressive races. It has opened up the whole of the countries lying near the coast-line of the Victoria Nyanza Lake to comparatively easy communication with the sea and with Europe."[3]

In this regard, the railway, though a single line, acted as a socioeconomic fence, enclosing and transforming the regions around it: local forms of economic production were destroyed, displaced, or incorporated as subsets of the growing international capitalist economy.[4] By 1907, white settlers were pouring in. Through force of law, taxation, and economic might these settlers took possession of what are now the highlands of central Kenya. From 1895 to 1903, British forces conducted regular "punitive expeditions." This use of force was central to wresting land from African hands, though not necessarily in the direct fashion of, say, the Belgian campaigns of violent theft in the Congo. More often than not, the actual transfer of land from Africans to settlers involved legerdemain, haggling, cooperation, and co-optation, all conducted against the backdrop of violence. In the process, some African elites even made out well.

John Lonsdale, another doyen of East African history, describes the nuance as follows: "What transpired on the battlefield then, when the Hotchkiss or Maxim was assembled or the bayonet charge went in; when the thatch was fired or the cattle captured—all this was of fundamental importance in establishing a sense of mastery or subordination. But force was not power. Power comes not by a single act of confrontation but by repeated transactions within some ordered set of social relations; its costs and benefits must at least carry the possibility of calculation and prediction."[5] In other words, states are born of violence, but they cannot be made solely of violence.

Along with colonial administration from Britain, white settlers established their own local government of sorts, the Legislative Council, which worked with London, but also against it. At their height, some 350,000 whites lived in Kenya. It was they who most antagonized and directly exploited the native population.[6] London and Nairobi bickered constantly about military expenses and the low economic productivity of the white farmers. "In its first nine years military costs swallowed nearly one-third of the Protectorate's budget; they exceeded local revenue, and were chiefly to blame for the tripling of the annual Imperial subsidy in the five years from 1896."[7]

Using Crisis, Seeding Crisis

Aiding British political consolidation—which is to say, the eventual formation of a modern state system in East Africa—was the ecological crisis
of the 1890s, when drought, livestock diseases, and smallpox killed almost
a quarter of the native people in central Kenya. The survivors were desperate for patrons both for defense against raids and for access to resources.
"In the devastated areas of Kenya the British happened to be the best patrons available. . . . They had also come as conquerors."[8]

As local modes of production spun into crisis, the settler class used its
money to buy up land. But the white farms were often ineptly run and un-
profitable. To protect themselves against economic competition, the settler-
controlled Legislative Council imposed harsh economic handicaps on
native farmers. For example, Africans were totally prohibited from raising
coffee. On top of that, the settlers demanded and received subsidies from
London, and thus the British economy as a whole.

The effect of these coddling, racist restrictions and subsidies was to re-
tard development of a functional capitalist economy within the colony. The
matrix of protection established by and for the settlers was only removed
in the 1930s, when the buildup to World War II triggered a global commodity boom. Britain needed raw materials and food imports more than it
needed a white African cowboy aristocracy. As Colin Leys has shown,
when black farmers were finally allowed to compete for and produce a
share of exports, Kenya's economic growth took off.[9]

Kikuyu Pushback

By the 1950s, the Kikuyu, who had been deracinated from the highlands
by white settlers, had nonetheless created something of a merchant, farming, and town-based intellectual leadership, and they began to agitate for
greater political rights. This was met with repression, and soon many
Kikuyu turned to guerrilla warfare.

The Mau Mau rebellion, as this uprising was known, provoked a brutal
and sophisticated counterinsurgency. Whites called it "the Emergency," and

the internal siege was replete with armed sweeps, terror squads, mass deten-
tion, torture, reeducation and the use of small, elite counterguerilla units.
The official casualty figure was 11,503 killed; however, scholars now put the
number much higher.[10] David Anderson settles on 20,000. Caroline Elikin's
Pulitzer Prize–winning *Imperial Reckoning: The Untold Story of Britain's
Gulag in Kenya* estimates the dead to have numbered 70,000 or more.[11] The
Mau Mau were crushed, but they put Kenya on schedule for full independ-
ence and the end for white minority rule in East Africa.

As decolonization approached, the authorities began negotiations with
their former adversary, Jomo Kenyatta. During the Emergency, white officials had demonized Kenyatta as a madman, a Mau Mau, and a communist and put him under house arrest. In reality Kenyatta was a liberal
nationalist, who, once released, acted as Britain's reasonable native inter-
locutor. The final arrangements of independence protected settler wealth
and gave settlers who wished to leave the option to sell their property at
market prices. To pay off these departing landlords, the new Kenyan government borrowed money from the United Kingdom. Acquired assets—
land and businesses—were mostly distributed to a new Kikuyu ruling
class, who were also heavily represented in Kenyatta's new government,
and the Kenya African National Union, which was the ruling party until
2002. This dominant position partially explains—but in no way justifies—
the pogroms against Kikuyus in 2007; once again, class antagonisms took
ethnic form.

Decline of Old Raiding

By 1909 colonial administrators had established the Collective Punishment Ordinance that attempted to stop raiding by levying punitive fines
on whole communities.[12] Colonial files at the National Archives in
Nairobi are full of reports from District Officers detailing an endless flow
of tit-for-tat attacks between the tribes. British officials routinely held
hearings, issued reports, detained suspects, levied fines, pursued fugitives,
and sternly admonished local subchiefs, who were usually leaders appointed
by the British.

The historical trend of East African cattle violence is difficult to measure with total accuracy—the records are incomplete, skewed, and tainted—
but there is evidence of a relative decline in raiding from about the late
1920s until the early 1970s. Steady expansion of the state's administrative
capacity and the absorption of ever more people into the formal labor market seem to have cut down on the violence. The British created legally de-
lineated "group ranches" designed to separate warring tribes and bring about
the economic integration of pastoralists. As more of them became wage laborers and commodity producers, the importance of cattle theft fell away.

An increase in police, courts, taxes, wage labor, identification papers,
conscription, jails, health care, water management, primary education, vet-
erinary services, and livestock-improvement programs—in short the matrix of governance—quelled the traditional raiding, even as it sometimes
gave rise to other, new forms of violence. The countryside was administra-
tively *contained* and thus controlled. The Turkana and other pastoralists
were partially absorbed into Kenyan society, and their traditional cultural
modes were subsumed by capitalist economic relations and the state's general regimentation of society.[13]

Yet in postcolonial Kenya, the pastoralists of the North remained pe-
ripheral—for better and for worse—largely neglected, though operating
within the half-present social and judicial confines of a modern state complete with schools, laws, clinics, roads, game parks, and a cash economy.
But the state's administrative grip on these lands and populations would
weaken considerably starting in the late 1970s, when a series of El Niño–
Southern Oscillation–linked droughts began. With that, cattle raiding
started to increase once again.

The Guns of Uganda

The British also controlled Uganda until the early 1960s. During the late
1970s it was from independent Uganda that the first flood of guns would
enter the Turkana region and much of northern Kenya. What is now
Uganda once comprised the former kingdom of Buganda plus a few other
African principalities and feudal states, all of which had fallen under

British suzerainty through a mix of coercion, cooperatation, and economic might.

By the mid-1950s, Uganda's old native elite and educated middle classes were watching the progress of the Kenyan Mau Mau, and the brutal campaign against them, with keen interest. The Kenyan rebels served as a cautionary tale for both Africans and white authorities. When Ugandans began agitating for greater political participation and full independence, British authorities wisely made preparations for a scheduled decolonization that began in the late 1950s. Uganda remained a British protectorate until 1962 but thereafter was an independent state.

The first president was an old African aristocrat, Sir Edward Mutesa, who had once been a regional king; his prime minister was the left-leaning nationalist Milton Obete, who nationalized large parts of the economy but was also known for corruption. In 1971 the infamous military officer Idi Amin Dada seized power, and there began a slide toward chaos.[14]

Born in about 1925 in northern Uganda, as a boy Amin went to primary school and tended his family's goats. In 1944, he enlisted in the Kings African Rifles, a British colonial regiment that served in East Africa and, during the world wars, elsewhere. Amin saw action in Burma and returned a corporal. He went on to become the local military heavyweight-boxing champion, participated in punitive expeditions against restive tribes in northern Uganda and, in 1953, fought the Mau Mau. Upon his return from Kenya in 1957, preparations for independence were under way in Uganda, and as a prominent noncommissioned officer, Amin was groomed for high rank in the Ugandan Army. By 1964, he was a top commander and ran secret missions into Congo/Zaire in support of the Simbas, a group of pro-Lumumba rebels fighting against the emerging kleptocracy of Mobutu Sese Seko. But mostly, Amin seems to have used his time in Congo to vacuum up ivory and gold.[15]

As soon as Amin had political control of Uganda, he began to threaten neighboring Tanzania.[16] Domestically, Amin's regime was marked by medieval savagery and modern weaponry. At first his repression had a political logic: violence was directed toward specific socioeconomic ends and served the dominant economic interests. But Amin was, ultimately, insane: a big, roly-poly, smiling, cherubic, khaki-clad sociopath in charge of what would become one of sub-Saharan Africa's largest armies. The Ugandan state quickly became personalistic, clique ridden, peculating, bribe taking, and vicious. In seven short years, Amin's Uganda would epitomize and foreshadow the kleptocracy that would dishonor much of postcolonial Africa. It was the worst of Mobutu-style, Big Man politics in which a leader's obligations are "first and foremost, to kith and kin, their clients, their communities, their regions, or even to their religion"—but not to the nation as such.[17]

Prior to 1971, Uganda had exported reasonable amounts of cotton, copper, sugar, and various other agricultural products. All that began to decline due to the military government's idiotic mismanagement and looting of the public sector. Soon state repression had spun out of control. In 1972 Amin attacked and expelled the country's South Asians, in a smash-and-grab pogrom called Operation Mafuta Mingi. The soldiers at the heart of the state now owned expropriated Asian businesses but did not manage them in any formal sense.

The regime's one concrete goal, in addition to the personal enrichment of its officialdom, was a colossal military buildup. The Soviets gave Amin generous aid toward that end, just as Western companies made money selling him weapons and training. It was a seemingly strange, but not unheard of, form of Cold War competition in which both camps courted the same client. As we shall see, Ethiopia, Somalia, and Afghanistan, to name but a few, enjoyed similarly mixed patronage.

Under Amin, Uganda's roads, ports, warehouses, farms, and factories fell into dilapidation. As *The Economist* wrote, "Expenditure to maintain the social and economic infrastructure, let alone to develop it, was reduced to a trickle. Scarcity and inflation were the harvest the regime reaped in a short period."[18] Labor strikes followed and were savagely repressed. The regime became increasingly isolated and vulnerable.

Finally, a horrified US Congress moved to impose economic sanctions. The Carter administration, despite a stated commitment to human rights, opposed the idea. Congress prevailed, nonetheless, and in October 1978 the

United States imposed a trade embargo on Uganda. In retaliation, Amin told American expatriates that they could not leave—essentially taking them all hostage.[19] As the Ugandan economy shrank further, the officer corps, fat on economic carrion, took to squabbling among themselves. To appease his henchmen, Amin created ten militarily run provinces, but these fiefs only weakened the state further. As the provincial governors smuggled coffee and stole revenue, the vaults of the central government emptied. By summer 1978, even soldiers were going unpaid. There were coup attempts and small mutinies, in which even the defense minister was implicated.

In October 1978, Amin resorted to the lowest trick of statecraft: he went to war. His invasion of Tanzania was, however, swiftly repelled, and Amin's army—a modern, motorized, state-of-the-art shambles—collapsed.

The Tanzanians and their anti-Amin Ugandan exile allies soon occupied Kampala.[20] A *New York Times* correspondent described the victory: "It did not take long for Uganda's liberators to discover that the dictator had left little behind. There was $200,000 in foreign exchange in the central bank, along with $250 million in foreign debts. There were mass graves throughout the land that held an estimated half million dead, most of them men who had been suspected of opposing Amin. It was a country of widows and orphans with no economy to speak of; a place of ruin."[21]

Armories Plundered

The capital was under occupation, but in the rural northeast no one was in charge. As the army melted away, the well-stocked Moroto Garrison near the Kenyan border and a smaller one in Kotido were looted by Karamojong and Jie tribesmen, who acquired "for the first time a significant supply of automatic weapons and ammunition." Many of these guns flowed into Kenya and on to other parts of the pastoralist corridor.[22] One report described Karamojong warriors looting a military armory in 1979, stealing 20,000 assault rifles and 2 million rounds of ammunition; more guns were dumped by fleeing soldiers.[23] A year into liberation, the *Times* described the crisis in Karamoja: "The natives stormed an army barracks in the town of Moroto during the revolution and took 15,000 automatic weapons. But

Karamoja has its own special tragedy. . . . For centuries the men among them have made their living with spears, stealing one another's cows, but with the acquisition of weapons, the cattle-raiding changed from spear-point to gunpoint."[24] Another press report called parts of Uganda "virtual war zones." "Bands of raiders, sometimes numbering in the hundreds and usually armed with automatic rifles, sweep into Ugandan and Tanzanian villages, kill those who resist and make off with livestock—the villagers' most valuable possessions."[25]

Thousands were displaced and hundreds killed before the new Ugandan president Yoweri Museveni could begin to restore some semblance of order. Today the Small Arms Survey estimates there are four hundred thousand illegal weapons in Uganda alone. And war continues there even today, now prosecuted by the sociopaths of the Lord's Resistance Army.[26]

Enter El Niño

Just as northeast Uganda was flooded with guns, a severe drought descended on the whole region. Famine swept the Karamoja, killing people and livestock. By the summer of 1980, *The Economist* described the crisis thus: "A disaster of huge proportions has hit northeast Africa. Hundreds of people, mainly children, are dying from starvation every day. In Somalia and Ethiopia, in northern Uganda and Kenya, in tiny Djibouti and in vast Sudan some 10 million people are at risk. All, to some degree, are victims of drought, but three million of them are also refugees from war and civil strife."[27] The preceding two decades had seen a series of droughts across the Sahel, and in the Horn of Africa, there had been famines in Ethiopia, Sudan, and Somalia. According to experts, most herders in the region lost up to 80 percent of their small stock and half of their cattle to starvation and disease.[28]

From 1980 to 1982 the weather got even more intense as one of the two worst El Niño events of the century occurred. By the end of it, the Karamojong's cattle holdings were only half what they had been in 1962; yet, their human population had doubled. As one press report explained: "The women stay behind and plant corn beside creeks. Last year, however, there was no rain and the creeks went dry. Cholera and famine spread quickly, and by late June of this year, an estimated 20,000 Karamojong had died." A UN relief program stopped after a few months because a food convoy was attacked.[29]

False Solutions

On the Uganda-Kenya border, the looted weapons provided the Karamojong with a social remedy to their ecological problems: large-scale raids against the agricultural Iteso. In short order, Karamojong gunmen took most of the Itesos' cattle. "Occasional raiding was a familiar enough experience, but the scale and consequences of these attacks were without precedent."[30] In revenge, the Iteso violently evicted those Karamojong who had settled in their area. Similar depredations befell other tribes, and with guns so cheap and plentiful, the cattle violence that had been in decline began a new upward trend. Some two thousand hungry and often armed Ugandans crossed into the Turkana region of Kenya in search of food and cattle.[31] Though relative stability has returned to most of Uganda, the country remains a source of illegal guns and ammunition for Kenyan tribesmen. And the damage of the late seventies and early eighties mayhem was never undone.

A greater source of instability to the whole region is, of course, Somalia, the textbook failed state. Today, Somalia is an anarchic warzone from which flow weaponry, piracy, and ethnic and religious radicalism. It supplies the Horn of Africa's bandits, raiders, militias, and guerrillas with guns, sanctuary, and markets. So, let us now address the history of Somalia's collapse—for it is a central element in the catastrophic convergence.

Chapter 7

Somali Apocalypse

> The statesman who yields to war fever must realize that once the signal is given, he is no longer the master of policy but the slave of unforeseeable and uncontrollable events.
>
> —Winston Churchill

In 1969 a left-wing military coup brought an end to newly independent Somalia's experiment with electoral democracy. The new strong man was Mohammed Siad Barre, who the following year proclaimed "scientific socialism" to be the official ideology, insisting it was "fully compatible with Islam and the reality of the nomadic society." All political opposition and any public mention of clans were strictly forbidden.

However, the early Siad Barre regime also brought some important social reforms. As I. M. Lewis, the preeminent scholar of Somali history, has explained, the new regime provided community health programs, rural education, and literacy campaigns and encouraged local communities to build schools, hospitals, and dispensaries. Cooperatives and tree planting were encouraged, and the roman script was adapted for the Somali language.[1]

Alas, Siad Barre was a virulent nationalist and irredentist. The Somali national space had been fragmented into five pieces by European and Ethiopian colonialism. Somali independence in 1960 reunited only the Italian (southern) and British (northern) controlled parts of Somalia. And,

for Siad Barre, that was not enough. In Mogadishu, nationalist intellectuals and political elites seethed with resentment as they coveted the So-
mali-speaking regions of Kenya, Djibouti, and Ethiopia. In particular, they
wanted the Ogaden, a poor, dry, rugged, Somali-populated wedge of
Ethiopia that juts into Somalia, giving that country its boomerang shape.
Siad Barre pledged to reunite the fragments of the Somali nation, and
when in the mid-1970s Ethiopia entered a period of political instability, he
saw an opportunity to begin his project.

The story of Somalia's implosion is a parable of how the Cold War's
grand ideas and noble alliances too often left only suffering and disorder.
More broadly, that dynamic is a constitutive element in the catastrophic
convergence.

Fall of the Lion

The pampered, autocratic Ethiopian emperor Haile Selassie—though
feted by western elites and, bizarrely, worshipped by impoverished, ganja-
smoking Rastafarians in Jamaica—was increasingly hated at home. His
pet lions ate meat while the people went hungry. Labor organizing of any
sort was banned until 1962.[2] The emperor enjoyed warm relations with
Washington and even sent a battalion of his best troops to aid the United
States during the Korean War. The American military had a communication outpost at Kagnew Station and trained Ethiopian troops. From
1953 to 1973, half of all US military aid to sub-Saharan Africa went to
imperial Ethiopia.[3]

By 1974, the emperor's rule was in trouble. The Sahelian drought was
decimating Ethiopian farmers, oil prices were quadrupling, and the global
economy was in the doldrums; inflation and fuel price hikes led to riots in
Addis Ababa. The emperor sent out his military to restore order—but the
troops mutinied. Chaos gripped the nation, and amidst this arose a leftist
revolutionary junta of lower-ranking officers called the Dergue, or "Committee." The new regime moved fast, implementing the largest land reform in Africa, nationalizing all industry, and establishing workers'
committees down to the local level. But for all its high-minded radical-

ism, the Dergue was beset by vicious, internecine struggles. Meanwhile in the countryside, there was resistance from landlords and multiple obscurantist revolts.[4]

Across the border, Siad Barre saw the chaos as an opportunity to seize the Ogaden. Never mind that both Ethiopia and Somalia were socialist states, both claiming to put economic development, solidarity, and the well-being of the masses above all else. Nationalism ruled the day.

Paved with Outside Help

In a pattern familiar around the world, Siad Barre began his war covertly, by training and arming Ethiopian-based Somali clans who became the Western Somalia Liberation Front. But, as these things so often go, the covert action soon escalated out of control.

At the same time this very local conflict was heating up, Cold War tensions across the region were also rising. The superpowers' grand strategy machinations found each competing for influence in the Horn of Africa, primarily by means of lavishing military aid on local allies. For its part, the Soviet Union sought to create a pro-Soviet alliance of four socialist states—Somalia, South Yemen, Ethiopia (which then included Eritrea), and possibly the soon-to-be-independent Djibouti. This alliance was important to the socialist camp, in part, because in 1972 Egypt had ejected Soviet troops and essentially switched to the US-led Cold War camp.[5] A socialist alliance in the Horn of Africa would allow the USSR to project power into the Middle East and out over the shipping lanes of the Red and Arabian seas and the Indian Ocean. Consider the strategic importance of this region: the Red Sea, passageway for so much of the West's oil, linked to the Mediterranean by the Suez Canal; Yemen, sharing a huge border with Saudi Arabia; Somalia, pointing out toward the mouth of the Gulf.[6]

This "Pax Sovietica" in the Horn of Africa, as worried Western observers called it, was championed in large part by Fidel Castro. In fact, it was Castro who first dragged the USSR into Africa—without asking them, it should be added—by dispatching Cuban troops to aid Angola's

MPLA (*Movimento Popular de Libertação de Angola–Partido do Traba-lho*), after South African forces, mercenaries, and CIA advisors invaded in 1975. The astounding facts of this strange dynamic were revealed in historian Piero Gleijeses's *Conflicting Missions: Havana, Washington, and Africa, 1959–1976.*[7] After victory in Angola, Cuba prodded the USSR to engage more fully with Africa. Castro took Africa so seriously for several reasons: one was his ideological commitment. Throughout the CIA and State Department documents quoted by Gleijeses, Castro is described as "first of all a revolutionary" and as "a compulsive revolutionary" with a "fanatical devotion to his cause," motivated by "a messianic sense of mission" and "engaged in a great crusade." There was also the matter of deep cultural ties between Cuba and Africa. As President Carter's UN ambassador, the former civil rights activist Andrew Young, told *Newsweek*, "There is no doubt that Cuba perceives itself as an Afro-Latin nation. . . . I don't believe that Cuba is in Africa because it was ordered there by the Russians. I believe that Cuba is in Africa because it really has a shared sense of colonial oppression and domination." It should be pointed out that Young was not championing armed socialist revolution in Africa and ultimately criticized the Cuban crusade as "contributing to destruction."[8]

Finally, there was the issue of survival. As one of the first Marxist-Leninist states in the Third World, Cuba needed friends. It needed a balance of power, a swarming of small states to the Red Banner. Just as he had in Angola, so too in the Horn did Castro play a leading role in the architecture and diplomacy of the Soviet strategy. He spoke of "a common anti-imperialist front" on the Red Sea. When the new government of Lieutenant Colonel Mengistu Haile-Mariam, head of the Dergue, embraced socialism, it expelled US military advisors and turned to the Warsaw Pact nations for aid. Soon the Soviet Union was aiding both Somalia and Ethiopia. This infuriated Siad Barre and his clique. The Soviets and Cubans tried to solve the Ogaden question and build unity between all the East African neighbors. Castro personally shuttled back and forth between Somalian and Ethiopian leaders trying to mend fences.

It was not to be. In Mogadishu, world socialism meant less than Greater Somalia. Local agendas derailed the grand plan, and when the strategic vision fell apart, so too did much of the region.

Ogaden War Forever

In the summer of 1977, the secret little war in the Ogaden boiled over. On June 13, about five thousand regular Somali troops, their insignia removed and working closely with the guerrillas of the Western Somalia Liberation Front, crossed into Ethiopia and went on the offensive.[9] By July, they had taken the towns of Jijiga and Harar, destroyed several important bridges, and severed the rail link between Addis Ababa and the Red Sea port of Djibouti. With that, over 40 percent of Ethiopia's exports and 50 percent of its imports were stalled.[10] All the while, Soviet and Cuban advisors and officers were in both Ethiopia and Somalia.

By November 1977, Somalia had confirmed that Cuban combat forces were not only in Ethiopia but fighting on Ethiopia's side! With that Siad Barre expelled the four thousand Soviet advisers who had been training his forces and maintaining his aircraft. Most of the departing advisors went straight to Ethiopia.[11] In February 1978, Somalia's military dropped all pretense of distance from the fight and formally joined the Western Somali Liberation Front in an "all-out bitter war with Ethiopia." The new offensive took huge swaths of the Ogaden.[12]

In Ethiopia, the Dergeu faced calamity: the loss of nearly one-third of the Committee's territory threatened national collapse. To stanch the bleeding, Soviet and Cuban aid came pouring into Ethiopia. The Soviets airlifted in millions of dollars' worth of sophisticated military hardware, while Cuba sent more infantry and pilots—twenty-four thousand troops in all.[13] Ethiopia's foreign-led counterattack crushed the invading Somali army and even pushed the air war into northern Somalia.[14]

Now, Siad Barre was on the ropes. Needing weapons to counter the Russian and Cuban forces, he went to the teetering shah of Iran, then called on the United States to "fulfill its moral responsibility" to help

Somalia. President Carter had said he would "aggressively challenge" the Soviet Union for influence, and the fighting between two socialist states gave the United States an opportunity to do that. With its regional allies, the United States now pulled Marxist Somalia into the so-called moderate Arab camp, though Siad Barre was neither.[15] US military aid during the short war totaled more than $200 million, while economic assistance exceeded $500 million.[16] With much of this assistance, Somalia bought weapons in Saudi Arabia, Egypt, Iran, and Pakistan.

By 1980, Siad Barre had abandoned scientific socialism, which, though it had led to some wealth redistribution, did not yield economic growth commensurate with population growth. By the mid-1980s, the Siad Barre regime was implementing International Monetary Fund–inspired economic liberalization. This led to a substantial increase in banana exports, with most of the benefits accruing to the main exporter and regime insiders. Siad Barre's wife and daughter both became plantation owners.[17]

Though US grand strategy was ultimately concerned with protecting market economies worldwide, the specific American interest in Somalia was not economic. Somalia's importance came *not* from the modest profits a few international firms might make there but rather because the country offered a political and military salient overlooking East Africa and the Indian Ocean. In addition, taking the Somalia Paladin broke up that developing "Pax Sovietica" in East Africa. American involvement was about the US versus Soviet balance of power internationally, as fought through regional proxies.

Fallout

Officially, the Ogaden War wrapped up in 1978 with tens of thousands dead. Yet, all through the 1980s Ethiopia and Somalia continued a low-intensity conflict, and the Western Somalia Liberation Front fights on to this day. The US Army maintained at least two training teams in Somalia, and Moscow poured $5 billion into Ethiopia over the 1980s, creating sub-Saharan Africa's largest army. The Cubans stayed in Ethiopia; and during the 1980s, Ethiopian troops would occasionally cross into Somalia or send planes to bomb towns.[18]

Somalia never recovered from its stunning defeat in the Ogaden, and that cataclysm set off the country's national disintegration. *Foreign Affairs* summarized war's the impact: "Soviet support enabled [Ethiopian] Mengistu to crush Somali aggression, humiliate Siad Barre and send half a million refugees and guerrillas back across the Somali border, many carrying the next wave of modern weapons in a rising tide. The Ogaden disaster would unleash serious domestic discontent against Siad Barre's increasingly brutal and discriminatory regime, leading to a 1978 coup attempt and the formation in 1981 of the Somali National Movement among northern Isaaq clans."[19]

The cost of war had crushed Somalia's small, agriculturally based economy. External debt tripled from $95 million in 1976 to $288 million in 1979.[20] The government's macroeconomic policy was described as "erratic, inconsistent," and often moving "from one set of objectives to another, thereby confusing the domestic market." By 1990, as the Somali state began its final descent into chaos, its external debt to Western lenders was $1.9 billion, or 360 percent of its GDP. The crisis had originated in the military expenditures of the Ogaden war.[21]

Into the Abyss

Siad Barre held on to Mogadishu until January 1991, when three loosely coordinated rebel groups forced him to flee. The dictator's military crumbled along clan lines, and his abandoned arsenals released a new wave of guns into Somalia, northern Kenya, and the whole Horn of Africa. As Terence Lyonses and Ahmed I. Samatar put it, "The demise of a state is inherently linked to a breakdown of social coherence on an extensive level as civil society can no longer create, aggregate, and articulate the supports and demands that are the foundations of the state. Without the state, society breaks down and without social structure, the state cannot survive."[22] A long-rotting structure came crashing down, and Somalia has not had a functioning government since. Worse yet, its war and constant instability have infected the entire region. The flow of weapons, ammunition, contraband, and armed men across borders has created a lawless zone that, increasingly, includes Kenya.

The Ogaden War, like the Ugandan invasion of Tanzania, was not initiated by the Cold War superpowers, but their compulsion to arm proxies badly exacerbated the conflicts. Put simply: imported weapons have brought Africa to its knees. Though it is not immediately obvious, all of this history came to bear when those Pokot raiders gunned down the Turkana herder, Ekaru Loruman, in a fight over cattle and water in the drought-stricken badlands of Kenya.

CHAPTER 8

Theorizing Failed States

The proceedings of civil and criminal jurisdiction . . . were finally suppressed; and the indiscriminate crowd of noble and plebeian slaves was governed by the traditionary customs which had been coarsely framed for the shepherds, and pirates of Germany. The language of science, of business, and of conversation, which had been introduced by the Romans, was lost in the general desolation.

—EDWARD GIBBON, *The Decline and Fall of the Roman Empire*

THE SKY OVER Kisangani is flat and gray, but it never rains. Down by the river, market women sell small heaps of edible caterpillars, but no one seems to buy them. The streets of this small city at the heart of the Congo Basin are strangely calm and almost devoid of cars, most of which were looted during two recent invasions.

The old art deco buildings of the colonial era have slid into ruin, slowly succumbing to the rain, mildew, and vegetation, as if fading away before one's eyes. No roads connect Kisangani to the rest of the Democratic Republic of Congo (DRC) or any other part of the world; the jungle has retaken the tarmac strips. At the riverfront, the muddy water flows past as it has for millennia; a further thirteen hundred miles from here, over a massive set of cataracts, the rough, churning, brown river spills into the sea, bringing debris and floating plants with it.

Kisangani began as a Belgian trading station. Henry Morton Stanley established it for King Leopold on the American's third bloody march through Congo in 1883.[1] Joseph Conrad used the spot as a model for his inner station in *Heart of Darkness*. It is the last navigable point on the river; the next 250 miles upstream are broken by cascading ledges and waterfalls. I was in Kisangani on my way to Isangi to report on logging in the world's second-largest intact tropical forest, but the police had detained me. Despite carrying five different forms of official documentation—including an *ordre de mission* and an *autorisation de reportage*—all stamped and signed by several different ministries, the cops insisted that I needed more paperwork, and while they prepared it I had to wait.

The next day, I visited the ramshackle provincial administrative offices. A dismal old clerk asked if I would pay $200 for the extra accreditation. I suggested $50. He agreed, but then each day brought more delays. I drifted around the city, befriended a man with a pet monkey named Johnny, drank beer at a bar owned by an Italian timber merchant, and sat on the steps of the church, looking out on the river Congo. There was no traffic on the water for lack of rain—the Intertropical Convergence Zone's problems extend to central Africa. Drought has made the Congo's water levels drop, and now it is full of dangerous shoals.

Finally, on the third day of waiting, I told the old clerk at the provincial offices that I would leave without the new authorization. That of course would mean he and his boss might go without the $50 "fee" they required. The clerk looked concerned. Suddenly, the document was ready. It was handwritten on old, brown paper but stamped and signed. On the verso was a different, older document: a typed travel authorization for someone else who was on a veterinary mission, also to Isangi. It read, "Congo Belge, District de Stanleyville, Secrétariat . . . 7 février 1957."

Anatomy of the Ruins

That document encapsulates how states fall apart and failed states, or semi-failed states, are important because they are so vulnerable to climate change. In failed states social breakdown is the norm; yet, governance and administration are never totally absent. They exist, but in spectral form. It is as if the failed state has reverted to older, tributary methods of domination and reciprocity. Because state failure is relative, in most so-called failed states government is a semifunctional ruin—the state as improvised afterlife. The "travel document" that the clerk in Kisangani gave me is a ludicrous, yet concrete example of this: a handwritten note on the backside of a fifty-year-old colonial document. One finds this type of bureaucracy amidst collapse in most failed states, where underpaid civil servants toy officiously with the components of a defunct colonial police apparatus, not for the sake of law and order but simply to extract survival-level bribes.

Most failed or semifailed states are like that—they have hollowed out governments. Each has a flag, a currency, and a seat at the United Nations, but there is little or no law and order or functioning infrastructure. Failed states are not always apocalyptic war zones of Somalia-style mayhem. Though racked by spasms of violence, everyday life in failed states is more typically defined by the type of kleptocratic jumble found in the DRC.

In places like Somalia, Afghanistan, Haiti, Guinea-Bissau, and Ivory Coast, the state is a ghost: it appears and then disappears. You can see its outline and feel its presence, but it's not really there. For example, in Kinshasa, capital city of the DRC, there is no real law enforcement, no public-safety program, but *there is* a strict, North Korean–style prohibition against taking photographs, and the police enforce it vigorously. I was once detained for two hours because I took a photograph of a huge, futuristic Space Needle–like tower that soars above the slums, a broken relic of Mobutu Sese Seko's architectural megalomania. During my detention, I slowly negotiated the "fine" down from $500 to $150.

So it is in failed states, among the ruins of modernity past, the institutions of sovereignty rot and fade like old documents and the colonial offices that house them. On these political frontiers of the catastrophic convergence, the state in its coherent modern form has collapsed but leaves behind many of its bureaucratic components: its uniforms, insignia, paperwork, ministries and officialdom, like the hungry clerk in Kisangani. Only now, these forces take on a strange phantom life, akin to the severed limbs of a spider, each of which keeps twitching and struggling as if the organism were still whole. The police in the Congo demand permissions, travel passes, registrations, and receipts as if they were the agents of some great, centralized despotic state. But in reality, there are no dossiers, no database, and no real oversight or project of extending sovereignty. There is not even sufficient electricity or paper.

Amidst this political rubble sprout superstition, ethnic hatred, tribalism, millenarian faiths, and violent instability. Entire national economies fall into the hands of organized crime. Conflict resources—like diamonds, timber, ore, and drugs—are the main products of these battered places. *Foreign Policy* magazine and The Fund for Peace maintain an index of failed states that uses thirteen criteria to determine a state's relative failure. They look at mounting demographic pressure, massive population movements, legacies of vengeance, chronic and sustained migration, uneven economic development and inequality, sudden economic downturns, corruption, criminalization of the state, deterioration of public services, arbitrary use of state violence and human rights violations, the relative autonomy of the security forces, factionalism among state elites, and finally, external intervention by other states or parastate forces. It is a descriptive collection of indices that is also explanatory.[2]

Development in Reverse

To travel in failing states, the front lines of climate change, has a hallucinogenic quality, as if one were passing through, in reverse, the arguments made by Max Weber in his famous lecture "Politics As a Vocation." In that essay Weber defines the state as "a human community that (successfully) claims the *monopoly of the legitimate use of physical force* within a given territory."[3] A modern state is defined by that and other features, crucial among them the depersonalization of politics. In the modern state, the head of state does not *own* the government, its armies, offices, equipment, revenue, and personnel. In the modern state the politicians and the administrators are legally separated from the means of administration and the real and implied repression they depend on. And they cannot, or should not, use these means of administration for personal profit. This depersonalization and legal rationalization of political power and administration gives a modern state legitimacy.

For Weber, political domination has three forms of legitimation: *traditional domination* rests on inherited patterns of age-old obedience; *charismatic domination* relies on the power, gifts, and personality of a specific leader; *legal domination* rests on "the belief in the validity of legal statute and functional 'competence' based on rationally created *rules*. . . . This is domination as exercised by the modern 'servant of the state,'" and thus by the modern state itself.[4]

Thus, the crucial factor in modern states is that the "means of administration" are not private property. And it is the *reversal* of this—the reprivatization of the state and the repersonalization of politics and the privatization of war—that marks the start of state failure. Consider again the operative passages in Weber: "All states may be classified according to whether they rest on the principle that the staff of men themselves *own* the administrative means, or whether the staff is 'separated' from these means of administration. . . . The question is whether or not the power-holder himself directs and organizes the administration while delegating executive power to personal servants, hired officials, or personal favorites and confidants, who are non-owners, i.e. who do not use the material means of administration in their own right but are directed by the lord."

A paragraph later the old Prussian explains the evolution toward the modern form of state:

> Everywhere the development of the modern state is initiated through the action of the prince. He paves the way for the expropriation of the autonomous and "private" bearers of executive power who stand beside him, of those who in their own right possess the means of administration, warfare, and financial organization, as well as politically usable goods of all sorts. The whole process is a complete parallel to the development of the capitalist enterprise through gradual expropriation of the independent producers. In the end, the modern state controls the total means of political organization, which actually come together under a single head. No single official personally owns the money he

pays out, or the buildings, stores, tools, and war machines he controls. In the contemporary "state"—and this is essential for the concept of state—the "separation" of the administrative staff, of the administrative officials, and of the workers from the material means of administrative organization is completed.[5]

In failed states it is the reverse. Power is repersonalized, the means of administration and repression reprivatized. Executive power—by which Weber means the power of decision making and execution—reverts from a centralized, legitimate institution back out to the institutional periphery, the officialdom that controls the apparatus of state: its offices, documents, dossiers, ministries, arms, checkpoints, and jail cells. These technologies are redeployed in a fragmented and parasitic fashion.

The failed state's bureaucratic disintegration produces a unique political geography: a patchwork sovereignty akin to the collage of authorities—king, church, cities, lords—that defined medieval Europe. The patchwork today appears to varying degrees, across parts of Latin America, Africa, and the Middle East and Central Asia. Perhaps the capital city is run by the "presidential guard" or some of the paramilitary forces of the interior ministry, itself the property of its head man. That would be a description of Kinshasa as well as Kabul or Baghdad. Outside the capital, a renegade commander's men control some crucial road to the border; you'll find this in Congo, Afghanistan, and Colombia. Foreign troops—perhaps wearing blue UN helmets or NATO insignia—secure the areas around their bases, a few government buildings, road links, and airports. Bandits and rebels control the areas beyond. In more distant regions or provinces with resources or lucrative trade links, one might find an armed and autonomous governor who pledges allegiance to whatever central government the great Western powers have propped up but who is, in reality, his own boss running an independent substate. In the port city, it will come as no surprise if the real power is the top import-export merchant, who, by means of his great wealth, bribes the cops and calls the shots with local politicians. These features again describe parts of Iraq, Colombia, Afghanistan, Haiti, Cote d'Ivoire, Guinea-Bissau, the DRC, and Somalia, to name a few.

These are the political patterns of fourteenth-century Europe, the political forms left by the collapse of Rome and in the wake of the plague.[6] They are not the patterns of underdevelopment but rather those of social breakdown and political collapse. They are the institutional and political rubble of a past modernity. And increasingly they define the present.

We see here a strange inversion of Walt W. Rostow's "stage theory" of development and his idea of "economic takeoff."[7] Collapse, like development, is gradual, each stage building sequentially upon the conditions created by the previous stages. Like development, it can become a self-reinforcing process. The slide toward entropy and chaos is like the virtuous cycle of modernization and industrialization imagined by the West's postwar planners—but in violent reverse.

States, War, Crime

If we read Weber in reverse, we would do well to consult Charles Tilly's classic essay "State Making and War Making As Organized Crime" in the same fashion.[8] According to Tilley, "War makes states," and "banditry, piracy, gangland rivalry, policing, and war making all belong on the same continuum."[9] He argues that organized crime–style protection rackets are, in many ways, akin to taxation by legitimate states. War, extortion, and plunder exist on a spectrum, separated by different levels of intensity and legitimacy. The main point of the essay is that as European war making became more expensive in the cost of ships, cannons, and fielding armies, so too did the project of taxation and administration become more developed and thus modern. As Tilley puts it,

> In an idealized sequence, a great lord made war so effectively as to become dominant in a substantial territory, but that war making led to increased extraction of the means of war—men, arms, food, lodging, transportation, supplies, and/or the money to buy them—from the population within that territory. The building up of war-making capacity likewise increased the capacity to extract. The very activity of extraction, if successful, entailed the elimination, neutralization, or cooptation of the

great lord's local rivals; thus, it led to state making. As a by-product, it created organization in the form of tax-collection agencies, police forces, courts, exchequers, account keepers; thus it again led to state making.[10]

If conventional war making produced the modern state, then asymmetrical warfare, social breakdown, intercommunal strife, brigandry, and open-ended counterinsurgency in the age of climate chaos may well be the modern state's undoing. As the means of administration and "extraction" collapse, "bands of armed men" fall away from the state and are released freelance into society to survive by their own devices. Taxation becomes theft as soldiers and police revert back to bribery, extortion, and banditry. Where the state is totally absent, gangs arise to govern slums like proto-city-states.

There may also be technological aspects to the breakdown of modern state power. As the Kenyan case illustrates, there is something particular about the proliferation of small arms: AK-47s, grenade launchers and machine guns. When these "democratic" means of violence are cheap enough, they undermine state power in a manner that is directly inverse to Tilley's argument in which expensive naval ships and cannons demanded (and thus created) elaborate, centralized, modern bureaucracies and taxation regimes.[11] If cannons and frigates made the modern nation state, the Kalashnikov and field radio might undo it.

III

ASIA

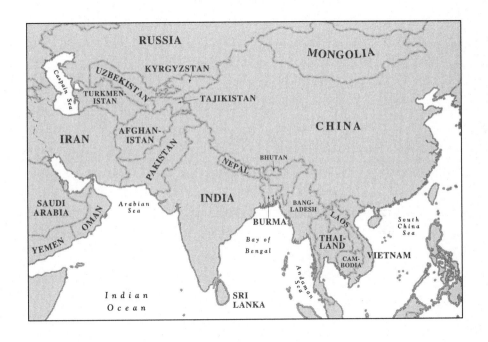

CHAPTER 9

Drugs, Drought, and Jihad: Environmental History of the Afghanistan War

A good year is determined by its spring.

—*Afghan proverb*

T HE OLD FARMER opened walnuts and pomegranates in the court-yard of his mud-walled fortress home and explained his troubles. Wazir, the farmer, grows opium poppy and marijuana in a border district of southern Nangarhar Province in eastern Afghanistan. The border, the Durand Line, runs along the ridges of a forbidding, snow-capped mountain range, which feeds the rivers that water Nangarhar's scorching valleys.[1]

When I visited in early September 2006, the area was in the midst of a very bad drought. As the United Nations had discovered during a survey four years earlier, wells had been running dry for most of the last decade, as Afghanistan suffered "the most severe drought in living memory."[2] Scientists link this desiccation to climate change, particularly rising temperatures in the mountains and a slight decrease in precipitation.

The drought in Nangarhar finally broke in 2010 when the colossal Arabian Ocean Monsoon that flooded some 20 percent of Pakistan brushed along the Durand Line. In Pakistan, the United Nations estimated that almost 2,000 people had died, 14 million needed humanitarian aid, 2.4 million hectares of crops were lost, 1.9 million homes were destroyed or damaged, and over 7 million people were homeless. Perhaps worse, the floods destroyed 50 years of infrastructure. The economic total for losses was estimated to be $43 billion.[3] By 2011 serious malnutrition gripped the flood zone.

In Afghanistan, the edge of the same weather system hit several eastern provinces, including Nangarhar, which was at the very periphery of the monsoon's reach. Typically, August in Nangarhar is bone dry, with precipitation of less than five millimeters for the whole month.[4] But that year, the skies opened, and the massive barrage of rain washed away crops, livestock, and twenty-five hundred houses, killing eighty people.

According to the security reports, Nangarhar is not only either parched or flooded but also violent: Twenty-three mostly war-related incidents were listed during the week I made my visit in September 2006. According to the Afghanistan NGO Safety Office (ANSO), that week saw kidnapping threats, ongoing counterinsurgency operations, and "reported infiltration of a new group of AGE/Insurgents" made up of "Arabs, Chechens and Pakistanis"; two vehicles used by "armed Taliban" were spotted in Sherzad District, and there were several rocket attacks. The ANSO reports portrayed a region beyond government control.

Only the drug trade has kept this region afloat economically, but eradication is a constant, if often distant, threat. Wazir recounted the panic of the local farmers when a poppy-eradication squad came down from Kabul. "The eradication campaign came, but they just took bribes," said Wazir as we sat in his *dera*, a shaded outside visiting area, on rope and wooden cots called *charpayi*. "When we heard that they were coming, we went to the district governor and negotiated a price." Wazir told me that the local commander, named Hasil, was chosen as the farmers' envoy. After taking bribes, for the sake of the cameras the police destroyed some old, dry, spent poppy fields.

"If the governor had not accepted the bribe, we were ready to fight. If a farmer loses his poppy he can't even have tea and sugar. He will borrow money from a rich person and lose his land." Wazir said that emergency loans carry 100 percent interest rates.

Climatic stress, an initial catalyst for Afghan instability, is now fueling violence. This is what the catastrophic convergence of poverty, violence and climate change looks like in Afghanistan: eroded soil, limited water, greedy police, foreign troops, popular anger, and an insurgency that protects poppy crops from eradication.

The Role of Drought

In 2008 the British government issued a report describing what climate change will do to Afghanistan: "The most likely adverse impacts . . . are drought related, including associated dynamics of desertification and land degradation. Drought is likely to be regarded as the norm by 2030, rather than as a temporary or cyclical event. . . . Floods due to untimely rainfall and a general increase in temperature are of secondary importance. However, their impacts may be amplified due to more rapid spring snow melt as a result of higher temperatures, combined with the downstream effects of land degradation, loss of vegetative cover and land mismanagement."[5]

Read the history of the war in Afghanistan closely, and a climate angle emerges. Central Asia is suffering water shocks—droughts and floods—that fit the pattern of anthropogenic global warming. Two-thirds of Afghans work in agriculture; yet, much of the country is desert, and its irrigation system is badly dilapidated. The extreme weather of climate change causes misery, which causes violence, which leads to more misery, and so on. At first glance, the most important cause of war in Afghanistan is the US presence there: the United States and its NATO allies are in Afghanistan to hunt down and destroy Al Qaeda and/or to build an Afghan state that will deny sanctuary to international terrorists. The Taliban, on the other hand, are fighting to eject the infidel invaders.

But there was war in Afghanistan before the United States intervened overtly and even before America's first covert intervention under President Jimmy Carter in 1979. There was war before the Soviet intervention of December 1979. In many ways the earliest origins of the current conflict are the 1973 coup d'état of Lieutenant General Mohammed Daud Khan against King Mohammed Zahir Shah. And within the story of Daud's coup lurks an element of hidden climate causality.

Yes, religious fanaticism, ethnic hatreds, and imperial ambitions are the larger moving pieces, but climate change also fuels the conflict in Afghanistan.

First, the violence began as the result of a drought forty years ago. Second, climate stress creates poverty and desperation, which now feeds the insurgency against NATO occupation. Third, climate change causes interstate rivalries, which play out as covert operations inside Afghanistan. Finally, and very importantly, opium poppy is drought resistant to an extent alternative crops are not, and NATO attacks poppy while the Taliban defends it. Let us begin the story with the drought and the coup that deposed King Zahir Shah.

Vacation King

In 1969 the rains in many parts of Afghanistan failed completely. During the next two years, they failed again. Then came a very severe winter; to survive, many farmers were forced to eat their seeds and slaughter their bullocks, leaving them little to plant and few animals to pull plows. As a result, the 1972 wheat crop was inadequate, and by April famine swept northern and central Afghanistan. According to Raja Anwar, it was "the most terrible famine in Afghan history."[6]

Ghor Province, in the remote interior of the country, was hardest hit. A thousand years ago the place was heavily forested, but its hills also held mineral deposits, so Ghor's trees were felled and burned to smelt the local ore. Then, the denuded region became the heart of medieval Afghanistan's cattle industry, but the cows, goats, and sheep destroyed the land. Now, Ghor almost looks like the moon—totally barren. Only along the rivers and streambeds is farming possible. For most people, small sage bushes gathered during the summer on faraway hills are the single source of fuel.[7]

The first journalist to break the story of the 1972 famine was Abdul Haq Waleh, editor of a local newspaper called *Caravan*. He traveled to Chakhcharan, the small dusty capital of Ghor, and found a terrifying scene: corpses littered the street; survivors could not dig graves fast enough to keep hungry dogs at bay; scores of children had been abandoned by parents who could no longer feed them or orphaned by parents who had starved.

The next journalist to visit was James Sterba of the *New York Times*. At first Sterba's editors on the foreign desk refused to run his story because it didn't contain enough statistics. How many people had died? He tried to explain that Afghanistan was not a land of statistics; no one even knew the population of Afghanistan; guesses varied by 5 million in either direction. Finally, Sterba sent back three rolls of film that he had shot in Ghor. The horror was undeniable, and the *Times* ran Sterba's story about the abandoned children of the famine. Here is an excerpt: "The boy's spindly body sank slowly to the dusty gravel road. He lowered his head to the pebbles, resting his sunken cheek on his hand. His dry, cracked lips did not close. He tried to cover his feet, but the torn, dirt encrusted rags he wore were not long enough. He placed an empty tin can, his only possession, near his stomach. And then he started to cry."[8]

While thousands starved to death in the mountains, little was said or done about the problem in Kabul. As one report put it, "What killed the people stricken by the drought, in the view of Afghan and foreign observers, was not only lack of food in their regions but also governmental indifference, and greed and official corruption."[9]

King Mohammed Zahir Shah had taken power in 1933 at the age of nineteen when his father was assassinated. Young, weak, and unconcerned with the plight of his people, Zahir Shah was dominated by his cousins and uncles; they ruled and used the young king as a ceremonial ornament and a key to the palace. From these arrangements emerged an inept and passive style of government, but as he matured Zahir Shah asserted more power. In 1964 he created an elected parliament, but it was a largely ineffective body dominated by landlords, religious scholars, and tribal leaders whose conservatism made them actively oppose any modernization.[10] Political parties were illegal. Almost comical gridlock and stagnation were the norm. During 1970 not a single piece of legislation was passed. Other years saw only one or two bills become into law.[11] Afghanistan remained isolated, economically stagnant, underdeveloped, impoverished, and politically unorganized. Five governments were elected and collapsed in less than a decade. One development proposal from West Germany worth $10 million in aid lingered in parliament for three years without action.

As drought became famine, the king and his squabbling little parliament lived in a fantasy world. When aid efforts were finally launched, corruption rendered them useless—just another scheme by which to steal from the people. In Chakhcharan, at the heart of the famine, frustrated and hungry farmers attacked a government building.[12] Meanwhile, in Kabul, the ferment of the late 1960s arrived; university students took to the streets and battled each other on campus—communists versus Islamists, Maoists versus Stalinists, all of them versus Spiro Agnew, who stopped by for a visit in 1970.[13] Among these activists were the men who in the 1980s would lead both the communist government and the mujahideen.

These student protests were not caused by the weather, or the climate, or the farmers' suffering, but they were related to all that. Especially as farmers began to die, famine in the countryside became a stark symbol of the king's incompetence and distance from the nation.

By the summer of 1973, the country was in its third year of drought and famine. The wheat harvest was again very bad. An ethnographic film made that year showed an Afghan farmer explaining the troubles: "The past two years have been hard. No one can explain God's will. No rain has fallen and many are hungry. We get up early in this hot climate. We have tea and bread and work until 4 in the afternoon."[14]

The *New York Times* reported, "There has been much discontent in Afghanistan over government efforts to deal with a famine brought on by a three-year drought. More than 80,000 people are said to have died in the famine."[15] Another *New York Times* report put it this way: "No one knows how many people live in Afghanistan—estimates range from 9 million to 17 million—and no estimate even exists of those who have starved to death."[16] The king, meanwhile, was vacationing off the coast of Naples, at the mineral springs on the island of Ischia. As it turned out, his vacation would last almost forty years.

The Famine Coup

On July 17, 1973, something finally snapped. Lieutenant General Mohammed Daud Khan, the king's cousin and brother-in-law, seized power in a coup d'état. Eight people were reported killed in small firefights between police loyal to the king and soldiers following Daud.[17] The bald-headed Daud had been Zahir Shah's closest adviser for much of the late 1950s and early 1960s. As prime minister during those years, Daud essentially ruled the country on the king's behalf. Daud was a modernizer, and he courted both the United States and the Soviet Union to build roads, dams, schools, and factories. But in 1963, Zahir Shah pushed aside Daud.

Once back in power, Daud declared martial law, abolished the monarchy, and set up a presidential republic with himself as head of state. Within days of the coup, food prices had dropped. His enemies were jailed, sometimes killed, often exiled.[18] An intense Pashtun nationalist and irredentist, Daud considered the Afghanistan-Pakistan border an illegitimate colonial imposition. Drawn up in 1893 by the British diplomat Mortimer Durand, the eponymous Durand Line ceded huge Pashtun-dominated swaths of royal Afghanistan (including the winter capital, Peshawar) to British India. After 1947 these lands became part of Pakistan.

As president, Daud started antagonizing Pakistan and talking of a greater Pashtunistan.[19] He set up a training camp outside Kandahar for Baluch rebels to foment trouble across the border in Pakistan, and he encouraged Pashtun nationalism inside Pakistan.[20] Later, under the communist government, Afghanistan would behave similarly. For example, it harbored and supported Murtaza Bhutto's red terror squad, Al Zulficar, which tried to overthrow General Muhammed Zia ul-Huq, the right-wing dictator who ran Pakistan from 1977 to 1988.[21]

Needless to say, Pakistanis do not see Afghanistan's claim upon their territory as legitimate, and Pakistan welcomed and trained radical Islamists from Afghanistan as soon as Daud came to power. Beginning in 1973, Pakistan supported Gulbuddin Hekmatyar and his party Hezb-i-Islami. This later became an anti-Soviet, Pakistani-based mujahideen force and has been allied with the Taliban since about 2005.

Since its inception, the Pakistani officer class has sought to keep Afghanistan weak so as to provide "strategic depth," or fallback room, in case of a major land war with India. On both sides of the border live Pashtuns. In Afghanistan, Pashtuns have always been the ruling ethnicity, but in Pakistan they are a large, poor, restive minority, making up about 16 percent of the population. The last thing Pakistan wants is for the Pashtun minority within its borders to link up with, or become tools of, a strong neighboring Afghanistan ruled by Pashtuns and allied with India.

Daud's new republican government included opposing elements of both the communists of the Peoples Democratic Party of Afghanistan (PDPA) and politically active Islamists. Both of these Red and Green revolutionary tendencies had gestated on the campus of Kabul University. In a fateful pattern reminiscent of Kasim in Iraq and other developmentalist strongmen, Daud tried to play the opposition forces off against each other, using a mix of political co-optation and repression. The PDPA had positions in government, but Daud also repressed them. The balancing act did not last for long.

Saur Revolution

In April 1978 a faction of the PDPA overthrew Daud in a coup, beginning the so-called Saur Revolution, named for the month of April in which it happened.

Afghanistan's Communist Party was dysfunctional, divided, and intoxicated by ideology. Almost immediately, the PDPA started attacking its own cadre. It also implemented well-intentioned but poorly planned land reform, which abolished bazaar moneylenders but did not provide farmers with an alternative credit structure. Other new laws enforced gender equality, universal education, and workers rights, but the headlong rush toward modernity proved too much for Afghanistan's deeply conservative rural culture. In April 1979, the military garrison in Herat rose in rebellion. By that autumn, the Afghan army had essentially fallen apart.

Since the 1950s Afghanistan had been the fourth-largest recipient of Soviet aid. The Soviets had fought Muslim rebels who had used a weak Afghanistan as their base until the mid-1930s.[22] After World War II, the USSR saw stability in Central Asia as hinging on stability in, and cordial relations with, Afghanistan. So, they pumped large flows of aid into their neighbor south of the Amu Darya. Watching the Afghan meltdown of 1979, the Soviets faced the loss of a client state and the possibility of renewed Islamic insurgency infecting their own Central Asian republics. Whether the Soviet Union invaded or was invited in, it then killed Hafizullah Amin, the extremist PDPA president who had summoned them, putting in his place the more moderate Babrak Karmal. Still, the war had begun.

The United States saw the intervention as a major Soviet blunder, and thus, as an American opportunity. The United States and Saudi Arabia were soon giving $8 billion in aid to the Pakistan-based and -supported mujahideen, who were fighting to overthrow the PDPA government.[23]

When the mujahideen finally won power in 1992, they immediately set to fighting among themselves, destroying half of Kabul in the process. Out of that civil war emerged the Taliban as a vigilante law-and-order force. When the Taliban secured the roads, it won the support of the Pakistani trucking mafia and then of the Pakistani intelligence services. When Osama bin Laden was ejected from the Sudan, he found sanctuary with the Taliban regime. By September 11, 2001, the Taliban controlled most of Afghanistan. And thus, the stage was set for the current war.

Droughtistan

British government researchers see a link between global warming and conflict in Afghanistan. They note how records since 1960 show that the mean annual temperature in Afghanistan has increased by 0.6°C while mean rainfall has decreased by about 2 percent per decade.[24] More important than rain is snowpack. For most of the year, snowmelt maintains a steady volume of water in the rivers, streams, and canals that feed the farms on Afghanistan's desiccated and brutally hot plains.

Meltwater accounts for as much as 70 percent of the Kabul River's dry-season volume. The Kabul flows west through Nangarhar, enters Pakistan and joins the Indus, which flows south to the sea.

In Kabul city, the river's plight is apparent to the naked eye. Through clouds of wind-whipped dust, one can see that the Kabul—a crucial source of water for the city's 3 million residents—has dwindled to little more that a trash-choked trickle. At numerous times over the last ten years, it has been completely dry.[25] The last decade of drought has brought Afghan agriculture to new lows. Some 80 percent of Afghans work the land, but, as a British government report called "Socio-Economic Impacts of Climate Change in Afghanistan" noted, "Most Afghan farmers are currently not self-sufficient in cereal production even in good years." The UK Department for International

Development reports, "The vulnerability of the agricultural sector to increased temperatures and changes in rainfall patterns and snowmelt is considered to be high. Increased soil evaporation, reduced river flow from earlier snow melt, and less frequent rain during peak cultivation seasons will all impact upon agricultural productivity and crop choice availability."[26]

The winter of 2010 was again "unusually warm and dry," stoking fears that drought "could cause food shortages, undermine efforts to slash poppy growing and worsen security problems." Across the mountains of central Afghanistan, the snowpack was only four to twelve inches deep, compared to the normal one to six feet. The imams asked people to pray for rain.[27]

A report from April 2010 noted that "below-average rainfall has hit food production in eastern and northeastern Afghanistan where some rain-fed fields have dried out." Hamidullah, a farmer from Nangarhar, explained, "I planted wheat on my land but it has failed due to lack of rain." Another farmer in a nearby district said, "I spent 70,000 Afghanis [US$1,450] on wheat and onion seeds but my fields have dried out." In spring of 2010, drought hit twelve of Nangarhar's twenty-three districts. Farmers begged for food aid and irrigation assistance. Then in May, the drought gave way to sudden torrential rains across parts of central and eastern Afghanistan; flash floods washed away crops, livestock, and topsoil, displacing thousands and killing scores.[28]

That was merely a preview. August brought more sudden, totally unexpected floods. "After hammering Pakistan, this weather system then crossed the border into Afghanistan," wrote Al Jazeera's weather presenter. "The high mountains to the south normally shield the country from the southwest monsoon altogether. This is usually the driest time and virtually no rain falls between June and October . . . but the mountains did help a little. Most of the rain fell over Pakistan. . . . Peshawar saw more than they would expect in the entire year."[29]

Merciful Flower

In the face of drought and flooding, one crop brings relative security: *Papaver somniferum*, the opium poppy. Why? The usual answer is that drugs command much higher prices than apricots, raisins, or wheat. But consider this: *poppy uses only one-sixth the water needed for wheat.* That fact alone can explain the drug trade in drought-stricken Afghanistan. Additionally, though grain prices have surged since 2008, poppy still earns more than wheat.[30] Afghanistan produces some 90 percent of world opium, and the opium economy is estimated to be about half the size of Afghanistan's official GDP. The Afghan province producing the most poppy is drought- and flood-battered Nangarhar, where Wazir lives.

Drought-resistant and valuable, poppy is nonetheless an outlaw crop, attacked by the NATO occupation and Hamid Karzai government but defended by the Taliban. Thus, drought-fueled poppy cultivation is one more factor pushing farmers toward the insurgents. As one journalist explained, "A poor harvest, especially if combined with lack of food support, would likely make the cash offered by the Taliban to its fighters more tempting, and undermine support for a central government already seen by many as remote and corrupt."[31] The International Council on Security and Development (formerly the Senlis Council) argued that US-backed eradication campaigns were "the single biggest reason many Afghans turned against the foreigners."[32]

Drought and flooding lead to increased poverty. Poverty fuels the sense of grievance and desperation among the people and creates ranks of unemployed unmarried young men. Destitute farm hands—unable to afford a bride price or to purchase land or even find work—drift into the ranks of the Taliban and become fodder for US drones, the war's human fuel.

As Ahmed Rashid has explained, "The United States and NATO have failed to understand that the Taliban belong to neither Afghanistan nor Pakistan, but are a lumpen population, the product of refugee camps, militarized madrassas, and the lack of opportunities in the borderlands of Pakistan and Afghanistan. They have neither been true citizens of either country nor experienced traditional Pashtun tribal society. The longer the war goes on, the more deeply rooted and widespread the Taliban and their transnational milieu will become."[33]

We might add, the longer climate change goes on with its causes unmitigated, and with no adaptation to its effects, the more pervasive this rootless, millenarian Taliban milieu will become. In this regard, the poppy economy and its armed defense are local adaptation mechanisms.

Sticky Sap

"Three years ago we didn't grow much poppy," said my host, a local farmer and former mujahideen fighter. "Now everyone grows it, even the police chief. Tomorrow I will get you some."

How does the poppy trade function within and fit into the war? In 2004 I traveled to Wardak, a province an hour outside Kabul. The guerrillas have since retaken Wardak, but it was then still in government hands. Wardak looks like New Mexico: green valleys with scattered poplars and clusters of adobe-style walled compounds, *qalas*, set back from the road. Looming above it all are huge, barren mountains and blue skies. I went to Wardak with photographer Teru Kuwayama and a man we'll call Mustafa, who introduced us to his family, or at least his male relatives. (As Pashtun custom dictates, the women were kept hidden from the eyes of strange men.) We sat in a carpet-lined, second-story sitting room, or *betek*. This room, in which we ate and slept, stood safely away from the family quarters. Our hosts were burly men with beards, many of whom had fought with the mujahideen warlord Gulbuddin Hekmatyar during the 1980s and 1990s. One of them had just come back from Iran, where he worked in an ice-cream cone factory. He was about to marry a woman he hadn't seen since she was twelve and he a few years older. The whole family was getting ready for the big day, so our weekend road trip turned into a party, with lots of eating, tea drinking, cigarette smoking, laughing and high-stakes, all-night gambling.

One of the men explained that a severe drought, then in its sixth year, had destroyed Wardak's more traditional crops, like grapes, apples, and wheat. The drought-resistant poppy was all they had left. "Everyone around here grows poppy," said a farmer called Nazir, whose relatives jokingly called him "Mr. Al Qaeda" because of his Taliban-style beard and skullcap.

The poppy boom was not unique to Wardak. All across Afghanistan the crop had made a comeback, in large part due to the drought. UN researchers believe that 1.7 million of Afghanistan's 28.5 million inhabitants

are directly involved in poppy cultivation, with many more working in processing, trafficking, money lending and laundering, and other associated
activities. Warlords tax farmers and traffickers alike, and thanks to Hamid
Karzai's policy of appeasement, many now hold official positions, further
facilitating their exploitation of the drug economy.

But the Taliban benefit as well. First of all, they tax the drug trade, just
as they tax all trade. Second, they do not destroy poppy crops. In areas loyal
to the Taliban, farmers do not have to worry about eradication or the abuse
and bribery that go with it.

In Wardak, as the night went on, with dinner, then tea, then cards and
more photos, the men became increasingly comfortable and explained the
details of the poppy industry. "Poppy is cheap to plant. You can find seeds
in any bazaar," Mahid, a veteran who lost a leg when he stepped on a landmine in the 1990s, told me. In Wardak, poppy has two seasons; in hotter
and colder climates, only one season is possible. The first crop, planted in
March and harvested in June and July, is always the better one. Of the
three flower colors—red, white, and purple—white is the best.

"After you plant and water the poppy, it sprouts in fifteen days," Mr. Al
Qaeda explained. "Then you must weed the crop and keep weeding until
the plants are bigger than the weeds. In three months, they blossom. Seed
pouches emerge and grow in the blossom, and then the flower falls away,
and the seed pouch continues to grow. Then we scratch the seedcase with
a *ghoza* [a small, homemade trowel with a serrated edge of six teeth. From
the wounds, sticky white milk emerges]. You scrape the poppy in the
morning and then collect the sap in the evening, when it is more sticky
and brown. A little from each flower and then you have a ball, and that
dries and is the opium," Mr. Al Qaeda said, grinning.

In most parts of Afghanistan, a farmer can milk each seed case up to
seven times. Eventually, it is tapped out and left to dry, before being harvested for the next planting. The seeds are also used to make edible oil and
are sometimes boiled into a tea that mothers use to drug their infants during the long hours of work.

To illustrate the economic influence of poppy, the one-legged Mahid
starts talking about land measurements. The unit here is a *jerib*, about half

an acre. The men in Wardak say that from one *jerib* farmers can usually get twenty-eight kilograms of opium, which they can sell for up to $5,000. Alternatively, one *jerib* of wheat might earn a farmer $100, or it might not bring in any money at all, depending on weather and prices.

In some areas, smugglers make loans that are repaid in opium. The system in Wardak seems to be more streamlined: farmers borrow from shopkeepers and repay them in cash when they've been paid by the smugglers. "In the last three years, many farms have got out of debt because of poppy. No other crop compares to it. And with the drought, we only have 10 percent of our apples and wheat. These crops use so much water compared to poppy. And the wheat is almost worthless," Mr. Al Qaeda said before turning back to the cards.

"We have many former Taliban and mujahideen commanders here who are getting angry at America because of what is happening in Palestine and Iraq and because the economy here is no good," Mr. Al Qaeda remarked. "Cutting down poppy will only make them more angry."

Out of Nangarhar

Sadly, the dialectical connections between climate change, war, and environmental degradation become mutually reinforcing. The Worldwatch Institute's Michael Renner summarized it well: "Three decades of armed conflict have displaced a large portion of the population, impeded access to farmland because of landmines, and destroyed many irrigation systems or rendered their maintenance impossible. Add recurring droughts and floods and the population's desperate coping strategies, and the net result has been a severe degradation of Afghanistan's natural environment and its water and farming infrastructure. Massive deforestation and heavy pressure on grazing lands has led to erosion and reduced flood resistance."[34]

The official rhetoric of poppy eradication is ridiculously ambitious when compared with facts on the ground. Among the five pillars of the strategy are "judicial reform" and "alternative livelihoods." None of that exists here. The only NGO in this district digs wells, but Wazir said that the corrupt drilling team charges a fee for what should be aid.

As the sun started to slide down in the sky, we headed out. Halfway to Jalalabad, five armed men emerged from behind rocks. One aimed a rocket-propelled grenade, or RPG, at our truck, while another stepped into the road, his AK-47 leveled at the windshield. The lead gunman approached and asked, "Is that police truck still down in the village?"

By freak luck we had passed a Frontier Police pickup truck going the opposite direction. Thinking fast, one of my Afghan colleagues answered, "Yes, and they will be following us in a few minutes." The gunman paused for one very long second, then allowed us to pass. We assumed these men were local thieves, or possibly Taliban, who lay in wait for us but choked at the last minute due to the random passing of the Frontier Police. Weeks later, my translator, Naqeeb, spoke with Wazir again and confirmed that these armed men were local thugs, desperate for money. Their plan had been to kidnap us and sell us to their Taliban contacts. In the face of drought, floods, and failed crops, we would have been an economic windfall.

CHAPTER 10

Kyrgyzstan's Little Climate War

People have suffered and have had such a hard time that it was impossible to go on like this. . . . Land tax has been increased. Prices for electricity and heating have gone up. . . . Young people do not have jobs. They just wander in the streets. We hardly give them an education.

—SHYNAR MAATKERIMOVA, *pensioner, Kyrgyzstan, 2010*[1]

SPRING WAS ON the way in Kyrgyzstan, the green buds and pale blossoms just pressing forth, the sky a beautiful overcast grey. Soft rain caressed the capital, Bishkek, leaving the wide Soviet-era plazas clean and fresh. Occasional birdsong carried through the moist air and across the city's empty streets.

But the calm was the product of crisis and fear. Soon the wide plazas filled with thousands of demonstrators. As the *Guardian* reported, "Protesters said they had been driven onto the streets by recent steep price hikes to communal services such as water and electricity. The hikes had been the last straw in a country already wrestling with huge unemployment and widespread poverty."[2] The *New York Times* also noted that crowds were "incensed over rising utility prices and a government they considered repressive and corrupt."[3] A week before the mayhem began in early April 2010, the government had announced a plan to boost utility prices by 20 percent.[4]

Why had it done this? Because the country is almost totally dependant on hydroelectric power and income from electricity exports, and that same prolonged Central Asian drought that was punishing Afghanistan and Pakistan had crippled Kyrgyzstan's power plants, thus its whole economy. In this regard, Kyrgyzstan encapsulates in the extreme how climate change can trigger violence. This chapter explores how that crisis occurred and why.

Power . . .

The crowds protesting price hikes soon turned into mobs and armed gangs and they attacked government buildings. Gunshots and stun grenades echoed in the streets. Canisters of teargas bounced across the plazas. Flames surged from the windows of government offices. First one building, then another, and then another were gutted by fire. Protesters grabbed and viciously beat the interior minister and took control of the security headquarters and state television. The police started shooting live rounds. Protesters shot back. The police advanced and retreated. The mobs ran away, then ran back. The wounded and dead were carried off in cars: sixty people were killed and hundreds more wounded. Soon Bishkek's main commercial district was burning, and a frenzy of unchecked looting was underway.

By early May 2010, President Kurmanbek Bakiyev—the pro-Western, free market "reformer" of the Tulip Revolution—had fled south to his hometown, Osh. The opposition had assumed power, and the new president, Ms. Roza Otunbayeva, promised to reduce utility tariffs and provide more aid to the poor. But there was no law and order. Neighborhoods erected barricades; militia formed. Amidst the looting, ethnic violence began—Kyrgyz against Uzbek and some of the opposite. The economic suffering of the people and their resentment of the kleptocrat overclass were quickly mutating into ethnic hatred. The murder and rape of ethnic cleansing drove many thousands of terrified Uzbeks to flight toward the border—but Uzbekistan was sealed closed.[5] President Otunbayeva called for Russian military intervention. The Kremlin declined.[6] As the rampaging slowly subsided, Kyrgyzstan seemed on the verge of bloody ethnic fragmentation.

On June 10, the violence flared again, this time in the southern city of Osh. A minor fight between Uzbeks and Kyrgyz in a casino quickly escalated into pogroms. This time, Kyrgyz elements of the state security forces were involved in hunting down Uzbeks. Historically, the southern towns had been home to sedentary Uzbek traders and farmers, while the mostly nomadic or seminomadic Kyrgyz moved with their herds. But forced collectivization in the 1930s ended that pattern as ethnic Kyrgyz settled in the valleys among the ethnic Uzbeks. Competition for water and land emerged. As a Human Rights Watch report explained, "The problems became more acute as the population grew. Grievances over land and water distribution increasingly took on an ethnic dimension during the perestroika and glasnost era in the mid-to-late 1980s, as ethnic, linguistic, and cultural identities became stronger."[7] Southern Kyrgyzstan saw interethnic rioting in the 1990s during the breakup of the Soviet Union. In 1990, Kyrgyzstan's Uzbek minority tried to gain autonomy and join neighboring Uzbekistan; the intercommunal violence that followed took 1,000 lives. In 2010, more than 350 died and thousands were left homeless.[8]

. . . and Water

The sudden spasms of violence reflected, at first glance, a rebellion against a corrupt, self-dealing president and the reignition of allegedly age-old ethnic conflict. But there is an environmental issue at the heart of the trouble. It was, in fact, the catastrophic convergence playing out as ethnic rampaging. In Kyrgyzstan, neoliberal economic shock therapy, imposed after the Soviet Union's implosion, and the political-military blowback of Cold War proxy fights meet the incipient crisis of climate change.

As noted above, a key grievance of the Bishkek protesters was the price and scarcity of electricity, and that was due to the long Central Asian drought. The dry weather plus bad management had crippled Kyrgyzstan's hydroelectric power plants. From the spring of 2008 onward,

Kyrgyzstan suffered rolling blackouts.[9] In some areas, ten-hour blackouts everyday were the norm. Then, in 2009, Uzbekistan made things a bit worse by pulling out of the regional power grid built by the Soviet Union.[10]

Ninety percent of electricity produced in Kyrgyzstan comes from hydroelectric power stations; the largest single source of its electricity is the hydroelectric dam at the base of the Toktogul Reservoir on the river Naryn. In fact, the Toktogul power station is Central Asia's largest. A monument to Soviet modernism, it was built between 1975 and 1982 during the Brezhnev heyday of high oil prices, the peak of Soviet prosperity. The drought, however, meant low water levels in the Toktogul Reservoir, thus reduced power production.

Drought was not the only form of extreme weather to fuel the crisis. A bitterly cold winter, compounded by bad management and greed, helped reduce water levels even further. The winter of 2008 saw a deep and prolonged cold snap; temperatures dropped to −31°C, or −25°F—twice as cold as normal. Due to the drought, there were also power outages during the cold snap. Thus, many places had no heat or hot water! Across the country, pipes froze, pensioners died, industry seized up, livestock perished, and schools closed for two months—the country effectively shut down.

The freezing cold forced the government to release more water than planned; it was the only way to generate electricity, to overcome the crippling power cuts. With energy prices on the regional market spiking up, corrupt officials released even more water—to generate extra power to pirate off to Tajikistan, Uzbekistan, and Kazakhstan.

The winter of 2007 had been the driest since Toktogul was built. And in 2008, the reservoir "received only 70 percent of the average inflows," and its volume dropped to half its 2005 level.[11] As one local political analyst put it, "The water level is lower than the critical mark. So the question of whether we have light and heating this winter, and whether large and small businesses will grow, depends directly on whether the requisite level of water builds up in the reservoir."[12] It did not.

A hardship in and of themselves, the power cuts also had a damaging knock-on effect for the whole economy, creating unemployment and shortages. As industry closed, unemployment rose, and demand fell, creating more unemployment. Most, if not all, economic activity depends on electricity; without it, an economy begins to collapse. A Bishkek baker illustrated the process: "I'm practically ruined because of the rolling blackouts. . . . There have been many times when I've made the dough mixture to bake buns and the lack of electricity has meant it's gone to waste. I took out a loan a year ago and things were picking up steadily. But I've suffered badly from the lack of power. I have to pay interest and every month I just can't work out where I can get the money." A power-starved garment manufacturer said he was working at only 30 percent of the previous year's capacity. "Our business partners are cross with us because we're falling down on delivery agreements. We don't know how we can repay our loans."[13]

Collapsing production led to a shortfall in tax revenues, which worsened the state's fiscal crisis. Dr. Nur Omarov, professor of international relations at Kyrgyz-Russian Slavic University, had it right when he told a reporter, "A social explosion is in the offing. It all depends on who organizes the protesting masses."[14]

Last Straw

In February 2010, even as top-ranking government officials illegally sold power, President Bakiyev *doubled* the cost of electricity, heating, and water and planned to raise rates *again* by midyear. Immediately, people in provincial cities like Naryn protested with placards reading, "We can't pay the new prices for electricity" and "Government, listen to us!"[15]

Bishkek's mayor, Nariman Tuleev, had earlier warned the central government that price hikes would have a damaging effect on the city budget and larger economy. The "lonely and elderly pensioners, disabled persons, many workers of public-financed organizations with low salaries" would be hit hardest, warned the mayor. He added that he feared "the wave of discontent" this might bring, and wanted to "prevent social protests" by increasing wages and subsidies to the indigent.[16]

The free market–loving president did not listen.

Post-Soviet Crisis

The drought that caused the power shortages, which in turn began to crip-
ple the economy and lent justification to Bakiyev's draconian price hikes on
utilities, was only part of the problem. The Kyrgyz system was already
weak before the extreme weather pushed it over the edge.

During the Soviet period, Kyrgyzstan's economy was structured by sub-
sidized integration into the greater USSR, in a pattern that one scholar
called "welfare colonialism." During the late Cold War, Kyrgyzstan became a major producer of weapons and military goods for the Red Army.
But it lost those markets in the chaos of the USSR's disintegration.

In the eyes of Ahmed Rashid, "The salient fact about Central Asia
today is that independent statehood was neither coveted nor sought by
the region's ruling Communist elites. It was thrust upon them when the
Soviet Union broke up in 1991. Thus the region's rulers were suddenly
compelled to fabricate a new identity for their five ethnically diverse states—
Kazakhstan, Kyrgyzstan, Tajikistan, Turkmenistan, and Uzbekistan—and
to contend for the first time with radically differing ideologies."[17] And,
one might add, new economies.

After 1991, Kyrgyzstan became one of Central Asia's smallest and most
liberalized economies. With the sudden loss of Soviet markets and subsidies, Kyrgyzstan went to the World Bank and International Monetary
Fund for aid. These institutions in turn demanded an array of neoliberal
reforms. The Kyrgyz political elites—high on the academic grog of neo-
classical economic orthodoxy—complied more than willingly. Kyrgyzstan
privatized agriculture, industry, and utilities; it moved to a freely convert-
ible currency and removed most trade barriers. By the end of the 1990s,
three-quarters of the economy had been privatized.[18]

This was supposed to spur growth, but it only deepened de-industrial-
ization: markets were now swamped by cheap foreign products that entered free of charge. Unable to compete with imports, many privatized
firms were simply stripped of assets. Unemployment soared, and workers
moved from cities back to the farms or out of the country. Between five
and eight hundred thousand Kyrgyz now work abroad, their remittances

forming an essential part of the economy. The Kyrgyz GDP fell by approximately 45 percent between 1991 and 1996 as industrial production collapsed and Soviet markets for Kyrgyz dairy products evaporated; inflation hit 1,200 percent in 1993.[19] Per capita income has not yet returned to its 1989 levels, and Kyrgyz income inequality is among the worst in the region. The collapse of public services, such as health care and education, has forced people to fend for themselves. Over 20 percent of the population lives on less than $2 a day. More than 40 percent of Kyrgyz are poor, meaning they struggle to meet life's basic necessities.

Three-quarters of the government's income from the sale of state assets went to paying off international debts. The privatization process was largely stopped and even reversed somewhat after the late 1990s. In 2010 the country had a GDP of about of $11.66 billion and (good news) an external debt of only about $3.4 billion.[20] Kyrgyzstan's mountains hold deposits of gold, rare earth, and other minerals, and its border with China means it could be pulled into the development vortex that is the PRC.

For now, however, Kyrgyzstan's people are mired in poverty and corruption.[21] Official unemployment is 20 percent, and with little prospect for a better future, elements of the population—its lumpenized, angry young men—turn to crime, drug running, nationalist xenophobia, and radical forms of political Islam.

Central Asian Jihad

The new states of Central Asia are defined by kleptocracy, despotism, dysfunction, and weakness. Over the last two decades, nonstate armed actors— ethnic warlords, drug traffickers, mercenaries, tribal militias, bandit gangs, and internationally connected terrorist networks, like Al Qaeda and the Islamic Movement of Uzbekistan (IMU)—have traversed the region, fought wars in it, and when pressured, moved south into the lawless regions of Afghanistan and Pakistan.[22]

Once economically and politically integrated and interdependent components of the Soviet Union, the Central Asian states now find themselves squabbling over previously shared resources and lines of communication and transportation. The ethnic populations that form these states' nominal basis are also scattered across national boundaries. For example, Uzbek minorities live all across Kazakhstan, Kyrgyzstan, and Tajikistan.

No place embodies these stresses more than the heavily populated Fergana Valley. Here, the boundaries between Uzbekistan, Tajikistan, and Kyrgyzstan bend in a convoluted pattern of political fragmentation. The area's economic infrastructure, however, follows the natural logic of the landscape. The drainage of the Syr Darya River links the three states and peoples. The river offers a Ratzelian logic of economic integration: the water and valley offer the promise of combined hydropower, agriculture, and transportation links. But the post-Soviet chaos, ethnic nationalism of political bosses, and economic suffering brought by neoliberal shock therapy have devastated the Fergana. Today, it incubates violent combinations of political Islam and ethnic irredentism.

We can see the future of Fergana Valley insecurity in its past. As early as 1917, local mullahs, landlords, and clan leaders in the valley and across Central Asia mounted an anti-Bolshevik resistance. These traditionalist, protomujahideen—called *Basmachi*, meaning "bandits," by the Soviets—described themselves as standing for Islam, Turkic nationalism, and anti-communism. One of these bands of Muslim rebels was led by Enver Pasha, the former Young Turk, Ottoman minister of war, pan-Turkish utopian, and early abuser of Armenians who had left Turkey to fight further east. Various *Basmachi* forces used northern Afghanistan as a sanctuary, and those led by Ibrahim Bek were not finally crushed until the early 1930s and only then with cooperation between the royal Afghan military and the Red Army.[23]

When war again broke out in Afghanistan during the 1980s, radical Islam also churned in Soviet Central Asia. An estimated thirty-five thousand Muslim fighters from all over the world passed through the Afghan war to fight for the mujahideen. Thousands more studied in radical madrassas in Pakistan.[24] Through this circuitry of jihad the volunteers flowed, concentrated in the war zone on the border, where they absorbed military skills and radical ideas. Among them were Uzbeks, Tajiks, and Kyrgyz from the Soviet republics.

In 1987 some mujahideen from Afghanistan—elements of the fanatic Gulbuddin Hekmatyar's Hezb-i-Islami—crossed into Soviet Tajikistan, attacked border guards, and rocketed the city of Panj.[25] At the time, the US press wrote, "The guerrillas announced March 24 that about two weeks earlier, they had fired rockets across the Amu Daryu River into Soviet territory, killing up to 12 people." On April 8, two Soviet border guards were killed during a second attack.[26]

Five years later the region imploded. The worst and most intense civil war of that decade was the Tajik conflagration. As many as sixty thousand people were killed, and Human Rights Watch described massive ethnic cleansing campaigns. At the end of the war, elements of an Islamic resistance party joined the extremist IMU and made incursions into Kyrgyzstan's portion of the Fergana Valley, parts of which are also controlled by Uzbekistan and Tajikistan. In 1999 and 2000, joint Kyrgyz-Uzbek military operations pushed the IMU into Afghanistan and then Pakistan.[27]

By the summer of 2010, with Kyrgyzstan smashed by its climate-induced unrest, the IMU was rumored to be moving back into the Fergana Valley. The Kyrgyz government had lost control of much of the South of the country. As the head of the International Crisis Group, writing in the *Independent*, warned, "No one should underestimate the potential for large-scale ethnic violence to spread throughout the Ferghana Valley." The region was primed for crisis.

The drought in Kyrgyzstan finally broke in 2010. The same weather patterns that brought Pakistan to its knees brought reprieve for hydropower-dependant Kyrgyzstan. By August 2010, heavy rains had restored the water levels in the Toktogul reservoir.[28] However, the Kyrgyzstan story is not over. The country remains divided, armed, and desperate. And the weather patterns upon which its hydro-dependent economy relies are increasingly eratic and very likely will become even more so as climate change intensifies.

CHAPTER 11

India and Pakistan: Glaciers, Rivers, and Unfinished Business

Water Flows or Blood

—*Protest sign in Pakistan*

PAKISTAN AND INDIA are famously locked in struggle. An important cause of this enmity is each side's need for water. An important method in the conflict is Pakistan's use of militant Islamist guerrillas and terrorists as proxies against India. One of this struggle's crucial battlefields is Afghanistan.

As climate change increases water stress in South and Central Asia, the India-Pakistan conflict, already unfolding on multiple fronts, is further aggravated. The India-Pakistan conflict is not reducible to water; nor is it caused by climate change. However, water and climate are key drivers of the conflict. As climate change brings more extreme weather, monsoon disruptions, flooding, drought, and rapid glacial melting, it plays an ever-greater role in shaping the India-Pakistan conflict.

Water Tower Karakorum

The India-Pakistan conflict pivots on Kashmir, in part because 90 percent of Pakistan's agricultural irrigation depends on rivers that originate in the region, much of which is occupied by the Indian military.[1] The conflict

123

began in 1947 during Partition. Under the British Raj, the princely state of Jammu and Kashmir had a Muslim majority but was ruled by a Hindu maharajah and his court staffed by Hindu outsiders.

The logic of partition was that India's Muslims and Hindus constituted separate nations. The Muslim League put this forward, and the Indian National Congress reluctantly agreed to the idea of geographic separation along religious lines. That process quickly turned apocalyptic as Hindus and Muslims turned on one another; 1 million people were killed and 15 million displaced. These intercommunal conflicts were religious in name but also involved displaced and distorted class conflicts. As a scholar of that era put it, "Communalism is more than a religious phenomenon. Its social and economic overtones appear when peasants who happen to be Muslims are oppressed by Hindu money-lenders or when Muslim weavers strike against Hindu mill owners."[2]

A central element in Partition was the fate of British India's 560 small, semiautonomous, so-called princely states. All were advised to accede to either Pakistan or India. Since the logic of Partition was that Muslim-majority areas should go to Pakistan, Kashmir seemed to belong there: it was more than 70 percent Muslim, and most of its trade links and communications lines tied it to that region. In one version of the original acronym that became the name Pakistan, the *k* stood for Kashmir.[3] Additionally, and very importantly, "its three mountain-fed rivers, the Indus, the Jhelum (which flows through the famed Vale of Kashmir), and the Chenab, join in a single stream to descend through the Pakistan lowlands and empty into the Arabian Sea at Karachi."[4]

Indian leaders, however, saw Kashmir as a resource frontier and geostrategic asset that was too valuable to concede—remember, along with huge glaciers, it had forests, minerals, and borders with Afghanistan, the Soviet Union, and China. As Alice Thorner, a leading historian of India, explained at the time, "Kashmir was conceived as both a gateway to greater Indian influence in Central Asia and a bastion of defense. India alone, it was argued, had the economic strength to develop Kashmir's so far untapped water-power potential and mineral resources."[5]

The Hindu maharajah and his court were reluctant to yield their autonomy to either state, and a three-way stalemate ensued. Then, on October 22, 1947, Pakistan made its move. In the predawn gloom, an armed column of approximately two thousand Pashtun tribesmen—the first generation of Pakistan's mercenary guerillas, recruited from the northwest borderlands with Afghanistan and led by a major in Pakistan's army—invaded Kashmir. They drove sixty miles beyond the border before meeting opposition from a small force of Kashmir state troops. The maharajah's government called for Indian military aid. As Indian troops were dispatched over the mountains by air, Kashmir's Hindu leader finally agreed to Indian control. When Indian soldiers touched down in Singar, they found the town unoccupied but soon fought approaching tribesmen. The Pashtun had faltered in their advance, as renegade groups broke away from the main column to plunder. India soon held half of Kashmir.

Pakistan immediately went on record as refusing to recognize Kashmir's accession to India, and both states publicly agreed there should be a referendum on the matter. However, in private, Jawaharlal Nehru opposed the idea.[6] India wanted, needed, felt it deserved Kashmir—a referendum would likely mean giving it to Pakistan. Two weeks later, India launched an assault that took two-thirds of the Pakistani-controlled territory.[7] By the middle of the next summer, Pakistan had regular military units in the fight.[8]

Thus, Kashmir's leaders went with India, while its majority Muslim population began to seethe under Indian occupation, and no referendum was held. Kashmir emerged from Partition divided and occupied. And beneath the Muslim-versus-Hindu conflict lurked the issue of water.

Riparian Politics

As far back as 1957, political leaders pointed to the centrality of water. Consider the comments of Hussain Suhrawardy, then prime minister of Pakistan:

There are, as you know, six rivers. Most of them rise in Kashmir. One of the reasons why, therefore, that Kashmir is so important for us, is this water, these waters which irrigate our lands. They do not irrigate Indian lands. Now, what India has done—it is not threatening—it has actually, it is building a dam today, and it is threatening to cut off the waters of the three rivers for the purpose of irrigating some of its lands. Now, if it does so without replacement, it is obvious that we shall be starved out and people will die of thirst. Under these circumstances—I hope that contingency will never arise—you can well realize that rather than die in that manner, people will die fighting.[9]

And so they did. In 1965 India and Pakistan went to war over Kashmir. Again in 1999 the armies clashed in that region.[10] India and Pakistan have conducted four wars during which Pakistan usually fared poorly. Two of them were fought over water-rich Kashmir. In 1971 Pakistan lost half its territory thanks to India. When a devastating cyclone in East Pakistan was met with a grossly inadequate government response, a secessionist movement launched a war for independence. Indian forces intervened to help them. Rebels captured ninety thousand Pakistani soldiers and helped midwife the new nation of Bangladesh.

Consider the conflict from the Pakistani point of view. Pakistan is long and thin, sandwiched between two hostile states, India and Afghanistan. It is arid with a large and growing population, most of which works in agriculture. As such, Pakistan is one of the most "water-stressed" countries in the world, and this fact helps animate the struggle with India over control of Kashmir and Jammu. The Indus and its main tributaries rise in Tibet, travel through India into Pakistan, then descend from the cold mountains onto the hot, fertile plains of the Punjab to water the nation's breadbasket.

The Indus is Pakistan's economic spine. Without the river, Pakistan's stock of groundwater and impounded reserves would only last a month. No river, no country. And atop the river sits the enemy, India: huge, economically dynamic, politically democratic, internationally respected, and atomically armed. To the west, sitting upon the Kabul River, which drains into the Indus, is India's unstable, often perfidious ally, Afghanistan.

Afghanistan has switched from monarchy to republic, from one-party communist state to multiparty democracy, but never—except during Taliban rule—has she left India's side. Imagine the stress this equation causes for Pakistan's military and political elites. Pakistan is simply overmatched by India.

Paradox of Scarcity

Within this story of rivalry, water serves as a cause of both destabilization and, surprisingly, cooperation.[11] One of the only transboundary water agreements in Central Asia is also the least likely: Pakistan and India are united by the Indus Water Treaty of 1960, negotiated under auspice of the World Bank.

According to the treaty, Pakistan receives exclusive rights to the waters of the Indus and its main western tributaries, the Jhelum and Chenab. India is allocated the eastern tributaries of Ravi, Beas, and Sutlej.[12] India can dam these rivers for power, fish from them, channel them for navigation, and so on, but it must release most of the water to Pakistan. In total, Pakistan should receive 80 percent of the waters that might otherwise reach the Indus. In the 1950s, as the treaty took form, India clearly had the upper hand, but it needed World Bank financing to develop its economy. So, India agreed to terms that favored Pakistan.[13]

Surprisingly, to date, the treaty has functioned. Why? One academic has argued that India and Pakistan cooperate because doing so is "water rational," meaning, "cooperation was needed to safe-guard the countries' long-term access to shared water."[14] But that tautology leaves unanswered the question: Why is conquest not water rational?

The central issue in the treaty is India's advantage. As the upstream riparian with the superior military, India could take more water. In fact, India could destroy Pakistan by turning the breadbasket of the Punjab into a desert. However, in the late 1950s, when the treaty was being negotiated, both countries needed World Bank financing, and only cooperation over water guaranteed that. Further, though Pakistan was in a weak position, India also faced significant constraints. Pakistan was closely allied to the

United States and was part of the US-backed Southeast Asian Treaty Organization. Pakistan was also growing close to China, India's rival. Two years after the treaty was signed, India and China even fought a brief war for control of other glacial peaks.

Numerous other aspects of the international equation stayed India's hand. For India to have launched an all-out war for Jammu and Kashmir and then built dams to divert Indus headwaters would have constituted an act of intolerable aggression.

Instead, India holds Muslim-majority Kashmir as occupied territory. An intifada-like popular resistance now grips the province. During the crisis summer of 2010, Indian forces killed a demonstrator or two every few days.[15] Indian officials in Kashmir are accused of ignoring "Kashmir's significant economic troubles, rampant corruption, and rigged elections" and of intervening "in Kashmiri politics in ways that contradicted India's own constitution."[16]

Rigged state-assembly elections in 1987 ignited widespread violent opposition. By 1992, as the jihad in Afghanistan wound down, some mujahideen pivoted from Afghanistan to Kashmir. The struggle for Kashmiri independence began to morph into an "Islamist crusade to bring all of Kashmir under Pakistani control."[17] The NATO occupation of Afghanistan since 2001 has not siphoned off militants from Kashmir but instead reinvigorated the entire Central Asian conflict system. Now the brutal tempo of drought and flooding exacerbates the tensions.

Bellicose Dams

In 2008 India inaugurated the 450-megawatt Baglihar hydroelectric dam on the Chenab and began restricting the flow of water to Pakistan. The Chenab rises in Kashmir and drains into Pakistan. Pakistan tried to stop construction of the Baglihar Dam by appealing to the World Bank in 2005. The project went ahead nonetheless, after India agreed to reduce the dam's height and promised not to restrict the river's flow.[18]

Yet, the Baglihar Dam is only one of several under construction.[19] The more paranoid and bellicose Pakistani activists say India has already constructed forty-four dams on "Pakistan's rivers" and has another fifty-two dams in process.[20] India maintains it is merely harnessing the energy of the water or clearing rivers for navigation and is not impounding and diverting more than its share. Pakistan disputes this and points to the decreased flows in its rivers.

In the summer of 2008, farmers along the Chenab reported lower levels of both the river and groundwater.[21] Under the Indus Water Treaty of 1960, Pakistan is to receive fifty-five thousand cusecs of water. (A cusec is a volumetric unit for measuring the flow of liquids, equal to one cubic foot per second.) In recent years, Pakistan has protested that India is cutting the water flow to a mere thirteen thousand cusecs during the winter and a maximum of twenty-nine thousand cusecs during summer. This damages both agriculture and electrical power generation, which in turn harms industry and manufacturing.[22]

To make matters worse, Pakistan reports declining rainfall and dangerous over-exploitation of groundwater. Water tables in Islamabad and Rawalpindi decreased between 1 and 2 meters per year, between 1982 and 2000. In Quetta, the parched capital of Balochistan, the water table is falling by 3.5 meters annually.[23] According to Pakistan's Water and Power Development Authority, the last 50 years have seen annual per capita water availability drop by almost 80 percent, from 5,600 to 1,038 cubic meters. By 2025 that figure is expected to fall to only 809 cubic meters per person, per year.[24]

Now, the India-Pakistan tensions—born in part of a water dispute and exacerbated by climate change—are being displaced onto, and played out as, religious war. The Muslim fanatics of Pakistan talk of water, god, and violence all in the same breath.

In 2010 the religious militant Hafiz Muhammad Saeed, head of the Jamaat-ut-Dawa (JuD) and founder of the outlawed Lashkar-e-Taiba, a terrorist group linked to Pakistan's military, accused India of "water terrorism" because it was building tunnels and dams on key Indus tributaries. India claims this does not impact water levels. But water volumes are decreasing, and Pakistani farmers have marched, warning, "Water Flows or Blood."[25]

Now militants of the JuD are building a water movement. A meeting they called in May 2010 was attended by representatives of most major political parties, including the Pakistan People's Party, Jamaat-e-Islami, and cricketer-turned-politician Imran Khan's Tehrik-e-Insaaf. At the meeting the JuD demanded the government stop India from building dams in Kashmir or give the "Kashmiri mujahideen" a "free hand" to address the problem.[26] "We have two options, either to accept India's water terrorism or wage a war against it," said senior JuD leader Hafiz Khalid Waleed. A leader of another party stoked anti-Semitism by claiming, "Israeli engineers are overseeing the building of dams blocking Pakistan's share of waters."[27]

Strategic Displacement

The climate-exacerbated water tensions between these two nuclear-armed states also get displaced onto, and play out as, religious and ethnic war in Afghanistan. For Afghans, the enmity between their state and Pakistan is rooted in Afghanistan's loss of territory to British India in 1893, when the Durand Line, now the Afghanistan-Pakistan border, was forced upon Afghanistan's "Iron Emir" Abdul Racman Kahn. In that bargain, Afghanistan lost a large amount of its Pashtun territory. Among Afghans that wound still festers. For Pakistan the issue is India.

India has courted Afghanistan with more than $1.3 billion in reconstruction aid since 2001. Its political influence expands via intelligence assets, a large diplomatic footprint, new hospitals, hydroelectric projects, and road building—lots of roads, some of them suspiciously close to the Pakistani border.

Pakistan wants India's ally, Afghanistan, to remain weak. So, as it has in Kashmir, it supports radical groups like the Taliban. Since the mid-1970s, Pakistan has been destabilizing its western neighbor. Even now Pakistani intelligence has links to elements of the Quetta Shura Taliban, the Haqqani network, and Hezb-i-Islami.

Ahmed Rashid details how this support continued late into the Afghanistan war in his excellent *Descent into Chaos: The United States and*

the Failure of Nation Building in Pakistan, Afghanistan, and Central Asia.
He writes, "The Pakistani army believed that Karzai's interim government
was profoundly anti-Pakistani. . . . To maintain its influence among the
Taliban and Afghan Pashtuns, the ISI [Inter-Services Intelligence] developed a two-track policy of protecting the Taliban while handing over al
Qaeda Arabs and other non-Afghans to the United States." The United
States remained suspicious, and so the Pakistani intelligence created "a
new clandestine organization that would operate outside the military intelligence structures, in the civilian sphere. Former ISI trainers of the Taliban, retired Pashtun officers from the Army and especially the Frontier
Corps, were rehired on contract. They set up offices in private houses in
Peshawar, Quetta, and other cities, and maintained no links with the local
ISI station chief or the Army. Most of these agents held down regular jobs
working undercover as coordinators for Afghan refugees, bureaucrats, researchers at universities, teachers at colleges, and even aid workers. Others
set up NGOs ostensibly to work with Afghan refugees."[28]

In 2007 it was discovered that much of the $5 billion the United States
had spent bolstering the Pakistani military's effort to fight Al Qaeda and
the Taliban had been stolen or diverted to build up the military's posture
vis-à-vis India. Meanwhile, elements of the Pakistani security forces continued working with the Taliban.

When I interviewed Taliban fighters in Zabul Province, Afghanistan, in
2006, they described themselves as based in, and supported by, Pakistan.[29]
"Pakistan stands with us," said one Talib. "And on that side of the border
we have our offices. Pakistan is supporting us; they supply us. Our leaders
are there collecting help. The people on this side of the border also support
us." A few days later I reached Taliban spokesman Dr. Mohammed Hanif
(later captured), who also confirmed Pakistani support.[30]

In June 2010, the ISI-Taliban link received further confirmation when
the London School of Economics' Development Studies Institute issued a
scathingly detailed report documenting how the Pakistani spy agency controls the Taliban as best it can—and not always with Afghan enthusiasm
or even consent. Written by Matt Waldman of the Carr Center for Human
Rights Policy at Harvard University, the report described an ISI-Taliban

relationship as going "far beyond contact and coexistence." It outlines how the ISI exerts control, deals with opposition from more-independent Taliban commanders, and has provided transportation, intelligence, munitions, fire support, and so on.[31]

Why does Pakistan do this?

Here is how US Director of National Intelligence Dennis C. Blair explained it in February 2010: "Militant groups are an important part of [Pakistan's] strategic arsenal to counter India's military and economic advantages."[32] Pakistan's proxies strike directly at Indian assets in Kashmir, India, and Afghanistan. Taliban terrorists have killed Indian engineers, police trainers, and diplomats working in Afghanistan. In July 2008, Taliban commandos with alleged links to the Pakistani ISI bombed the Indian embassy in Kabul, killing 41 and wounding or maiming 130 others. In October 2008, another suicide car bomb hit the Indian embassy, killing 17 Afghans who were waiting in line for visas. In the autumn of 2009, men with links to Lashkar-e-Taiba attacked two Kabul guesthouses full of personnel from the Indian army's medical and educational corps.[33]

Triage

Pakistan security forces will not end their support for the religious radicals who make war on India and Afghanistan. There will be no rollback of Taliban-style fundamentalism and no end to the struggle over Kashmir unless Pakistan's security vis-à-vis India is guaranteed. That security, increasingly, pivots on the issue of water, and the 1960 Indus Water Treaty is now fraying badly.

CHAPTER 12

India's Drought Rebels

The man who has gotten everything he wants is all in favor of
peace and order.

—JAWAHARLAL NEHRU

B ARREN FORESTS COVER the hills of northern Andhra Pradesh
on the edge of India's Deccan Plateau. It is February, summertime
for this region, and the deciduous trees have dropped their leaves in the dry
heat. The landscape is peculiar: flat-topped hills with steep ridges run in
long lines often marked by horizontal cliffs. Between these lie broad valley plains, containing occasional piles of volcanic rubble.[1]

Life for the farmers here is difficult. "There is declining rain, and this
affects yields, and the prices are still low," says Linga Reddy Sama, a cotton farmer in the village of Jaamni, a few kilometers from the Sathnala
Reservoir not far from the border of Chhattisgarh and Maharashtra states.
Most of the people in this area are *Adivasi*, or "tribal people," the Gonds of
the Adilabad District. Others are Hindu migrants who came down from
the state of Maharashtra.

On that day in 2009, when I sat in the shade of a roughhewn wood arbor
with a group of farmers, none of them had yet heard of greenhouse gases
or anthropogenic climate change. However, they all thought the weather
was changing. They said that in the last ten to fifteen years, regular drought

and strangely timed rains had become very common. Many of them speculated that deforestation was the culprit.

"This generation has done something wrong to affect the rains like this," said a farmer named Mohan Rao. "When I was a child, the forests came right up to here. You couldn't see those hills; all of this was covered in trees. We used to have two rainy seasons. In June we planted irrespective of rain; we planted between the fifteenth and twenty-eighth, and by September we harvested." He said typically the summer rains fall for three or four months and are then followed by lighter, shorter rains in the late autumn.

That pattern is common across South India. The summer monsoon blows in off the Indian Ocean, usually making landfall in southern India about June 1. These mighty rains arrive because the rising summertime temperature of the Indian landmass sucks moist air in off the ocean. The moisture rises, cools, and falls as rain. The monsoon is split into two branches by India's coastal mountain ranges, the Ghats, and most of the rain falls on western coastal India, leaving much of the central region quite dry. The monsoons travel north until September; then, as the sun begins moving south, the weather system begins its retreat back in that direction, creating the winter monsoon. The summer monsoons account for four-fifths of India's total rainfall; the lighter, retreating or northwest monsoons deliver the rest. But things are less stable than in the past. The farmers say recent years have seen only light winter rains. That makes it impossible to plant a second cotton crop.

To make matters worse, this area has been in the grip of a nasty little guerrilla war. India, the world's largest democracy, is also home to one of the world's oldest guerrilla movements—a Maoist insurgency known as the Naxalites. The Maoist's war began in 1967 in West Bengal. Their parties have fragmented and reunited as the war has ebbed and flowed.[2] Today, this low-intensity conflict runs the length of eastern India and has a variety of geographically specific causes. In Bihar and Chattisgarh, the heart of the violence, large-scale mining on tribal lands is the immediate cause of troubles. But elsewhere, we find the catastrophic convergence.

If one compares maps of precipitation with those of violence, a disturbing pattern emerges: where drought advances, so do Maoists. This geography runs down the Eastern Ghats, from Bihar and West Bengal, through Orissa and Chattisgarh, into Andhra Pradesh and even further south and west. This "Red Corridor" is also the drought corridor. Drought produces a chain reaction of debt, land loss, hunger, suicide, banditry, and Maoism.

Why this neat correlation? The link is not "natural" but rather historically produced. In the years of the Naxal rise in Andhra Pradesh, drought was also intense: 1984–1985, 1986–1987, 1997–1998, 1999–2000, and 2002–2003 were all drought years.[3]

As India's weather patterns have grown more disjointed, so too have its economic policies shifted rightward to effectively abandon the peasant farming class and create greater inequality. If the catastrophic convergence in East Africa pivoted primarily upon Cold War militarism, then in India the story foregrounds economic neoliberalism. The Maoist fire burns not only due to drought but also because of free-market government policy. The rest of this chapter traces the connections between climate, economic history, and political violence in Andhra Pradesh.

Deep Roots of Rebellion

The language of the guerrillas permeates political discourse among the Gonds of Telangana, as the northern part of Andhra Pradesh is known. Repression makes the farmers reticent, but any discussion of the weather and economy soon yields hints of Naxalite ideology.

"Jal, jungle, zameen," said one of the farmers in Jamni village. It means "water, forest, land" and has been a rallying cry for the social organizations of the local Gonds. It is also a Naxalite battle cry, a defense of the commons against all who would encroach. But the concept goes back further, to a tribal rebellion against the nizam, the old Muslim ruler of Telangana. During the 1940s, tribals, led by Komaram Bheem, and communists rebelled against their feudal overlords. During the British Raj, Telangana remained nominally free as one of the semiautonomous princely states.

Atop the old order sat the nizam, the Muslim head of state ruling from the city of Hyderabad. From the seventeenth century until 1948, a succession of nizams ruled, but always in league with a class of Hindi landlords, the *dora*. Together, the nizam and dora, the landed aristocracy, extracted heavy agricultural rents from the rural population but invested little in infrastructure. By the early twentieth century, the British had insinuated themselves into the nizam's court and controlled its finances and external relations. Nonetheless, the nizam still did well. In fact, the last nizam, Osman Ali Khan Bahadur, who ruled from 1911 to 1948, was for a time the wealthiest man in the world and even made the cover of *Time* in 1937.[4] But in 1948, with the cataclysm of Partition as backdrop, the arrogant noble overplayed his hand when he dallied during accession negotiations with India.

As with Kashmir, newly independent India saw it as entirely unfeasible to accept a somewhat hostile Muslim-ruled state wedged into its southeast. On September 13, 1948, negotiations ended when Jawaharlal Nehru decided unilaterally and by force that Telangana would join India. The massive Indian army rolled in and crushed the nizam's palace guard, plus a supporting cast of Muslim irregulars called *Razakars*. This four-day "war" was called Operation Polo in a mocking reference to the nizam's many well-appointed playing fields. Thus, the Hyderabad state was annexed to the Republic of India.

For Telangana farmers, however, the fundamentals did not change. The region remained isolated and economically stagnant, and its peasants continued to live in a matrix of risk, caught between the vicissitudes of markets, state policies, and weather. The last of these factors, weather, tends to matter most in the arid and semiarid regions that cover 60 percent of India.[5]

The various Naxalite factions trace their origins to the Communist Party of India (Maoist) and an obscure 1967 massacre in the eponymous West Bengal village of Naxalbari, in the famous tea-growing subdivision of Darjeeling.[6] In 1969, the Naxalites congealed into a political party called the Communist Party of India (Marxist-Leninist), but the party was outlawed. That forced the Naxals to hide in remote backwaters where they tended to fragment into factions, without centralized leadership.[7] From the beginning, Naxals were found in West Bengal, Bihar, and Andhra Pradesh.[8]

Naxalism Now

Over the course of the conversation with struggling farmers in Jaamni, it finally comes out that this village has had Naxalite-connected mass-based organizations. Through these movements, the villagers have repeatedly protested, staging *darna*, or traffic stops, to demand government investment in their water systems. Collectively, they want borehole wells and lift irrigation to bring water from the Sathnala Reservoir. Individually, many of them just want to leave for Hyderabad and its promise of work on constructions sites or to go north to Maharashtra, where they can work as agricultural laborers on large farms.

The Naxalite war is a strange affair that mixes open political advocacy by students and urban intellectuals with nonviolent direct action by peasant organizations (such as road blockades), and the terrorist methods of the guerrilla cadre (such as assassinations and mining of roads). The Naxals hardly seem capable of taking state power, but neither did their fight wind down with the end of the Cold War. In recent years the state has pushed back with a classic, increasingly violent counterinsurgency, hunting down and killing both insurgents and their civilian supporters. The war is creating centrifugal forms of violence that leave the social fabric weakened and infected with corruption, crime, and pathology.

In this district, the little war against the Naxalites has mostly been won, at least for the moment. Yet, civilian Naxal supporters still close roads with blockades, and the people here still observe the anniversary of an infamous April 20, 1981, massacre in which police shot dead as many as one hundred tribals at the village of Indervelli.[9] The Naxals also pass through, sometimes killing informants (real or imagined). A local student, a Gond tribal who was showing me around, said that the previous year guerrillas had accused a cousin of his of informing and killed him. Other Adilabad locals have died at the hands of the Greyhounds—the state police special forces.

In 2008 Naxals even attacked a police boat on the Balimeda-Sileru reservoir near the Andhra-Orissa border. In that fight, fifty-nine Greyhounds on "combing operations" decided for some reason to cross the reservoir in a single boat, only to be attacked by Maoists firing from nearby hills. The police boat capsized, and thirty-eight of the commandos were killed.[10]

Climate, Water, and War

In Telangana, water is political; to manage water is to manage society. The region is bound by the Godavari River to the north and the Krishna River to the south. Both began as rain-fed rivers, not glacier-fed ones, like the Ganga and Indus. As such, Telangana's rivers are extremely vulnerable to climate variability and local deforestation. The Godavari and Krishna both rise in the Western Ghats—the mountains and escarpments that catch the greater part of the summer monsoons—and drain east across the Deccan Plateau, through Telangana, eventually discharging into the Bay of Bengal. When the monsoons fail, the rivers are reduced to mere memories. Even in the epic monsoon of 2010, Adilabad still had a 25 percent deficit below the regional norm.[11]

Climate scientists predict *cataclysmic* physical changes for the subcontinent in the very near future. The Fourth Assessment Report of the Intergovernmental Panel on Climate Change (IPCC) made an infamous and very serious error in predicting the speed of future glacial melt.[12] But after all the science had been subject to hostile vetting, the IPCC Fourth Assessment Report's core findings remained true: "The entire Hindu Kush–Himalaya ice mass has decreased in the last two decades." And it continues to do so at an alarming rate.[13]

Now consider this: two-thirds of Indians are farmers, most of whom depend on Himalayan glacial runoff or the monsoon rains. And the region's hydrological system is sliding into crisis: monsoon variability is increasing; the rains are late or too light, or they come heavily all at once. In the winter, some areas get no rain.

When I interviewed one of India's top climatologists, Dr. Murari Lal, he was distraught: "The political class are in total denial. They are not dealing with the issue of climate change. They think it is a rich man's problem. Nothing can get in the way of 'India Shining.' You understand? They are thinking, 'Development first, then address the environment.' It has only been due to pressure from the international community, and only in the last three years, that they have even begun to realize that there is a problem." A few months later, India's environment minister, Jairam Ramesh, shocked the world when he accused rich nations of needlessly raising alarm. "Science has its limitation," said the minister.[14]

Lal's specialty is the monsoon system, and he is a crucial player in the IPCC. He says the monsoons are "exhibiting increased variability" with a slight increase in overall precipitation, but in such an erratic fashion that, in combination with bad land management and inadequate attention to water harvesting, the general direction is toward increased desertification and drought despite more rainfall. "Ten years ago I predicted the decline of the winter rains in the north, and already that's happened," said Lal in sad exasperation.[15]

The US intelligence community has also noticed. In February 2010, National Intelligence Director Adm. Dennis C. Blair told Congress, "For India, our research indicates the practical effects of climate change will be manageable by New Delhi through 2030. Beyond 2030, India's ability to cope will be reduced by declining agricultural productivity, decreasing water supplies, and increasing pressures from cross-border migration into the country."[16]

The core issue is water, both its quantity and quality. *When* the rain comes and *how* it falls is almost as important as *if* it falls. In other words, monsoon variability is bad news for Indian farmers. It has a negative effect on crop yields beyond what aggregate and average precipitation data can reveal. In social terms, monsoon variability manifests as increased debt, immiseration, migration, and social conflict.

India's other source of water is the Himalayan ice pack—the so-called third pole—and it is melting fast. The Himalaya's 46,298 glaciers hold water in frozen reserve for hundreds of millions of people in Asia.[17] If greenhouse gas emissions continue to increase unabated, and world temperatures continue to rise, and these masses of ice completely disappear, the Ganges, Indus, Yamuna, Brahmaputra, and other rivers that traverse the northern Indian plain will become mere seasonal waterways flowing only when the monsoons unleash.[18]

For example, the Ganges—or *Ganga Ma*, Hinduism's most sacred river, the water source for some 500 million people—has a dry-season flow that is 70 percent meltwater from the Gangotri Glacier, a vast channel of ice 5 miles wide and 15 miles long. The Gangotri is shrinking at a rate of 40 yards per year, nearly twice as fast as it was two decades ago.[19] This is typical of the "super-rapid decline in the glaciers of the region."[20] The Ganges is now in such serious decline that it is considered among the 10 most endangered rivers of the world.[21]

In the short term, this Himalayan melting will lead to increased runoff, but in the long term, Asia's glacier-fed rivers will largely vanish.[22] Meanwhile, population and water demand increase: by 2050, India will likely have a population bigger than China's, and some 900 million of these people will still be working the land.[23]

Hydraulic States—in Theory and Practice

Back in the village of Jaamni, in Adilabad District, the talk still turns on the issue of water. Some farmers here irrigate from small wells, some from a local river, but most depend primarily on rain, nothing more. They live by the mercy of the monsoon, much of which is kept off the Deccan by the Western and Eastern Ghats. Not far from the village is the almost completely dry river, which the locals simply call the Big Stream. It flows into the Sathnala reservoir, which is the product of a dam built in decades past.

In such a climate, rainwater harvesting and irrigation are essential parts of the landscape. In Andhra Pradesh and Tamul Nadu, most agriculture has traditionally been dependent on water impoundment and storage; "rainfall is diverted, captured, stored, and controlled in a large number of reservoirs," known locally as tanks, formed by blocking the drainage of natural depressions with crescent-shaped earthen dams.[24] Canals feed out from the tanks, and elaborate rules govern how and when water is allocated.

The irrigation systems of southern India were famously, and somewhat incorrectly, theorized in both Marx and Weber as the products of well-organized, stable, autarkic states. A long line of scholars following these foundational thinkers has assumed that large-scale irrigation is normally accompanied by despotism and stable state bureaucracies that absorb the surplus created by the society. This link between irrigation and state power is essential in Marx's theory of the "Asiatic mode of production."

In his classic *Oriental Despotism: A Comparative Study of Total Power*, Karl Wittfogel described water's political imperatives thus: "No operational necessity compels [a farmer] to manipulate either soil or plants in cooperation with many others. But the bulkiness of all except the smallest sources of water supply creates a technical task which is solved either by mass labor or not at all."[25] Another scholar explained, "The need to control corvee labor and competition between societies requires ever larger works; larger works require heavier corvees of labor, heavier corvees require higher levels of integration and co-ordination and therefore large permanent systems ultimately require permanent specialized bureaucracies who will decide how many people are needed for what, and where. These must be 'vertically' organized."[26] In other words, the argument behind the idea of hydraulic despotism or the Asiatic mode of production: large-scale canal irrigation systems seem to require mass organization, and that seems to require a centralized powerful state.

In reality, India's old irrigation systems seem to have evolved slowly, piecemeal, haphazardly, through a succession of political arrangements that were often unstable and punctuated by violence. Viewed over the long term, plenty of social change and instability existed, especially at the political and geographic margins of states.[27] As the anthropologist David Mosse argued contra the old consensus, in southern India war and the rule of warriors was always bound up with irrigation and water rights—but that did not always mean stability. Political conflict was ongoing, and irrigation systems most likely have always existed in a state of relative crisis and ill repair.

British representatives of the East India Company latched on to this fact and used it as an ideological prop in their larger mission. They took great pains to note the dilapidation of water works in their reports; as Mosse explains, "These officers were the first to put into place a representation of tanks as part of the noble tradition of the ancient community eroded by contemporary exploitative rulers. And from this damaged landscape, they read justification for the extension of a British rule of order and property."[28]

Thus, water, irrigation, and extreme weather have been central to Indian politics, power structures, property arrangements, and traditions of repression and resistance for centuries. Climate change—and the catastrophic convergence by which it is expressed within the social world—is only enhancing water's significance.

Neoliberalism and Death by Cotton

The farmers in Telangana all grow genetically modified *Bacillus thuringiensis* (Bt) cotton, a product of the agricultural giant Monsanto. The new cotton became available a few years back. Although advertised as not needing pesticides, it does. At first it boosted output and incomes, but after a few years, incomes fell and the new cotton became a curse. Its roots penetrate deep into the soil, sucking up all the nutrients. Before long the farmers need large amounts of artificial fertilizer—and that means taking loans. Scholars call this the "vicious cycle of chemical agriculture."

"We know that after three or four years, the land will be dead," said Linga Reddy Sama, whose family are Hindu migrants rather than of the local tribal Gond people. The farmers in these villages know they are mining the soil, extracting and exporting its nutrition in the form of cheap cotton. While their crops decline, their debts increase. And in the worst of cases, farmers are killing themselves. This is the catastrophic convergence at the local scale, at the scale of specific crops and actual families.

Had anyone committed suicide in Jaamni? Yes, a man named Anjanna, who was about forty-five years old and had killed himself the previous year by drinking pesticide. "He killed himself to escape his debts," said one of the farmers. "Now his wife and grown son are in Maharashtra State working as farm laborers."

The problem, again, comes back to water. In recent years, irrigation has suffered under a wave of neoliberal disinvestment. The state has removed important subsidies from small farmers; as result, thousands of them have killed themselves.

The process went like this: Starting in 1991 the Indian government began a process of economic liberalization. Efficiency became the watchword; the state cut power subsidies to farmers. With that, running pumps for wells and irrigation became more expensive. To cope, farmers started taking loans from local banks or usurious moneylenders.[29] The neoliberal withdrawal of developmentalist policies meant that local irrigation systems fell into dilapidation. With bad irrigation works soon the norm, farmers turned to drilling privately-funded wells and taking groundwater. This was typically done on an ad hoc and individual or village-by-village basis, with little planning or proper water management. As a result, the aquifers soon fell into decline. These private coping strategies require private capital. To drill wells, farmers had to borrow from local moneylenders—often at exorbitant rates. Now, when crops fail or wells run dry, which is becoming more common due to climate change, farmers cannot repay their debts.

By the late 1990s, many farmers had run out of options—they were too far in arrears to borrow more, too broke to produce crops. For thousands, the only escape from this debt trap came in the form of suicide—often by swallowing pesticides. According to data from the National Crime Records Bureau, 150,000 Indian farmers killed themselves between 1997 and 2005. But as Anuradha Mittal reports, "Farmers' organizations believe the number of suicides to be even greater."[30] In Andhra Pradesh, an estimated 2,000 to 3,000 farmers killed themselves between 1998 and 2004. As one creditor told the *New York Times*, "Many moneylenders have made a whole lot of money. . . . Farmers, many of them, are ruined."[31]

When the links between drought, irrigation, debt, and suicide were becoming clear a dozen years ago, the *Political and Economic Weekly* investigated. "A study of 50 deceased farmers in Warangal District [near Adilabad] shows that well [water] is the largest source of irrigation for about three-fourths of the farmers. Only about one-third of the wells were dug under the subsidy schemes of the government. In the rest of the cases farmers themselves have borne the expenses for digging of wells. Besides this the depletion of groundwater in recent years has necessitated deepening of wells and laying of in-well bores."

The cost of such a well in the late 1990s averaged between $1,400 and $3,000.[32] As a World Bank study on drought and climate change in Andhra Pradesh found, that means debt. The Bank noted, "Household responses to drought have been largely reactive and do little to build longterm drought resilience. Credit remains the most common coping response to drought." In fact, 68 percent of households in the study took loans due to drought, with large landholders borrowing "from formal sources (such as banks), while the landless and small farmers borrow from moneylenders at inflated interest rates."[33] Not only are the rates usurious, but these more informal contracts rely on brutal and humiliating enforcement mechanisms.

The Green Revolution

Another cause of debt is seed purchase. The zenith of this trap is Monsanto's genetically modified Bt cotton. The story of Bt begins back in the halcyon days of modernization theory and the Green Revolution, when Walt W. Rostow's 1960 *The Stages of Economic Growth: A Non-Communist Manifesto* held the intellectual high ground among Western scholars and policy makers.[34] The general goal of the moment was to industrialize agriculture, thus boost yields and free up labor that could be harnessed in cities as part of the new manufacturing sectors. Toward that end, new seed varieties were introduced.

The term *Green Revolution* is attributed to William Gaud of the US Agency for International Development (USAID) and dates back to about 1968.[35] In a strict sense, the Green Revolution comprised a set of planned and targeted agricultural-intensification programs supported by the World Bank and USAID. Experts introduced high-yield-variety seeds, synthetic fertilizers, chemical pesticides, and intensive, groundwater-dependant irrigation. Governments and foundations supported farm extension and education programs to inculcate the methods of these new technologies among the farmers. More broadly, the Green Revolution refers to the unplanned spread of these same methods and technologies throughout the Global South.

In Andhra Pradesh, the official wing of the Green Revolution was confined to the coastal deltas. The first crops targeted were rice and wheat. The program's goal, in India as a whole, was to achieve food self-sufficiency and to create surpluses of labor and capital in the countryside that could be urbanized and facilitate industrialization. According to Rostow, this would enable economic "takeoff"—the onset of rapid, modernizing industrialization and economic growth.

Environmentalists have greatly criticized the Green Revolution in India for its wanton use of toxic chemicals, while Marxists have attacked it for creating greater inequality among farmers.[36] But this modernization drive had the support of many populists and involved redistributive forms of government aid, like price-stabilization programs and basic income support for farmers.[37] By comparison to the neoliberal austerity of today, the state played a robust, almost socialistic role. A government-owned company, the National Seed Corporation, provided financing and guidance, and yields did increase, essentially doubling during the 1960s. These yields, however, were a function of greater capital investment. Farmers required more capital to buy fertilizer, pesticides, irrigation piping, and machinery.[38] Thus, debts rose along with output.

Soon cotton became one of the main crops. Now the issue was no longer food security but instead victory and profit on the international commodity markets. Very problematically, cotton also needs large amounts of water. Within a decade yields began to drop as the soil was stripped of its nutrients and poisoned by pesticides. The only solution for many farmers was to double down: borrow more and invest more, use more technology, take on more debt.

The Green Revolution came to the Deccan Plateau indirectly and informally, when prosperous farmers of the Kama caste migrated inland from the coast in search of land on which to farm cotton and chili peppers. The migrants settled together and maintained strong marriage links with the coast, but they brought with them and disseminated the new capital-intensive farming methods.[39] Again, the pattern repeated elsewhere: at first yields were good, but then invariably declined.

With the rise of capital-intensive cotton farming in Telangana over the last thirty years, two strange contradictions have arisen.[40] First, the primary cash crop, cotton, continues to decline in value; yet, farmers continue to plant more of it. Why do the farmers not shift to other crops? Second, while the region's overall growth in agricultural output has been robust—more than 4 percent per annum for many years—the incomes and consumption of most farmers have declined precipitously, and this manifests as farmers' suicides and support for the Naxals.[41] The question now becomes: Why do farmers go into debt so as to plant a crop (cotton) for which the price is falling?

A brilliant young economic historian, Vamsi Vakulabharanam, has identified and explained the politics of this contradictory, seemingly nonsensical set of facts. The answer, he writes, lies in the credit system. The moneylenders demand that cotton be planted with their capital because cotton is *inedible*, so during times of crisis, producers cannot "steal," that is eat, it. Moneylenders essentially give advances on crops, then receive the harvest. If a farm family is dying of hunger and their crop is grain, chances are they will eat the collateral crop to stay alive, rather than give it to the moneylender. Cotton avoids that problem. Thus, even when food crops, like grains, command higher prices, they carry greater risks *for the moneylenders*. Cotton is the moneylenders' biological insurance; they steer farmers away from food crops, even if the potential for profits is higher, because only cotton is guaranteed collateral. Using this insight, Vakulabharanam shows that since 1980, farmers in Telangana have moved away from planting coarse grains, like jowar, barley, and millet, toward growing cotton, even as the price signal should have them doing the opposite.

This shift has coincided with the neoliberal reforms that removed from agriculture many legal protections and government subsidies—including public credit and public investment in irrigation.[42] In response to the relative withdrawal of the state, farmers took on more expenses themselves and, in turn, had to raise capital wherever they could—that meant from moneylenders. The more farmers turned to private moneylenders, the more they were under pressure to grow more cotton. And the more cotton they grew, the lower its price sank.

Thus, Telangana farmers become trapped in a downward economic cycle: they need expensive inputs and capital to produce a crop that drops in value even as they invest more heavily in it. And the central equipment—especially as climate change makes the region drier, due to extreme weather and frequent drought—are the well and irrigation systems. So, the farmers borrow. Vakulabharanam calls it "immiserizing growth"—agricultural output rises but incomes sink. Others have described the same set of contradictions as "modern poverty" or a form of "development-induced scarcity."[43]

Irrigating Corruption

Recent mismanagement and political meddling have compounded the climate-change-driven water problem in Andhra Pradesh. In particular, the neglect of the traditional water-management system is due to the interventions of N. T. Rama Rao. A Telugu-speaking film star, N. T. Rao, as he was known, scripted himself into the political scene by founding the Telugu Desam Party, a Telangana regionalist party that sought greater development in northern Andhra Pradesh and governed throughout much of the 1980s and 1990s. He made his charismatic appeals directly to the people with a populist mix of ideas from the Left and Right.

On the one hand, he fought vigorously against the Naxalites, presiding over the creation of the Greyhounds—those police counterinsurgency forces. On the other hand, he did much to disrupt old power groups and deliver services to the popular classes of the region. As part of this attack on established and inherited privilege, he abolished the feudal *munasob* and *karanam* system in which local dignitaries inherited tax-collection, water-management, and irrigation maintenance jobs—all opportunities to shake down the farmer. The film star did away with these village satraps— a bit of justice but also just one more layer of political interference between himself and the masses—but, unfortunately, nothing better fully replaced them. Some village committees, *raitu sangam,* were organized but not funded. The transition to a different, more democratic system of water management remained incomplete and disorganized, so local irrigation has suffered.

Corruption is also a problem affecting water management. In the village of Patagvada, a few kilometers down the road from Jaamni, across the Big Stream and up a small hill, the people are in thrall to the Congress Party. The reasons for that are very concrete (forgive the pun): Congress paved the village's main street with cement and has promised to legalize and upgrade the jerry-rigged electrical connections that the village has been using to pirate power. The villagers tell me how five boreholes were promised, and five boreholes are listed in district records as having been drilled, but only one was actually completed. And so, the people suffer diminished yields, lower incomes, greater stress, illness, fear, and frustration. The winter rains having failed, the Big Stream is but a few stagnant pools.

Dry Cocktail of Rage

All these social factors—the withdrawal of the state, the rise of capital-intensive farming and the depredation of moneylenders, and the incompetence and corruption of the local state, all in a semiarid climate—make up the preexisting crisis upon which climate change now descends. This, like counterinsurgency and war, contributes to the catastrophic convergences of climate, poverty, and violence.

From under the arbor, I can see why Linga Reddy Sama and the other farmers in Jaamni are so pessimistic about farming. They have a clear a set of ideas about the environmental politics of what they are doing: the Bt cotton they use is killing the land. A few say that population growth has led to overharvesting of the forest, which they (correctly) believe is adversely affecting rainfall. Further away in the hills there's been commercial and often illegal logging. Here, though, the deforestation is a by-product of their local fuel and construction needs.

In the remote forests of Chattisgarh, Naxalite activity is so intense that the paramilitary state police are largely pinned down, restricted to their fortresslike compounds—redoubts reinforced with sandbags, wire, log walls, and gun turrets. When the police venture out, the Naxals ambush. The guerillas also mass their troops for large attacks that sometimes overrun the paramilitary police compounds and detention centers. For example, in November 2005 Naxalite guerillas stormed a jail in Jehanabad, Bihar, "firebombing offices and freeing several hundred prisoners." In March 2006 "they attacked a police camp in Chattisgarh, killing fifty-five policemen and making off with a huge cache of weapons." They have bombed railway stations and transmission towers. During the 2009 elections, they took a whole passenger train hostage and attacked a multibillion-dollar iron ore slurry pipeline.[44]

The Naxalite weapon of choice is the command-activated landmine. As these are not pressure-detonated mines, they can be planted in a road months before use: rain, mud, traffic, and sunshine bake the road above the mines into perfect camouflage. The buried mines become impossible to detect under the hard-packed tracks, but the explosives are active and linked to long wires that can be connected to detonators and triggered whenever the guerillas are ready.

Like improvised explosive devices, or IEDs, in Iraq and Afghanistan, the Naxalite landmines are effective on several levels simultaneously. Tactically, landmines maim and kill the paramilitary police. Psychologically, the explosives wear down and demoralize the enemy. Politically, the mines function as a social barrier between the counterinsurgency forces and the people whom they seek to control. The situation is so bad that elements in the Indian air force are lobbying to start an aerial bombing campaign upon the parched lands of the Red Corridor.[45]

Dark Arts of Repression

Instead of robustly embracing new, green agricultural technologies and supports for farmers facing an uncertain climate, the state is focusing on repression. The relative victory over the guerillas in Telangana results from a near-perfect mix of classic guns-and-butter counterinsurgency. At the thin end of the wedge are the above-mentioned Greyhounds, the paramilitary special forces of the state police. Established in the early 1990s, this counterinsurgency force has been highly effective, never hesitating to use violence but also investing enormous energy in intelligence. That is to say, the Greyhounds target their terror effectively. Often they travel in civilian dress, out of uniform, heavily armed but undercover, passing among the population unannounced, largely unseen, as teams of assassins rather than as occupying soldiers. They are part special forces, part death squad.

For years, the Greyhounds conducted search-and-destroy operations in the forest belt of northern Telangana, and they still do. Sometimes they confront armed *dalam* (the cadre) in firefights. More often, they kill unarmed guerrillas and civilian supporters.[46] Aided by a network of paid informants, tribal irregulars in service to the state, and former Naxals who have switched sides, the Greyhounds spent half a decade combing the hills, mapping both the physical and social terrain, observing the comings and goings of activists, learning the social networks in the villages, and then—in the style of the US Army's Operation Phoenix in South Vietnam—breaking the key social links between the guerrillas and the people. That is to say, they killed both the *dalam*, the armed cadre, and the unarmed *sangam*, or activists. The strategy continues, though not as intensely. Always, when the dead are displayed to the press—blood smeared and dirty, laid out, two or three at a time, on reed mats—the Greyhounds ascribe the assassinations to self-defense. The euphemism describing the killings is always the same. They are "encounters" or accidental collisions between armed bandits and the forces of order. In the Red Corridor, this is the nomenclature of state terrorism.[47]

The zenith of Naxalite activity in Andhra Pradesh occurred in October 2003, when the chief minister of the state, N. Chandrababu Naidu, was visiting the famous Venkateswara Temple to attend part of a Hindu festival. As his convoy left the temple, a series of six remote-controlled claymore mines lifted the earth beneath the vehicles in a deafening shock of linked explosions. The minister's bulletproof ambassador car was mangled and flipped off the road. But, to the credit of Hindustan Motors' retrofitting, Naidu survived with only light wounds to the face and chest. His driver and four other members of the legislative assembly, however, were very badly hurt. The assailants were cadre of the outlawed People's War Group (PWG), one of the largest and oldest Maoist parties in India.

"The attack on Naidu shows that there really is no alternative but to revive dialogue and peace talks between the PWG and the government," said one of the Naxals' aboveground spokespeople, the popular left-leaning folk singer Gaddar, who uses only one name.[48] Indeed, the attack was one of the Naxals' most spectacular assaults yet, not because of its size but because of its target; they had almost decapitated a state government. The *Political and Economic Weekly* lamented the implications:

> With the state government panic-stricken by the attempt on the life of Chandrababu Naidu and the PWG peeved by the failure of its attempt, both sides are hardening their vengeful attitudes and Andhra Pradesh is likely to go through another cycle of vicious killings. The victims will be fall guys. The police will target poor villagers and human rights activists as "suspected Naxalites" (as they have done by raiding the house of the veteran civil liberties movement leader K G Kannabiran) and arrest or kill them in false encounters. The PWG, in its turn, will take it out on some village "pradhan" or subordinate government employee, branding them as "informers," and let off steam by setting fire to a few railway stations or bus depots.[49]

After the bombing against Chief Minister Naidu, the police in Andhra Pradesh turned up the heat. Naidu's government reopened negotiations with the PWG. (Talks had been under way starting in June 2002, but a massive attack on a bus full of police ended them.) The police were ordered to pull back and the rebels were implored to do likewise. "We have reports that squads are roaming in villages with arms. We are requesting them not to move around with weapons," said Andhra Pradesh's home minister.[50]

Initial talks were conducted via emissaries, one of them a famous Naxalite writer, Varavara Rao, who gave me his account on a hot afternoon in Hyderabad. "The government was not serious," said the old writer. "They were using the talks to research the Naxal networks." By 2005, Varavara Rao himself had been arrested, accused of murdering policemen. As the hammer of the state was descending again, he told the press, "The Congress is like sweet poison. While the TDP [regionalist party] government always ruled out talks with us, the Congress is talking of peace but killing revolutionaries in stage-managed encounters."

The Andhra Pradesh cease-fire and those in other states were ultimately part of a ruse, a larger strategy to flush out the underground networks of the PWG so as to liquidate and jail them. The federal government had finally begun promulgating a three-pronged counterinsurgency: strengthened intelligence at the state level; sustained, intelligence-driven police repression; and accelerated economic development in Naxal-affected areas. Between 2003 and 2005, over fifteen hundred casualties were reported every year from *each* of the eleven states affected by Naxalite violence. Just over three hundred police were killed during that time.[51]

Sowing Chaos

The Naxalite violence in Andhra Pradesh peaked just after 2005.[52] Ultimately, the Greyhounds proved too much for the Naxals of Telangana; the Maoists fell back into the forest of Chattisgarh and there multiplied. In that province, police had developed a force of civilian vigilantes, called the Salva Judum, which in the local Gond dialect means "peace march." Initially an organic self-defense organization, the Salva Judum was co-opted by the state. Participation became mandatory, and this "third force" became an armed auxiliary of police repression.[53]

The new paramilitaries include many former Naxals and, in this regard, resemble the civil patrols of the Guatemalan counterinsurgency or the early paramilitaries in Columbia.[54] In January 2009, the Andhra Pradesh Civil Liberties Committee reported that one "encounter" in Chattisgarh was actually a massacre of eighteen tribals by armed Salva Judum backed up by police.[55] Critics say the government-sanctioned vigilantism of the Salva Judum has forced more than fifty thousand people into roadside refugee camps.[56]

India's internal war is a stark example of the catastrophic convergence. Poverty made worse by neoliberalism meets counterinsurgency and repression meets climate-driven ecological crisis. If the monsoons fail or hit too hard, the Maoists, the Greyhounds, and the Salva Judum all threaten to play an increasingly destabilizing role in the coming years. They are precisely the types of centrifugal, unaccountable, violent criminogenic forces that insurgency and counterinsurgency leave in their wake to degrade the already battered social fabric. Total war at the grass roots—now the preferred response to social crisis and violent chaos—releases political sepsis that produces devastating corruption, anomie, trauma, and pathology—none of which are useful in confronting climate change.

The Naxals are only one source of instability. Prime Minister Manmohan Singh was correct when he called India "fissiparous." Despite the strong win of the Congress Party–led coalition in the 2009 elections, the country's parliamentary politics are defined by fiercely independent regional political parties and locally powerful charismatic leaders.[57]

Across rural India, social tensions are intense. There is spasmodic intercommunal violence between Hindus, Muslims, and Christians. Mass migration of Bangladeshi Muslims into Hindu-dominated regions of India is fueling religious nationalism in both communities. The Bharatiya Janata Party (BJP), the *Hindutva* fanatics, traffics in cryptofascist Islamophobia. Meanwhile, Pakistan sponsors Muslim terrorist groups, and in the northeast armed secessionists are fighting for an independent state of Assam. Across the rugged dry north, social banditry continues, and in the growing megacities, like Delhi, criminality is on the rise. These problems wait on the horizon of Indian history, threatening to grow much worse as climate change intensifies.

In the cities of the south, the information technology and business process outsourcing boom has produced a class of new billionaires.[58] Yet, the Indian political leadership cannot, or will not, deliver electricity, water, basic health care and education to the majority of the population. According to the United Nations' new multidimensional poverty index, more poor people live in eight Indian states than in all of sub-Saharan Africa. The Indian ruling classes need to wake up, or climate change will destroy them. How should India fight the Naxals? By adapting to climate change with economic redistribution, social justice, and sustainable development.

IV

LATIN AMERICA

CHAPTER 13

Rio's Agony: From Extreme Weather to "Planet of Slums"

> The death of the contemporary forms of social order ought to gladden rather than trouble the soul. But what is frightening is that the departing world leaves behind it not an heir, but a pregnant widow. Between the death of one and the birth of the other, much water will flow by, a long night of chaos and desolation will pass.
>
> —ALEXANDER HERZEN, *on the failure of the 1848 revolutions*

THE BLACK POLICE helicopter floated above Rio. Ahead of us loomed the huge mountaintop statue of Christ, arms outstretched to the city; below us lay the long, wide expanse of Ipanema Beach. Inland from the posh neighborhoods on the water rose abrupt mountains of solid rock topped by lush jungle. Stacked up haphazardly along these steep slopes were the favelas, the densely packed unplanned neighborhoods of the poor and working classes.

If the contrast of white beaches and dark mountains defines Rio's postcard-perfect geography, it is the surreal inequality of luxury condos overlooked by impoverished slums that defines Rio's social landscape. Originally built by squatters from the rural northeast and named for a hardy weed of that region, the poverty- and crime-plagued favelas are the open sore on Rio's welcoming smile.

To live in a slum that looks down on a wealthy beach community is a provocation of unique intensity. This contrast makes Rio the geographic embodiment of "relative deprivation." Sociology reveals that absolute deprivation, poverty alone, does not cause violence. Rather, it is deprivation experienced *in relation* to the status of others, or in relation to what could be, should be, or once was, that hurts the most and drives crime, rebellion, and violence.[1] Thus, relative deprivation destroys the social cohesion within communities.[2]

The police were giving me an airborne tour of this strange geography and explaining how they manage it with violence and about their new offensive against the favela gunmen. As we approached Favela Vidigal, the pilot steered the chopper out over the water in a wide defensive arc. Vidigal is "hostile," under the control of the Comando Vermelho (CV), one of Rio's gangs known to shoot at police helicopters. The cocky young pilot, wearing a blue jumpsuit and dark shades, made sure to point out three freshly patched bullet holes near its tail rotor just before we took off. Damage the tail rotor, and the chopper spins out of control.

In October 2009, favela gunmen shot down a police helicopter during a daylong firefight between two rival gang factions and the police. Three officers were killed and four were badly injured. Twelve civilians were also killed, and in the surrounding area young men firebombed ten buses. A year later it happened again: police raids killed thirteen, and then gang members burned fifteen buses during four days of violence.[3]

Indeed, the gangs of Rio run the favelas and the city's retail drug trade. Inside the communities they carry machine guns openly as if they were the police, tax local economic activity as if they were the revenue service, and operate informal courts and mete out punishment as if they had a legal code. Steal a cell phone? Get shot through the hands and feet. Snitch someone out? Expect execution.

Roughly the size of New York, Rio has a murder rate six times higher. In 2009 about five thousand people were slain here. The police enter the favelas only for short and brutal raids—arriving at night in armed columns to ransack, torture, and kill. In most slums, they have not established police stations. According to a 2009 Human Rights Watch report, the Rio constabulary kills more than eleven hundred people every year. Only four Rio police officers have been convicted of abuses in the past decade. But Rio's cops face other risks: almost ninety died in the line of duty in 2009.

If that weren't enough, now a third source feeds the violence: off-duty police, firefighters, and prison guards have formed militias to check the gangs. These vigilantes can be just as criminal as their enemies. In 2008 such militias even tortured journalists from the city's biggest newspaper. The situation increasingly looks like a low-intensity war.

Catastrophic Convergence Urbanized

Why are there so many people in Rio? Why is it so violent? And what will climate change do to places like Rio? I decided to explore this megacity because it reveals how climate crisis in the countryside is expressed as urban violence. One of the most dramatic transformations of the last fifty years has been our planet's rapid urbanization. The process continues, and climate change is now helping to fuel migration from the countryside to the city. Rio allows us to forecast political issues linked to climate change because, in many ways, it is a city produced by extreme weather elsewhere. A brutal rhythm of drought and flooding hundreds of miles away in Brazil's arid Northeast, or *Nordeste*, has fueled Rio's growth. As weather patterns grow more chaotic and extreme due to global warming, outmigration from the countryside will increase.

Already disruptions in the patterns of the Intertropical Convergence Zone are leading to new weather shocks—prolonged drought punctuated by violent flooding—that are making subsistence farming in the *Nordeste* even more difficult. Displaced farmers of that region—internal climate refugees—make their way south to the megacities like Rio and São Paulo. There, they become trapped in the favelas, and many of the youth are pulled into the vortex of the sub-rosa economy, that carnival of guns, drugs, money, sex, music, solidarity, and respect. Thus, by displacing people into the favelas, the extreme weather associated with climate change fuels Rio's crime wars.

Rio, too, faces extreme weather. Just after I visited, a freak storm dropped eleven inches of rain on the city in about twenty-four hours—the worst downpour in its recorded history. The streets flooded with sewage, traffic seized up into daylong jams, slabs of shantytowns slipped away down hill-sides, and more that one hundred people died. In January, São Paulo had seen similar weather; two rivers broke their banks, thousands were tem-porarily homeless, and sixty-four people drowned.[4] But the real front line of climate change in Brazil is the dry *Nordeste*.

New Climatic Normal

Since the 1970s the *Nordeste* has suffered increased drought; now, it is also regularly hit by flash floods. The summer of 2010 saw devastating floods, as had the year before. They killed almost 50 people, made 120,000 home-less, wiped out 1,200 miles of roads, and destroyed at least 80 bridges. The crisis was bad enough for President Luiz Inácio Lula da Silva to skip a G20 conference.[5]

This new normal of flooding, drought, and freak storms forms part of a larger pattern of extreme weather that scientists say is the product of anthro-pogenic climate change and predict will hit northeastern Brazil very hard. Though they are careful to point out that no single weather event can be de-finitively blamed on climate change, the larger pattern, on the other hand, can be. Consider the findings of the Intergovernmental Panel on Climate Change (IPCC) Fourth Assessment Report: "Over the past three decades, Latin America has been subjected to climate-related impacts of increased El Niño occurrences. . . . The occurrence of climate-related disasters increased by 2.4 times between the periods 1970–1999 and 2000–2005, continuing the trend observed during the 1990s."[6] Later the report notes, "Prolonged droughts in semi-arid north-eastern Brazil have provoked rural-urban mi-gration of subsistence farmers" and increased outbreaks of disease.

Many favela residents are from the *Nordeste*. Dejacir Alves, whom I met on a stairway in the favela Do Morro dos Cabritos, is typical. He migrated to Rio from Varjota, up in Ceará. "I came here to work, about twenty years ago. My family was in farming. We have a big family, but only two of us still work the land. They do subsistence farming. It is very hard to survive there, and now it is getting harder; there is so much drought there."

Alves has done "all sorts of work" in Rio—construction, services, taking tickets on a bus. Talking on this concrete-covered hillside, inlaid with walled paths and a warren of hand-built homes, he wears flip-flops and a green football shirt; farming and the land seem far away in the past.

In colonial times the *Nordeste* hosted a coastal plantation economy and cattle industry. Then, droughts in the late 1870s and early 1880s provoked the steady outmigration of the region's poor. During much of the twentieth century, Brazilian agriculture remained backward and underdeveloped. Unlike many Latin American countries, such as Mexico and Bolivia, Brazil never had a proper bourgeois revolution to check the power of the feudal landed oligarchy and impose land reform. The redistributive programs of the 1930s *Estado Novo* only affected urban workers and the middle classes.[7] The military takeover of 1964 brought a government-led program of rapid modernization in agriculture, but that did not include land redistribution.

To this day, about 3 percent of the population owns about two-thirds of all farmland.[8] Agricultural modernization in the form of the Green Revolution and mechanization caused rising rural unemployment, thus a mass outmigration to the cities. By 1972, major crops, like wheat and soybean, were nearly 60 percent mechanized. Displaced rural workers moved to the cities and built the favelas.[9] In 1940 only 15 percent of the country's population lived in cities; by 1970 that ratio had reached 50 percent.[10] Today, over 80 percent of Brazilians live in cities. And now, we see harbingers of a new wave of migration driven by the strange weather of the unraveling climate system.

Repression in the Megaslums

Social pressure in the cities—driven to some extent by socioclimatological crisis in the rural Northeast—is expressed as criminal violence and state repression. After leaving the favelas to fester for decades, the state is moving to retake them. The strategy runs as follows: First, Rio's military police special forces—known by their Portuguese acronym, BOPE—invade the favelas and suppress the gangs. Then regular military police units establish permanent bases and begin patrols. Once an area is secured, government services—such as health care, education, cultural facilities, and civil courts—move in. Or that is the plan. They call it pacification; it is classic counterinsurgency except the enemy is a specter, an amorphous threat, a milieu of crime, gangs, and chaos rather than a coherent insurgent foe.

When I was in Rio in early 2010, about ten of the city's roughly one thousand favelas were undergoing pacification. The people of the favelas were of a mixed mind about the occupations. The gangs, however, were not pleased, and they were taking revenge on the larger society by firebombing commuter buses down "on the pavement," as nonfavela Rio is called. "Whoever has the guns is the law," explained Claudio Carvalha, president of the resident association in Do Morro dos Cabritos. For years this favela was subject to a constant struggle between the CV and a rival gang, Amigos dos Amigos (Friends of Friends).

"When one of theirs was wounded, they would dump the guy—bleeding, half dead—at the association, and we were expected to take them to the hospital," explained Claudio.

In Dona Marta, the first favela occupied back in November 2008 and said to be a showcase of social programs, I met a group of unemployed young people. They may or may not have been enrolled foot soldiers of the CV, but they saw the occupation as all stick and no carrot.

"They are just beating people up," said a short, tattooed twenty-three-year-old named Max. He wore red shorts and plastic flip-flops and leaned on the wall of the old wooden shack where he lived with his wife, Amanda. A small radio blared a tinny stream of baile funk, essentially Brazilian hip-hop, as Amanda did dishes by an outdoor tap just off one of the main stairways. A few other young men, shirtless and wearing baggy shorts in the heat, gathered as we talked.

"Most people just want the cops to go away and find someone else to harass," said Amanda. "They treat us like criminals. They force us inside after eleven. If you have what they think is too much money, they take it from you."

"They push us around when we leave or enter the community," said another guy, his arms heavily tattooed, who went by the nickname The Moor. "They take us in for minor crimes; they kick us, grab our crotches, search us, kick in our doors, beat us up. They do whatever they want. And we can't fight back, or we get killed."

"This whole 'social vision' is not well thought out," said Max. "They promised day care, clinics and jobs. But all I see are cops."

Blowback Brazilian Style

Scholars argue that Brazil's crisis of violence is rooted in its history of slavery and frontier conquest. This is true, but more recent origins lie in the country's intense economic inequality and the violent class struggles it has provoked. Workers' organizations were long met with brutal repression. From 1964 to 1985, Brazil suffered outright military dictatorship and a decade of "dirty war"; from that age of rebellion and repression, it now experiences a form of blowback. In this history, we see two elements of the catastrophic convergence at play: neoliberal economic restructuring and Cold War violence.

The story of the largest and oldest Rio gang is rooted in the armed struggle of the Cold War, specifically in the story of right-wing military dictatorship and the Marxist resistance to it. According to its veterans, the Comando Vermelho was founded during the mid-1970s in the Cândido Mendes Prison on Ilha Grande, when captured guerrillas were housed with common prisoners.

Like most Latin American countries in the late 1960s and early 1970s, Brazil saw the rise of urban guerrillas opposing economic exploitation and political repression. In 1968, commandos from the tiny MR8 even managed to kidnap the US ambassador, Charles B. Elbrick. The man who coordinated the kidnapping, Fernando Gabeira, is now a famous journalist, author, and leftist politician. The film *Four Days in September* is based on those events. Another prominent former guerrilla and political prisoner of that era is Dilma Vana Rousseff, Brazil's first woman president.

Not all the revolutionaries had such illustrious careers. The dictatorship met the Left with the extreme violence of death squads, torture, and incarceration. More broadly, it applied a sweeping national security law that allowed the detention of anyone who gave off the slightest whiff of bohemia—long hair and a guitar could get one arrested. A very complete history of the repression exists thanks to the Catholic Archdiocese of São Paulo, which assembled a secret team of lawyers to illegally copy and publish documents from 707 secret military-tribunal cases, involving 7,367 defendants.[11] The purloined dossiers show that torture and murder were widespread, and when a synthesis and summary was published as *Brasil: Nunca Mais*, it became a sudden bestseller.[12]

While some elements of the revolution later rose in politics, other lumpen cadre became the first-generation leadership of Comando Vermelho (other gangs later formed by splitting off from the CV). As Ben Penglase writes, "In a fairly direct sense, the Comando Vermelho was the bastard child of the dictatorship's attempt to repress armed political opposition."[13]

From Guerrillas to Gangs

Behind bars, the political radicals of Galeria B of Cândido Mendes Prison organized themselves and then united with the general-population inmates. The common criminals saw how the political prisoners maintained unity and, through it, had strength and a higher standard of living. The jailed radicals were "sharing any food or money that they received from outside the prison and enforcing strict discipline that banned inmates from attacking or stealing from each other, practices which were common in the prison. The political prisoners also joined together to defend any political prisoner who had been assaulted by guards or by other prisoners and to demand better conditions."[14]

The first written account of this history was *Four Hundred Against One*, the memoir of William da Silva, who as a young prisoner helped start the CV. He describes how the first "red" prison gang was the Falange LSN, which in 1979 killed off the leaders of several rival apolitical organizations, assumed control of the whole prison, became the Comando Vermelho, and then imposed new revolutionary rules. These, according to da Silva, included "death to anyone who assaults or rapes fellow prisoners; conflicts brought from the street must be left outside of prison; violence only to attempt to escape; constant struggle against repression and abuse."[15]

This discipline and unity was soon extended to the favelas. The notion was to support returning prisoners and control the communities, including the drug trade, in preparation for a revolution in Rio and beyond. The CV functioned as a political organization and a beneficent society for prisoners and ex-convicts. It reached into communities, armed in the name of self-defense and revolution, and started taxing the drug trade.[16] The first generation of radical CV leaders was soon wiped out, and by the mid-1980s Comando Vermelho had become just another drug gang, albeit very big and well organized.

As the CV was beginning its rise, Brazil's larger political economy began a process of brutal, neoliberal transformation. It was the concatenation of the early stages of the catastrophic convergence taking form: political violence met a new wave of poverty.

Neoliberal Brazil

It was 1983, the lapels were still wide, the sideburns long, and the protesters furious. Newly unemployed industrial workers—thousands of them—marched down São Paulo's streets. *Screw the military government!* These people had reached their limit. Some chanted, "The people united will never be defeated," but others just screamed, "We're hungry!"

As the Comando Vermelho was moving into the favelas, the Brazilian economy was falling to its knees; the protests were a symptom of that. In the first two weeks of January, 14,860 workers in São Paulo were fired. At the same time, the government was implementing austerity measures: cutting public services, aid to the poor, and support for industry. In early April, the rage boiled over: the unemployed marched, only to be met by 10,000 riot police. The protests and chanting soon gave way to rock throwing and looting. The police answered with volleys of tear gas, charges, and vicious beatings. For three days the violence went on, and at least 11 supermarkets and dozens of bakeries were looted; thousands of protesters, shouting for jobs, even attacked the state governor's palace. Police arrested more than 450 people; damages reached $1.5 million.[17]

Brazil was entering a period of painful economic restructuring. Mired in debt, the government turned to the International Monetary Fund (IMF) and World Bank for new loans, but emergency help came with strict new economic conditions. To balance the books, Brazil would suffer a wave of pauperization, unemployment, hunger, homelessness, and desperation.

This was the context for the rise of the drug trade and the Comando Vermelho's pivot from Rio's prisons out into the favelas. To understand the catastrophic convergence, we must first understand the foundational crisis of violence and poverty into which is now added accelerating climate change.

From ISI to IMF

Like many developing economies, Brazil had followed a model of state-directed import-substitution industrialization (ISI) from the 1930s onward. Arrived at as a reaction to the collapse of markets for traditional exports during the Great Depression, this state-led form of capitalist development involved an uneasy compact between business and labor brokered by an interventionist state. In exchange for discipline on the shop floor, the state created social security programs and allowed rising wages for the aristocracy of labor. Investment and finance were regulated, and banks were often state owned. Throughout the 1930s and 1940s, in response to the Great Depression and World War II, forms of corporatism took root in many places. Sometimes corporatist policies were enacted by democratic states; witness the American New Deal. More often the developmentalist pact between labor and capital was delivered by "relatively autonomous" and authoritarian states, such as mid-century Italy, Spain, Portugal, Japan, Bolivia, and Argentina.

Domestic industry and markets were heavily protected. For example, in 1960 Brazil's tariffs on manufactured imports were almost ten times as high as those charged by the European Economic Community (EEC)—a 165 percent markup in Brazil versus 17 percent in the EEC.[18] Both infant and well-established industries were heavily guarded against foreign competition. Under this regime, industry grew robustly but unevenly. Some sectors were dynamic, efficient, and innovative, "a group of leading firms gained a competitive edge in the manufacturing sector," while others languished due to the artificial monopolies allowed by ISI. Overall—and contrary to the assertions of today's economic orthodoxy—labor productivity, living standards, and the economy as a whole increased under ISI.[19]

David Harvey described the age of state-led development as follows: "This system had delivered high rates of growth in the advanced capitalist countries and generated some spillover benefits (most obviously to Japan but also unevenly across South America and to some other countries of South East Asia) during the 'golden age' of capitalism in the 1950s and early 1960s."[20] In the early 1970s, the model in its various iterations hit trouble—partly due to internal problems and partly due to a worldwide crisis of overproduction and overaccumulation.[21]

The so-called golden age of capitalism, roughly 1945 to 1973, was essentially the story of postwar reconstruction: the long boom was the big rebuild following the devastation of World War II. The war destroyed not only 59 million human lives but also vast amounts of existing capital: factories, cities, farms, docks, gas works, water mains, roads, rails, and communications systems. For six years the scientific genius and herculean industrial might of the major economies was fed wholesale in the maw of war. The overall costs are variously estimated as at $1.5 or $2 trillion, but we'll never know the real total.

The post-1945 economic boom was essentially the big rebuild or big recovery. The war's end meant there was pent up demand and plenty of investment, and industrial planning enjoyed broad legitimacy. During the big rebuild, wages, taxes, and profits all grew together. However, during the mid-1960s there started to be too much stuff and not enough demand.[22] By 1970, 99 percent of American homes had refrigerators, electric irons, and radios. More than 90 percent had washing machines, vacuum cleaners, and toasters.

As one economist put it, "Saturation in one market led to saturation in others as producers looked abroad when the possibilities for domestic expansion were exhausted. The results were simultaneous export drives by companies in all advanced countries, with similar, technologically sophisticated products going into one another's markets. . . . Increasing exports . . .

from developing countries such as Taiwan, Korea, Mexico and Brazil further increased the congestion of mass markets in the advanced economies."[23]

By the early 1970s, capitalism was suffocating from industrial success.
Around the world and across industries, firms found it increasingly difficult to maintain their amazing (if not aberrant) postwar profitability.[24]

Continent of Debt

By the early 1970s, a new factor had entered the equation: there was a
global glut of liquidity—too much capital was competing for too few investment outlets. That translated into very inexpensive and abundant
credit. Brazil had always borrowed to fund its industrialization, but now
growth slowed, and capital became cheap.

In 1973, the other shoe dropped: Arab defeat in the Yom Kippur War
led to an oil embargo by many key exporters. The price of oil quadrupled
in less than a year. That hit Brazil hard. Though now a major oil producer,
it then imported 80 percent of its petroleum. Before prices could subside,
the Shah of Iran fell to a revolution, precipitating a second oil shock in
1979. Prices nearly doubled again. By the early 1980s, the Brazilian government was desperately trying to stimulate its economy by borrowing and
spending. The *Miami Herald* business section pointed out the unfairness of
the macroeconomic situation: "In contrast to Argentina and Mexico, a very
high proportion of the billions borrowed here went to productive projects,
analysts say. Many were the projects of 'Brasil Grande'—nuclear power
plants, hydroelectric dams, jungle highways, petrochemical complexes, an
export-oriented arms industry, steel mills, and a $3-billion railroad to fa-
cilitate steel exports."[25] But Brazil was subject to the same austerity as
those who had borrowed less productively.

Then, a third layer of the crisis hit. The world's leading economy, the
United States, also faced deep trouble. Overcapacity globally meant a collapse in the rate of return on investment—a collapse of profits. "From a
peak of nearly 10 percent in 1965, the average net after-tax profit rate of
domestic non-financial corporations plunged to less than 6 percent during
the second half of the 1970s—a decline of more than a third."[26] After

twenty years of continual expansion during the long postwar recovery, profits began to sag in 1966 and continued to decline steadily until 1974, until they reached a low of around 4.5 percent.[27] The same pattern was visible from Germany to Japan, as all advanced capitalist countries experienced an after-tax profit decline of between 20 and 30 percent.

Robert Brenner, a leading scholar on this history, put it this way: "Due to the onset of over-capacity and over-production, world manufacturing prices had been unable to grow in line with product wages and the cost of plant and equipment: the result was falling profit shares and output-capital ratios, making for falling profit rates."

How was this to be dealt with?

Fundamentally, for profits to recover, wages had to fall, and not just wages, but the social wage—the share of national production redistributed to the working class in the form of public goods like government-funded education, health care, and welfare. Rescue arrived in the form of Paul Volcker, the new chairman of the US Federal Reserve. Beginning in 1979, Volcker began a dramatic rise in interest rates from 7.9 percent in 1979 to 16.4 percent in 1981. This had the effect of cutting borrowing throughout the economy, and with that, investment and consumer spending also ratcheted down abruptly. Unemployment reached 10.8 percent by December 1982.[28] At the same time, both Reagan and Thatcher launched offensives against the power of organized labor, cut social spending, and slashed taxes on the wealthy. As a result, the US economy plunged into what was then the most severe recession since the Great Depression.[29] In the process, it dragged down many of its trading partners with it, as US imports shrank radically.

In Latin America the new monetary policy also meant that interest payments on existing debt soared. Thus began the Latin American debt crisis. From 1978 to the end of 1982, total Latin American debt more than doubled, from $159 billion to $327 billion. Debt servicing—that is, interest payments—grew even faster: the average Latin American country used more than 30 percent of its export earnings just to service its debts. Brazil paid nearly 60 percent.[30] Journalist Andres Oppenheimer explained, "As the old debt gets more expensive it begets new debt; to meet their interest payments the major Latin American countries have had to rely more and more on emergency loans from the International Monetary Fund and commercial banks. In effect, they are receiving with one hand and paying back with the other."[31] As public debt soared, the Brazilian currency lost value until chronic inflation became hyperinflation, hitting 1,765 percent by the end of the 1980s.[32]

Austerity

The solution to the crisis came in the form of IMF- and World Bank–enforced austerity. In 1983 Brazil had the largest foreign debt of the developing world: $83.8 billion. Just to service its debt, it had to borrow more and more in a downward spiral. In early 1983, Brazil went to the IMF for $6 billion, then the single-largest loan in the Fund's history. In return, Brazil agreed to a brutal austerity program: to cut inflation, growth was strangled, public spending cut, the currency devalued, imports restricted, public assets privatized, and exports boosted.[33] In São Paulo, workers soon rioted.[34] Over the next decade the crisis dragged on.

Brazil's military government did push back a bit, resisting the Bretton Woods institutions' more draconian stipulations. As Finance Minister Dilson Funaro explained in 1986, "The way out of the debt crisis is through growth, and the IMF formulas don't provide growth."[35] But, in the end, neoliberalism won; deflationary austerity, deregulation, privatization, aggressive exporting, unemployment, suppressed wages, hunger, corruption, crime, and migration all defined the economic landscape.

Unfortunately, Brazil's export drive took place amidst falling commodity prices. Two factors contributed to this. The Bretton Woods institutions were simultaneously pressuring other Third World debtors to export more; meanwhile, deep recessions and high interests rates in the richer countries held down consumption. Increased supply plus reduced demand meant plummeting prices. Sugar, copper, aluminum, and other raw materials all hit deep lows.

The IMF's structural-adjustment program resulted in higher unemployment, rising poverty, and growing urbanization as the rural poor went to cities in search of work. From 1980 to 1990, Rio's overall population growth rate was 8 percent, but the favela population surged by 41 percent. As economist and Latin America expert Mark Weisbrot explained, "From 1960–1980, income per person—the most basic measure that economists have of economic progress—in Brazil grew by about 123 percent. From 1980 to 2000, it grew by less than 4 percent." Weisbrot estimates that, had Brazil not embraced neoliberalism, "the country would have European living standards today. Instead of about 50 million poor people as there are today, there would be very few. And almost everyone would today enjoy vastly higher living standards, educational levels, and better health care."[36] Even if Weisbrot overstates the case a bit (Which Europe? Rural Greece or urban Holland?), his larger point about neoliberalism's damaging impact is valid.

Human Costs

Had Brazil not embraced neoliberalism, violence would surely be less of an issue. As poverty increased and the favelas grew, social relations within them frayed. Amidst this neoliberal transformation, the Comando Vermelho and other gangs grew to become guerrilla armies *minus* the ideology or political cause, employing only the methods and organization of war.

"By 1991 the CV had become purely criminal. There was no ideology anymore," explained Commander Rodrigo Oliveira of Rio's Civilian Police Special Forces when I met him in his office to discuss the gangs and the war on them. "Now their goal is power, plain and simple—not even huge private fortunes for the slum 'owners,'" he said, using the colloquial term for the gang leaders. "Mostly it's just about organizational power, weapons, and status."

Academic analyses of Rio's gangs often note the absence or failure of state institutions. Others, most notably Enrique Desmond Arias, argue that the criminal structures in the favelas bring together gangsters, police, community leaders, and mainstream politicians in a matrix of mutually beneficial relations. Such an arraignment, essentially the criminalization of the local state, has evolved out of the crisis of neoliberalism.[37] To the extent that Arias is correct, criminality in the favelas becomes a matter less of state withdrawal and more of societal rot—a whole society infected by the gangrene of sub-rosa economics, corruption and violence.

Nordeste

The red flag of revolution whips in the hot wind atop a roughhewn pole. Below it sits a small squatter camp where poor farmers occupy land belonging to a distant and wealthy rancher. Welcome to the hot scrublands of the *Nordeste* and the tiny village of Boqueirão in Brazil's Ceará Province. The village sits on a dusty one-lane track at the bottom of a long valley, hemmed in on either side by looming mountains of dark, barren rock. If you look on Google Maps, Boqueirão is, roughly, due north of Iracuba, which sits on the road BR 222. The long valley shows up like a pale scar amidst the dark hills.

On one side of the road is the village of solid little whitewashed homes, with smooth cement floors and red-tile roofs. On the other side is the camp of peasant activists, members of the landless people's movement Movimento dos Trabalhadore Rurais Sem Terra (MST). The MST is a social movement of some 370,000 people organized in more than 1,000 communities across Brazil. Their objective is simple: redistribute land to hungry farmers. And in the last twenty years they've had remarkable success. Their methods are also simple: move in and start using the land. That is what is happening here. The MST cadres have used heavy black plastic and wood to build two long, collective shacks called *barracos*, or "barracks." One is for cooking, eating, and meeting; the other, strung with hammocks, is for sleeping. The camp is never left unoccupied.

Drought Land

The *Nordeste* is semiarid, receiving very little rain. Severe floods punctuate its frequent droughts. In 1877 to 1879, a catastrophic drought killed more than five hundred thousand people and sent the rural Northeast into political crisis.[38] Now, fear of drought is etched in the region's culture. For example, in parts of Ceará, the year traditionally ended with drought-prediction rituals. On December 13, the eve of St. Luzia's Day, an old man would set six pieces of rock salt out on a banana leaf, each piece representing a month of the upcoming rainy season. The following morning, the salt pieces that had melted away in the dew symbolized the months of the coming season that would receive rain. The farmer who explained this tradition to me also said, "It doesn't seem to work well anymore." In any event, research indicates that the drought cycle "has become more frequent over the last century, with five droughts recorded during the current decade."[39]

The rainy season in Ceará runs from January to June, with much variability in duration, timing, and intensity and between localities. The rain is delivered as the Intertropical Convergence Zone moves to its southernmost position.[40] A study in the *Journal of Applied Meteorology* finds that sea surface temperatures are the primary factor responsible for "the interannual variability of rainfall in northeast Brazil," meaning among other things that droughts "tend to coincide with the warm phase of El Niño–Southern Oscillation (ENSO) episodes."[41]

More broadly, regional studies of temperature trends in the region "show changes that are in line with expected warming, most notably warmer nights." The majority of climate models find that northeast Brazil "is expected to experience more rapid warming than the global average during the 21st century." Depending on the model and the potential amounts of greenhouse gases loaded into the atmosphere in coming decades, projected temperature increases for this century range from 1°C to 6°C. In more concrete terms, most forecasts predict northeastern Brazil will be a region of *very severe* water stress by 2050.[42]

Rio's favelas are largely populated by people from these dry lands. Despite its harsh climate, the Northeast is densely populated.[43] As climate change grinds down subsistence farmers, more *Nordestinos* leave to search for work either in the depressed cities of their nearby coastal areas, like Fortaleza and Recife, or down south in the megacities of São Palo and Rio. Thus, the social dimensions of the ecological crisis in the *Nordeste* (a frontline region for climate change) are expressed in cities as unemployment, makeshift housing, the narcotrade and violence.

In this light, we can read the struggle of the farmers in Boqueirão as an inadvertent struggle against violence and social breakdown in the cities. At the same time, their struggle to stay on the land is a struggle for social justice in one of the most unequal countries in the world. It is also a struggle to adapt to climate change in an already extreme environment; as such, it encapsulates the possibilities and perils of Brazilian life in the face of the catastrophic convergence.

Technologies of Adaptation

"Thank God we are all strong people. We don't take loans," said Osmar Careinro Araujo. We were sitting in the shade of the MST camp's kitchen shack; around us the afternoon landscape was still and hot. Everything seemed to be waiting for the sun to relent. Osmar, the de facto community leader, was in his early forties, short and dark, with squinty, thoughtful eyes and a full black mustache. He had come up with the idea of the land occupation. He said,

> We had a few years without bad drought. And then last year—we have never seen a winter like that. It rained until August. As for the temperature rising, we can't measure this, but it feels much hotter. We feel the increase over the years. And for agriculture this is bad. Last year we had a really bad year. Because it flooded, we lost 50 percent of our beans. The fava did well. But there was a bumper crop, so prices were low. A real farmer always keeps back some seed. We are okay despite last year. But if the weather is really bad again we will have a hard time to recover.

This community has twenty-seven families, most of them related to each other. In face of drought and flooding, they have begun to adapt both technologically and politically. First, they switched from monocropping cotton and beans, which require burning the fallow fields and using expensive chemical inputs, to a form of mixed-crop agroecological farming, agroforestry, and integrated pest management that uses few or no chemical pesticides or fertilizers. They are also using inventive forms of low-impact water-capturing and rain-harvesting technologies.

Osmar and some of his compatriots take me across the road to show me "the system" and some of their alternative water-harvesting techniques.

One method involves building "underground dams." It goes like this: First the farmers find a dry streambed or natural area of drainage. At the bottom of this feature, below and away from the slope of the hill, they dig a long ditch across the natural path of drainage. The ditch may be one hundred or three hundred feet long and deep enough to hit solid rock—here, about five to ten feet down. Then, within the ditch, they build a cement and rock wall—or dam—lined with heavy plastic. Then the ditch is filled in, and the wall is buried. This underground dam greatly slows the natural drainage and creates a moist and fertile field "upstream."

The agroforestry crops are a mix of fruit trees, corn, cover crops, and climbing-vine crops. The fields seem abandoned due to the tangled mix of plant species. This lush mesh captures moisture and creates a balance of competing insects, limiting or eliminating the need for chemical pesticides. During the first three to five years, yields decrease, but then they increase as soil health improves. And the produce, as organic, commands higher prices.

For individual plants that need irrigation, they attach punctured empty plastic soda bottles to stakes above the thirsty plant. With this form of low-tech drip irrigation, a farmer can feed an individual plant little bits of water, allowing the precious liquid to drip out slowly and only onto the plant that needs it. The farmers' list of ingenious methods is long and evolving, thanks in part to groups like the Catholic NGO Caritas, which works to spread knowledge of best practices among the communities.

Altogether, these agroforestry or agroecological methods, which revive and enhance old ways, are in use all over the world. The IPCC mentions them in the Fourth Assessment Report: "Agroforestry using agroecological methods offers strong possibilities for maintaining biological diversity in Latin America, given the overlap between protected areas and agricultural zones."[44]

"The system," as the farmers call it, preserves and enhances the land's fertility and moisture, and because the fields are never left as bare ground, it helps prevent erosion. "People talk about sustainable farming, but that takes money and time," Osmar said. "We need land reform and help with water harvesting and storage facilities."

Politics of Adaptation

During my time in Boqueirão, I noticed a contradiction. While Osmar and the others championed "the system" and used the green farming methods on the side of the road where they *owned* land, they were still burning and monocropping on the land that they merely *occupied*. The reason for this reveals how *adaptation* and *social justice* really are linked: agroforestry takes three to five years to become profitable. Without land rights—without legal title—these families could not afford to invest their minimal capital and precious effort in the long-term and labor-intensive project of land restoration and stewardship. In another village, further north along the dirt track, I found further confirmation that land reform *is* climate adaptation.

In the village of Bueno, I met Antonio Braga Mota. "The system is a balanced system. I was really surprised that we actually did not need fertilizer and pesticides to do this," said Antonio as we tour his vine- and tree-covered crops. "The traditional method was destructive. Burning depletes the land. Unfortunately, I did a lot of that." He said even tapirs and rare birds are returning. He could be passionate about the system because he owned his land. He was not rich but had enough land to make the transition from mainstream methods to green farming.

At the MST camp I also found an example of reverse migration, from the favelas back to the land. Marcio Romero de Araujo Braga, a lean young farmer, had left the valley in March 2003 for the bright lights of São Paulo, where he worked painting buildings.

"It was good and bad in the city," he explained while taking a break from uprooting small trees on the newly occupied land. In São Paulo he met and married a young woman, originally from rural Bahia, and they had a kid. "But it was dangerous. My wife had to cross a favela every morning to get to work. There was too much violence, always drugs around. I prefer working the land."

Marcio's desire to come home was only possible once the occupation of the unused ranch began. Now there is land for him to work. "My dream would be to stay here and keep farming," he said when I ask him how he saw his future. "When we win this struggle"—he gestured to the field that he and a dozen other men were clearing—"I can do that."

Rolling Back Neoliberalism

During his eight years in power, President Luiz Inácio Lula da Silva took seriously the task of economic redistribution and development of Brazil's infrastructure—that is, he sought to roll back neoliberalism in Brazil. He promised something like Roosevelt's New Deal but delivered something closer to Johnson's "war on poverty"—providing real benefits to the poor but leaving the rich unmolested. Lula did not address the climate crisis with an ambitious program of mitigation and adaptation. Yet, he laid the groundwork for real adaptation efforts that may come later.

Under Lula, Brazil paid off its external debt and built up reserves of $240 billion. In 2005, Brazil announced it would pay off both the Paris Club (that is, nineteen of the world's biggest economies) and the much-loathed IMF.[45] That, in effect, redirected huge streams of revenue away from wealthy international creditors (who make money by owning the debts of others) back toward social and economic investment within Brazil.

One of Lula's central economic programs has been the Bolsa Família, which gives payments of up to $104 a month to poor families. Mothers with children are paid for sending kids to school, getting vaccinations, and following proper nutrition. The program gives food not only to the destitute but also to the solidly working class and thus enjoys wide support. The Bolsa was actually started in the 1990s by state governments and expanded under President Fernando Henrique Cardoso, then expanded again very widely by Lula. By 2010 one in four Brazilians depended on the Bolsa, which had helped lift 21 million out of poverty. The cost is minimal: Brazil spends less than half of 1 percent of its $1.6 trillion GDP on antipoverty programs. This is redistributive social justice, but it is not transformative of underlying social relations.

Lula's other big initiative was potentially more profound. The Growth Acceleration Program (PAC), a macroeconomic and infrastructural policy—classic Keynesianism—began in 2007 with an initial investment of $4.2 billion and aimed to revamp Brazil's infrastructure. The PAC has built roads, rails, power lines, and housing; in the *Nordeste*, it mostly helps agroexporters with water impoundment, irrigation, transportation, and port facilities.

The PAC helped maintain Brazil's robust economic growth: even during the worst of the recent world economic slump, Brazil did well and inequality decreased. Under Lula the top 10 percent of Brazilians has grown 11 percent richer, but the bottom tenth has seen incomes rise 72 percent. But the PAC's focus on large-scale, capital-intensive projects means relying on well-connected businesses, and this tends to reinforce old hierarchies.[46]

Climate change and the harsh task of adaptation at the grass roots require an expanded economic role for the Brazilian state. Yet, even simply redistributive actions by the state can inadvertently reinforce the five-hundred-year-old client-patron dynamic that has fettered Brazil. Will climate-adaptation aid in the *Nordeste* force poor people to depend on local elites—political bosses—to act as brokers with the state? Or will it work with the social movements? Time will tell.

As Donald R. Nelson and Timothy J. Finan, two experts on the matter, have found, government actions now provide food, water, and cash to victims of drought. The Northeast has been targeted for both emergency drought aid and big water-storage infrastructure projects for more than one hundred years. "As a consequence, drought-related mortality is no longer apparent and forced migrations have significantly declined, suggesting that the state has been successful in mitigating the worst of the impacts. Nonetheless, as a result of the high levels of vulnerability, farm families remain dependent on the state political apparatus (and the local elite) during times of crisis."[47]

Just as MST and CV represent two contradictory grassroots adaptive responses to suffering, Lula's tropical New Deal and the paramilitary assaults of the BOPE upon the favelas are examples of the Brazilian state's conflicting potentials. The social problems of poverty and violence in Brazil will become more intense as climate change takes hold. Some amount of repression is inevitable. The question is, Which tendency within the state will dominate future policy: the move to alleviate suffering or that to violently contain and repress it?

CHAPTER 14

Golgotha Mexicana:
Climate Refugees, Free Trade, and the War Next Door

A new day has begun and it looks like night.

    —CHARLES BOWDEN, *Murder City*

T HE WIND OFF the Mexican desert was cold and gritty. A pale winter sun slipped away, and the shadows of Juarez reached long across the streets. I was riding with a Mexican army patrol in a military truck that bounced and lurched across the broken terrain. Cinderblock shacks sat scattered haphazardly over the steep little hills and gullies. We were driving around and around waiting for violence. That is what the soldiers do here: drive in loops, then stop for snacks, then drive some more. Soon a bullet-ridden corpse would turn up. Several do every night, because this is one of the most violent cities in the world.

A gum-chewing soldier in the back of the truck, holding his G3 rifle in a gloved hand and the truck roll bar with the other, had a plan for Juarez: "martial law." He scanned the flat rooftops through pale yellow wraparound shooting glasses. "A curfew. House-to-house searches. Take all the weapons. No mercy."

They say there is a war in Mexico, and the body count makes it look that way. Close to thirty thousand people have been killed here since 2006, when President Felipe Calderón deployed the military into the border cities to fight the drug war.[1] By 2009, more than eleven hundred of the dead were soldiers, police, and security officials. A classified Mexican government report described 2009 as the deadliest year to date with over ninety-six hundred killed; the next year was even worse.[2]

At the end of 2009, when I spent some time drifting around the border region, Juarez—shabby, grime smeared, semiabandoned—clocked a staggering twenty six hundred killings.[3] Many of these incidents also involved kidnapping, torture, and mutilation. El Paso, on the other hand, counted only four murders. Some Juarez murders happened one at a time, some in massacres of up to eighteen victims at once.[4] Some happened in the dead of night, others during noontime traffic jams. New Year's Day 2010 began with a mass killing: more than a dozen gunmen attacked a house party of middle-class high school students, killing thirteen and wounding two dozen.[5] Then two US embassy officials were ambushed and murdered. By late April 2010, twenty-nine police officers had already been killed in Juarez; then gunmen ambushed two police vehicles in the middle of town, killing seven more cops. Around the same time, gunmen raided the customs office on the Mexican side of the international bridge linking Camargo, Mexico, to Rio Grande, Texas. The same day, in La Union, Guerrero, police were attacked with grenades. A police chief and two deputies were executed in the farm town of Los Aldamas, Nuevo Leon. The police chief of a nearby town was decapitated. Then, around the same time, gunmen ambushed and killed the assistant police chief of Nogales, Sonora, and his bodyguard. In the states of Tamaulipas and Nuevo Leon, dozens of narco gunmen launched simultaneous attacks on two army garrisons; eighteen of the attackers were reported killed. A car bomb went off in Juarez, and seventeen migrants were massacred in Tamaulipas about one hundred miles from Brownsville, Texas.[6] These days, Mexican mayors, police officials, and drug-rehab patients are all routinely murdered in shockingly large numbers. The list of strange atrocities could go on and on.

Political Teleconnections

At first glance, this crisis of violence seems to have little to do with climate change—drug dealers do not murder cops because the Intertropical

Convergence Zone is off kilter. But, on closer examination, the meltdown of northern Mexico provides another illustration of the catastrophic convergence: policies that create poverty and violence are now colliding with the new realities of climate change, and together these three forces are creating socially destructive forms of adaptation.

As I explored Juarez, it became clear that climate change is already an important factor in the crisis. First and foremost, climate change is undermining agriculture and fishing. Along with neoliberal economic policies, it is driving rising unemployment and pushing people north, toward the United States, and into the traps of the underground drug economy.

Mexico is being hammered by climate change. The northern half of the country is in the grips of the worst drought in sixty years, while the southeastern areas are being deluged. A recent study found that for every 10 percent decrease in crop yields, 2 percent more Mexicans will leave for the United States. The same study projects that 10 percent of the current population of Mexicans aged fifteen to sixty-five could attempt to emigrate north as a result of rising temperatures.[7]

The year 2010 saw more freakish weather: rains destroyed much of the bean harvest in the Pacific Coast states of Nayarit and Sinaloa; rivers burst their banks and flooded crops in Michoacán. Hurricane Alex soaked northeastern Mexico, killing at least thirty people and destroying crops. Mass flooding hit Tabasco for the second time in four years; in 2007, floodwaters inundated 80 percent of that state.[8]

Migration

In 1990 the Intergovernmental Panel on Climate Change predicted that "the gravest effects of climate change may be those on human migration." Increased storms, droughts, flooding, proliferation of pathogens, and rising seas will wreak havoc upon the world's urbanized coastlines and agricultural economies. This suggests a future in which millions of people will be on the move. A one-meter rise in sea level—almost certain by the century's end, barring some strange intervention by Mother Nature, like a radical solar minimum—will inundate terrain currently housing about 10 percent of the world's population. Many other people living far from the sea, on semiarid agricultural lands, will be unable to adapt and forced to move.

In this light, the US-Mexico border becomes a template for understanding dangerous global dynamics. All over the world, borders and policing regimes are hardening as restrictive immigration policies are matched by a xenophobic style of politics.

By 2050 global population is expected to peak at 9 billion, and global temperatures are likely be close to 2°C hotter than today, or more. How many environmental refugees will there be? A report from the International Migration Organization was realistic about the uncertainties, noting, "Current estimates range between 25 million and 1 billion people by 2050." The report also explained that "as is already the case with political refugees, it is likely that the burden of providing for climate migrants will be borne by the poorest countries—those least responsible for emissions of greenhouse gases."[9]

Britain's 2006 Stern Review estimated that between 200 and 250 million people would be uprooted by climate change. That is 10 times the current number of refugees in the world.[10] Let that sink in for a moment. Bangladeshi academic Atiq Rahman had it correct when he warned, "Millions of people will be moving. No amount of nuclear submarines will be able to stop that."[11] Another report estimated there are 214 million international migrants in the world today. "If this number continues to grow at the same pace as during the last 20 years, international migrants could number 405 million by 2050."[12]

Migration unfolds in a series of knock-on effects that mask causal relationships. In poor countries, it is not necessarily the poorest and hardest hit who migrate the first and furthest. "The ability to migrate is a function of mobility and resources (both financial and social). In other words, the people most vulnerable to climate change are not necessarily the ones most likely to migrate."[13]

Here the catastrophic convergence reveals itself again: the climate crisis adds its propellant power to the already unfolding, highly destructive legacy of neoliberalism and Cold War military adventures. Climate change acts as an additional causal factor in shaping already-established migration flows. And in the face of rising migration, the borders between wealthy core economies and the developing world harden and militarize.[14]

Who Is a Climate Migrant?

On the south bank of the Rio Grande I met José Ramírez. Squat and ruddy faced, dressed in jeans and a hooded sweatshirt, he was unemployed and gazing across the river at the United States. He had been a fisherman in Michoacán but was displaced by the economic aftershocks of 1997–1998's El Niño. His story reveals the connections between environmental and economic crises.

"The sea became red, and all the fish just disappeared," Ramírez said in explaining why he left his home. The coast of Michoacán was becoming warmer, both the land and the sea. At first he hung on, but El Niño had put him into debt. Ramírez's family had run a little restaurant but had to close it when everyone took an economic hit. Eventually, he had to sell his skiff and outboard motor. Then he worked on a large shrimp fishing boat, but the income was minimal. So a couple years after the weather shock of El Niño, he moved north to Juarez, aiming to come to the United States, which he did. For about a year he worked illegally as a roofer in Las Cruces, New Mexico, but then he was caught and deported.

Now he is waiting to go back. "I even talked to my old boss on the phone. He said he has work for me," Ramírez said, looking across the dry Rio Grande into downtown El Paso. But it is difficult to cross the border these days. He needs money to hire a professional coyote. And there is no work here in Juarez. Between the global economic downturn and the city's extreme drug violence, industry is in decline. Ramírez makes just enough to survive from occasional day labor.

"The killings around here make it very hard. I saw a child killed right in front of me. Not far from here at a store, they shot a man and then the child. I don't want to get involved in drugs. I just want to do honest work," Ramírez said.

What happened to José Ramírez? In simple terms, the El Niño pushed him into debt, which in turn forced him to migrate north. As I have repeated throughout this book, it is impossible to say that a warmer globe has caused any single weather event. But the pattern of association is clear: increased surface temperatures correlate with more El Niño events.

Climate change unfolds as part of a matrix of causality. The warm water of the El Niño triggered the poisonous red tide algae bloom that killed and pushed away the fish and thus began Ramírez's sojourn in the north. But the toxic algae bloom was not produced by warm water alone. It was also created on land by rampant development of tourist hotels, golf courses, and agroexport fruit plantations, all of which discharge more sewage and organophosphates into the sea, feeding toxic algae blooms.

Compounding this increase in organic pollution is the decline of natural defenses in the form of mangrove forests and wetlands. Mangrove forests grow on tidal flats and clean freshwater runoff by absorbing the nutrients that otherwise feed algae blooms. Their decline means more algae. The same uncontrolled development that adds organic pollutants to coastal waters also clears away mangroves. According to the United Nations' Food and Agricultural Organization, Mexico had 1.4 million hectares of mangrove forest in 1971. By 1999, those coastal woodlands had dropped by almost half to only 733,000 hectares.[15]

Likewise, the social impacts of the red tide were not inevitable but were created in part by political economic policies. For example, why were the fish stocks not more robust? Because Mexico's fisheries are badly managed and in decline; catches have been level since 1980 despite ever more investment.[16] Why was there no public system of support for José Ramírez during his difficult times? Because Mexico is now a social laboratory of radical free market orthodoxy.

Neoliberal Fish

The Mexican Revolution was broadly progressive in character. Among its many reforms, it reserved the best fish stocks for small individual fisherman and state-sponsored cooperatives. "Throughout the 1930s co-operatives were progressively awarded concessions to national fish stocks, a process that culminated with the 1947 Fishing Law granting them exclusive access rights to the nine most important inshore marine and shellfish fisheries."[17] Subsistence or artisanal fishermen got the rest. How fish were caught, processed, and sold was, like much of the economy, encased in layers of regulation defined by economic nationalism. A parastatal enterprise called Productos Pesqueros Mexicanos, or Propemex, controlled fish packing and processing, price regulation and marketing.[18]

During the Latin American debt crisis of the 1980s, Mexico steadily liberalized its economy. The end goal of the process was a free trade agreement with the United States and Canada. As part of that, Propemex with all its canneries, processing factories, and vessels, was privatized. Deregulation of the banking sector allowed private firms to push aside government financing of the fishing sector.[19] In 1989 foreign ownership of up to 50 percent of fishing and fish-processing industries was allowed.[20] The monopoly of the co-ops was ended, forcing them to compete with the private sector for formal access rights. The state reduced public expenditures by selling the main state-owned fish processor and exporter to a private bank and reducing subsidies to small fishermen. More broadly, between 1982 and 1994, 940 of 1,155 publicly owned businesses throughout the economy were privatized or liquidated. And previously closed markets were opened. In exchange for all of this, Mexico got greater access to US markets.[21]

The neoliberal model of fisheries management has come at a high social and environmental cost. Stocks have plummeted and poverty has risen among fishing communities. As the state downsized its role and private capital moved into a heavily regulated sector, official corruption and marine-resource poaching grew.[22]

The little regulation remaining is often circumvented in what veteran *Times* reporter Tim Wiener called "the great divide between Mexico's laws and its law enforcement." Officials have estimated that as many twelve thousand unregulated fishing boats work the Sea of Cortez alone.[23] Foreign boats take much of the fish: Mexico's fleet accounts for less than 10 percent of the total catch, with the rest going to boats from the United States, Canada, and Japan.[24] This bad management of fish resources has made people like José Ramírez vulnerable to the new freak weather and helped push them away from their original livelihoods and toward Mexico's cities and the United States.

The story of José Ramírez, multiplied across the country, is the story of climate change expressing itself through the political economic realities of neoliberalism. While it is impossible to say that climate change caused the 1997–1998 El Niño, we know that a hotter planet will likely lead to more extreme weather events like the El Niño–Southern Oscillation and more toxic algae blooms. Combined with bad economic policies, climate change is already creating climate refugees.

Pushed from the Sierra

On the southwestern edge of Juarez, where the slums creep up into the Sierra Madre, I met other climate migrants in a *colonia* of Rarámuri Indians. Also known as the Tarahumara, these famous long-distance runners come from southern Chihuahua's Sierra Madre Occidental. Their urban *colonia* replicates a mountain village centered around a plaza and a yellow-walled catholic church. Above them looms a cold, grey massif. On a fence hung two drying cowhides from animals slaughtered for the holidays. Many of the Rarámuri men were out of work or had only intermittent day labor, and many were drunk. The Indians moved here because jobs pulled them north, but drought back home is also pushing them.

"We have no rains there, so many people are coming here," said Celso Nava Galindo. Thirty-six, he moved from a village seven hours away called Bocoina. "No rain, no people," said Galindo. "Back home we survive by farming and speak our own language. But the drought makes it very difficult."

In 2008, travel writer Richard Grant noted the same: "The Tarahumara had moved out of the area now. It was climate change as much as anything. There had been twelve drought years in the last fifteen. And it was becoming impossible for subsistence farmers to keep themselves alive. Of all the problems and challenges the Tarahumara are up against, this was the most intractable."[25]

When farming gave way to drought, Galindo became a full-time logger, but when the trees were cleared, he lost his job. So he came to Juarez—like the timber from his homeland—and worked in construction. Like the other men in the plaza, he explained the drought in local and empiricist terms: "Too much logging."

Indeed, the forests of the Sierra Tarahumara are under strain; almost 90 percent of the lumber produced in Chihuahua State comes from there. Mexico as a whole, never heavily wooded, has cut down more than one-third of its forests. The 1980s, the decade of steady liberalization leading to the North American Free Trade Agreement (NAFTA), saw rapid deforestation. Between 1990 and 2005, Mexico lost 6.9 percent of its forest cover.[26]

The men on the plaza may be correct that deforestation is a cause of the drought. However, the problems extend beyond their sierra. Much of Mexico is suffering dry and erratic weather, including sudden flooding in otherwise drought-plagued areas. Increasingly, climate change will be the central dynamic in migration. The World Watch Institute reports, "Desertification affecting [Mexican] drylands is leading some 600,000 to 700,000 people to migrate annually." In 2009 and 2010, thanks to an El Niño, Mexico was gripped by the worst drought in decades. In many parts of Mexico, ownership of water has been even more important than ownership of land.[27] "Almost 40 percent of the farm land inspected by the government has been affected by the drought, causing shortfalls in the harvests of corn, beans, wheat and sorghum," reported a business wire. And the Mexican government spent more than $100 million on emergency crop-insurance aid to farmers.[28] It announced that drought had reduced the 2009 harvest of the staple white corn by 10 percent but insisted that "the supply for human consumption will be guaranteed."[29]

CARE International examined desertification and migration in Mexico, finding more evidence of climate-driven dislocation. "When our harvest is bad, we have to rely on ourselves," explained one farmer. "Many of us had to leave, to Canada or the United States. . . . The money I made there . . . was a big help for my family. Without that income, it would have become extremely difficult." Another farmer told CARE, "My grandfather, father and I have worked these lands. But times have changed. . . . The rain is coming later now, so that we produce less. The only solution is to go away."[30]

Further south, similar conditions obtain. The warming of the Pacific off Peru has meant that Guatemala faced its worst drought in three decades. In 2009 corn crops failed in four provinces, and four hundred thousand peasant families needed food aid. The government pleaded for $100 million in emergency donations. In El Salvador, Hurricane Ida brought massive flooding: fifteen thousand people were displaced, and more than two hundred died. But the real devastation from that storm would arrive later as eroded soil, failed crops, and mounting household debt drove people off the land into cities and beyond, to Mexico and then north again.

When displaced populations meet with more poverty and unemployment, slum living, the lure of the underground narcotics trade, state corruption, inequality, and a media landscape full of materialism, narcissism, sexism, and blood lust, the resulting anomie and relative deprivation they experience fuels crime. Crime justifies Mexican state repression and, as we shall see latter, a xenophobic hardening of policing in the United States. In this fashion, a crisis of natural systems becomes a crisis of urban violence and border repression.

The catastrophic convergence as it unfolds in northern Mexico links migration, economics, violence, and climate. To understand the social breakdown that is the Mexican drug war and into which climate refugees now flow, we must understand the country's economic history, because the strange new weather that drives people off the land is articulated through the economic realities history has bequeathed. This is evident in the case of José Ramírez, the fisherman from Michoacán, and Celso Nava Galindo, the Rarámuri farmer turned logger, then urban day laborer. Migrants like them are not merely *pushed* away by drought, floods, and algae blooms; they are also *pulled* into the vortex of migration and border politics by the lure of industrial work. Thus, making sense of climate change in Mexico and at the militarized US border requires a foray into the economic history of the Mexican Revolution and the transformations wrought by NAFTA.

Insurgent Mexico

From 1920, when the guns of the revolution fell silent, until the early 1980s, the Mexican economy developed along inward-looking, state-led corporatist lines in a pattern similar to Brazil's and common throughout Latin America. Under Porfirio Diaz, Mexico was said to be the mother of foreigners and the stepmother of Mexicans.[31] As *The Nation* correspondent and historian Carlton Beals described in his biography of Diaz, "His group had only one basic idea, to steal, much, often and scientifically."[32] This was particularly so after the US war with Spain in 1898, when under commercial pressure from the north, Diaz slipped into the authoritarian *caudilloismo* for which he is best known. Economic depression in 1903 made it worse. Strikes during the recovery in 1906 and 1907 were met with vicious repression. His methods—*pan o palo*, "bread or stick"—combined repression and corrupt patronage. During his last decade in power, economic policy was in disarray, and in response to the international economic crises of 1893 and 1903, Diaz borrowed heavily and at high rates of interest.[33]

By the eve of the revolution, power relations in Mexico were rotten. Beals painted a picture (perhaps exaggerated) of unbearable humiliation: "Everywhere, the *hacendado* had first right to women. Frequently the *hacendado*, or foreman, after enjoying a girl just entering puberty, would call in some young peon, with the remark 'this is your wife' such was the marriage ceremony."[34] At the top of this heap was Diaz.

When the revolution against him finally broke out, it was a chaotic affair, pitting geographically and ideologically heterogeneous forces against Diaz and his backers: hacienda landlords, the corrupt officialdom, and large foreign capitalists, mostly British and European.[35] The rebels included Liberals, demanding free politics; Indian peasants, demanding land; cowboys and gangsters, demanding loot; and nationalist entrepreneurs, seeking a path toward modern economic development. As Frank Tannenbaum put it in his contemporary classic *Peace by Revolution*, "The Mexican Revolution was anonymous. It was essentially the work of the common people. No organized party presided at its birth. No great intellectuals prescribed its program, formulated its doctrine, outlined its objectives."[36]

Article 27 and the Corporatist State

In victory, the revolution settled on an agenda of economic modernization and capitalist development that pivoted, interestingly, on the world's first socialist constitution.[37] More specifically, Article 27 of that 1917 document read, "In the Nation is vested the direct ownership of all natural resources." That meant all lands, minerals, and forests, all the waters and all the fish. The actual text goes on in great detail to enumerate "precious stones, rock-salt and the deposits of salt formed by sea water . . . petroleum and all solid, liquid, and gaseous hydrocarbons."[38] (Even the rock salt!) At the heart of Article 27 was land reform, which liberated much of the peasantry from debt peonage. By 1940 almost 23 percent of all land was collectively owned in the *ejido* system, up from 1.6 percent at the end of the revolution.[39] In 1960, about 20,000 *ejidos* with about 2 million members worked "slightly less than half of all cultivated land."[40]

The relatively autonomous state sought to spur economic development through policies of import-substitution industrialization (ISI). Like Brazil and many other Latin American states during the twentieth century, Mexico forged a limited labor-capital compact. The state owned some industries and imposed controls upon others. Ultimately, this semisocialist set of interventions formed part of "an alliance for profit" with business.[41]

In exchange for cooperating and negotiating with trade unions, Mexican capitalists were allowed to form monopolies and cartels. They were also forced into state-managed business chambers. The state supported business with subsidies, protective tariffs, and regulations designed to blunt the most ravaging effects of unbridled interfirm competition and protect Mexican companies from foreign rivals. Partial state ownership allowed stronger sectors of the economy to support weaker sectors.[42]

The state provided cheap and stable credit as "foreign ownership of the banking system was progressively replaced by national and state ownership."[43] The new credit system facilitated "the progress of the agrarian reform" and developed a crop-based, rather than land-based, credit system for small individual proprietors and "peasants holding communal lands in villages." By these arrangements they could access ready credit, but communal lands would not carry mortgages or be foreclosed on.[44] Meanwhile, trade unions won legal rights, although organized labor's more radical elements were marginalized. Union agitation and collective bargaining increased wages, which in turn spurred consumption and the growth of internal markets, and that encouraged more productive investment, creating further employment, consumption, profits, and so on.[45] All these progressive reforms allowed Mexican industry to compete with the more powerful British and American interests that had dominated business and trade (but not agriculture) under Porfirio Diaz.[46]

Cárdenas and Oil

This Mexican version of corporatism deepened significantly in the late 1930s under President Lazaro Cárdenas, who accelerated land reform and the nationalization of basic industry. "The assumption underlying Cardenas' policies was that while capitalism was necessary for development, capital, like labor, could be controlled and regulated by the state."[47] Cárdenas "emphasized programs to improve the lot of the lower classes, especially the Indians, through education, redistribution of land, collective farms (ejidos), curbs on foreign capital, and a larger role for state-run enterprise."[48]

By 1937, Cárdenas had nationalized the railroads and set his sights on the ultimate prize: petroleum. That brought him into direct confrontation with Standard Oil of New Jersey, Shell, and the US government. But Cárdenas prevailed and expropriated the Mexican operations of the international petroleum firms to create the state oil company Petróleos Mexicanos, or Pemex.[49]

But the system had its problems. By centralizing power and excluding, but not smashing, capital, the Mexican state opened the way for serious corruption. The idea was that the state should be the "rector of the economy." Business was excluded from politics and denied access to decision-making circles; owners of private businesses were not even allowed to be part of the ruling party.[50] Yet, formal exclusion of the private sector from official channels of influence encouraged businessmen to cultivate informal influence and access. Corruption and clientelism resulted.

By the 1960s, some industries had founded autonomous chambers that opposed state involvement in the economy. The most powerful of these were the Businessmen's Council, formed in 1962, and the Businessmen's Coordinating Council, created in 1975. Within these elite factions, pressure for a rightward turn in economic policy would grow.

Oil's Cursed Boom

The corporatist model fell upon hard times during the 1970s. Sagging growth and rising inflation were coupled with increasing public debt. At the same time, an oil boom began to distort the Mexican economy. In 1973, just as new oil reserves came into production, prices surged, going from $3 to $12 per barrel.[51]

At the same time, social pressure was growing throughout Mexico: farmers, workers, and, most of all, students and urban youth were forming active social movements. Their protests were met with arrest, torture, murder, and even massacre. Ten days before the 1968 Summer Olympics opened in Mexico City, soldiers opened fire on a student protest at La Plaza de las Tres Culturas at Tlatelolco. Some two to three hundred were killed, hundreds more wounded, hundreds arrested and beaten, with scores of bodies taken away and hidden by troops.[52]

Amidst the rising tension, Luis Echeverría began his six-year term as president in 1970. Personally implicated in the slaughter of protesting students at Tlatelolco in 1968, President Echeverría attempted to shore up the state's legitimacy with a neopopulist program of political and social reforms. "Shared development" was the catch phrase; a massive expansion in public spending, the means. Among other things, the number of university students increased by 290 percent between 1970 and 1976.

The stimulus was paid for with oil income, which was rising as international petroleum prices spiraled upward. But Echeverría needed more revenue. He needed to collect more taxes from the rich but could not because too many were hiding their wealth abroad. So, the government increased borrowing on foreign markets.[53] Under Echeverría, foreign debt shot from $3.2 billion to $16 billion. With the stimulus came inflation. In

August 1976, Echeverría's debt bubble burst, and the peso was devalued 45 percent. Mexico had been a low-inflation country, but in the early 1970s, prices began to rise from an annual average increase of 3.6 percent between 1965 and 1970, to 30.5 percent between 1977 and 1982. By the mid-1980s inflation averaged 90 percent.

The next president, José Lopez Portillo, continued the balancing act: he repressed the radical Left but allowed the Communist Party to run in elections. He spent lavishly on development projects and invested in neglected sectors like agriculture, housing, health, and education. Again, oil prices were surging. Between 1979 and 1980, Mexican oil income grew by almost two-thirds.[54] Yet, the government still had to borrow to pay its bills. The economy was growing by 8 percent per year, many companies were operating at full capacity, and Mexico's small stock market was booming. From the early 1960s through the 1970s the number of primary schools doubled, and the illiteracy rate fell to 15 percent; the infant mortality rate fell by half, thanks to a nearly tenfold increase in the number of public doctors.[55]

Logic of Loans

In theory, the strategy of taking loans against future oil incomes was sound. As international oil prices increased, so too did the value of Mexico's untapped petroleum. Mexican planners sought to avoid the "resource curse" of developing into an unbalanced, petroleum-fixated economy. Mexico's leading politicians wagered that while credit was cheap and oil income high, they could renovate the nonoil sectors of the economy with petroleum-collateralized debt. Because of the oil boom, credit was cheap: financial markets were awash in liquidity because most petrostates lacked the capacity to invest their windfall earnings internally. These so-called petrodollars were recycled through international financial markets. Diversified and balanced economic growth would allow Mexico to generate tax revenue with which to repay the loans. With this strategy, Mexican technocrats sought to avoid the "mistakes of Venezuela," which had spent most of the century exporting oil and squandering the income. The trick was to *invest* the petroleum-collateralized income in production, not just *spend* the money on imports.[56]

Alas, imports did not decline, and domestic production did not surge. The peso's value rose, making imports cheap: grain imports doubled between 1979 and 1980; the oil and service sectors drew away talent. Agriculture, the heart of Mexican society, stagnated amidst the boom, as did other nonoil sectors. Poverty remained severe and widespread. By the end of 1980, Mexico owed $33 billion to foreign banks. As crisis loomed, President José Lopez Portillo insisted, "Our economy is not petrolized." In fact, it was: nearly 75 percent of Mexico's export earnings came from petroleum.[57]

The Mexican economy was now like a waiter rushing forward with a tray full of dishes: keep moving and you are okay. But, as the bankers say, "It's not speed that kills; it's the sudden stop."

Crash

The sudden stop took the form of that disciplinary recession unleashed in 1979 when the US Federal Reserve, under Paul Volcker, jacked up rates. This triggered (but did not cause) the Latin American debt crisis. As the crisis worsened, the International Monetary Fund (IMF) and World Bank stepped in. As chapter 13 on Brazil explains, assistance from the Bretton Woods institutions came with strings attached: emergency loans were given only if austerity was imposed and exports increased. But increased exports meant an oversupply of primary commodities and therefore declining prices. Thus, the debt crisis begat the commodity crisis, a prolonged period of low prices for primary commodities such as timber; metal ores like iron, bauxite, and tin; grains and foods like sugar, coca, coffee; and, to some extent, oil. By one estimate, commodity prices declined 35 percent during the 1980s.[58] As a result, many economies in the Global South—the ones now feeling the first effects of climate change—suffered relative stagnation for nearly two decades. Only the overflow of the long Chinese boom and the early impact of climate change finally broke the torpor beginning around 2004 and accelerated to the food crises of 2008 and 2010.[59]

The commodity crisis essentially had three causes: (1) the economic slowdown in the developed countries; (2) the rise of synthetic subsidies in part as a result of the oil-price hikes of the 1970s, which raised incentives for new industrial engineering techniques; and (3) the structural-adjustment policies of the IMF and World Bank that forced debtor nations to increase exports and devalue their currencies.[60]

In the summer of 1981, as the effect of Volcker's monetarist squeeze went international, oil prices began to slide, and Mexico faced badly diminished revenues and the world's largest foreign debt: $70 billion. Mexican economists had projected the country would have oil revenues of $20 billion in 1981 and $27 billion in 1982. Both borrowing and domestic spending were based on those figures. In 1981, however, oil brought in a mere $14 billion, and the next year was also below target.[61] The cost of debt servicing now consumed most of Mexico's projected petroleum sales, thus most of its foreign earnings.[62] By the summer of 1982, Mexico owed almost $81 billion to foreign banks, and that sum was growing. To avoid default, the peso was devalued, and the government imposed limited capital controls. It was the second devaluation of the year.[63] Rich individuals and private firms began to panic and shift their wealth out of the country.

On August 12, 1982, Mexico announced that it could not pay its bills and took the first steps toward default, declaring a ninety-day moratorium on repayment. The peso was devalued 30 percent and before year's end would drop another 53 percent.[64] As the *New York Times* explained, "A default by Mexico could have serious effects on the American banking system and on banks throughout the world. According to one American banker, some United States banks have as much as 90 percent of their capital on loan to Mexico. Even at banks with relatively small exposure, the Mexican loans represent 30 percent of their capital."[65] In early September, President José Lopez Portillo nationalized the country's private banking system, freezing negotiations with the IMF.[66]

Bailout '82

The eventual compromise involved the US Federal Reserve, the IMF, and most of the 800 banks to which Mexico owed money.[67] In exchange for $12 billion in credit, Mexico began economic liberalization and imposed austerity. Out went Keynes; in came Hayek. The government sold 106 state-owned companies and agencies. These included sugar mills, shipyards, textile and power plants, as well as the parastatal processing plants and the export-marketing firm Ocean Garden Products, to which the unemployed fisherman José Ramírez would have sold his catch.[68]

Privatization brought new owners who broke unions, fired workers, and drove down wages. By decade's end, 1,155 state businesses had shrunk to only 400. The government earned less than $2 billion from these privatizations, which went to service debts.[69] At the same time, food subsidies were slashed; those for eggs, milk, cooking oil, sugar, beans, and rice were eliminated completely. The retail price of gasoline and natural gas doubled.[70] By 1986, the purchasing power of the average Mexican was about half of what it had been in 1982.[71]

President José Lopez Portillo, however, retired to a $30 million mountaintop mansion, a monument to venality and arrogance that included a walk-in "refrigerator for furs," a library with space for a million volumes, and "an astronomical observatory that is better equipped than National University's."[72]

NAFTA

Mexico's trial by debt began the long march to the North American Free Trade Agreement. The agreement culminated a process of liberalization born of the 1982 debt crisis. Along the way, Article 27 of the 1917 constitution was eviscerated; among other things, it now allows greater foreign investment. On January 1, 1994, NAFTA took effect.[73] At the same time, in the southern Mexican state of Chiapas, the Zapatista National Liberation Army, a group of mostly indigenous peasants, rose up against the government, calling NAFTA a death sentence for Indians.[74]

According to its main booster, former Mexican president Carlos Salinas, NAFTA would empower Mexico "to export goods, not people."[75] The rural economy would be modernized, and farmers who could not adapt would find work in the expanding industrial and service sectors.[76] But what did free trade really do for Mexico? An almost quizzical article published in the *New York Times* in 2009 answered this as follows: "In some cases, NAFTA produced results that were exactly the opposite of what was promised. For instance, domestic industries were dismantled as multinationals imported parts from their own suppliers. Local farmers were priced out of the market by food imported tariff-free. Many Mexican farmers simply abandoned their land and headed north."[77] The piece went on to note that, although the value of Mexico's exports had quintupled in fifteen years, almost half a million people each year were outmigrating in search of work, a disproportionate number of them from the countryside. With only one-quarter of Mexico's total population, the countryside accounts for 44 percent of all Mexican immigrants moving to the United States.[78]

Under NAFTA, the government dismantled most of the agencies that offered assistance and administered subsidies to small farmers. "Lending by both government and private-sector rural credit programs declined 75% after 1994, when NAFTA took effect, while rural bankruptcies increased six-fold."[79] The reformed Article 27 now allows sale of *ejido* lands, which has increased landlessness.[80] According to a 2010 report by Oxfam, Mexico has spent $80 billion on food imports and now has a deficit in food trade of $435 million.[81] Mexican agricultural production has turned away from food for people and internal markets toward animal feed for export.[82] Markets for corn, the staple food, protected by government policy until NAFTA, have been completely opened.[83] Peasant organizations have demanded a renegotiation of the treaty.[84]

Since 1994, Mexico's economic growth has slowed. It now averages only about 3 percent. From 1921 to 1967, annual growth averaged 5.2 percent, and for much of that period, it was over 6 percent.[85] According to World Bank figures, "in 2004, 28 percent of rural dwellers were extremely poor and 57 percent moderately poor."[86]

The suffering and social polarization produced by neoliberalism has fostered corruption and exacerbated relative deprivation. This is the stage, preset, onto which now enters the issue of climate change to converge with the economic crisis and the legacy of political repression. In combination, all of these factors help drive migration to the United States and to northern Mexico, where the chaotic drug war now eats away at society.

Narcoguerra: Countdown to Chaos

Tanila Garcia's shack looks out upon the United States of America from the western edge of Juarez. The view takes in a kaleidoscopic political landscape defined by the social chasm between the underdevelopment of the Global South and the dazzling wealth of the Global North. The shack has a dirt floor covered with strips of salvaged grey office carpet. Its walls are lined with layers of flattened cardboard boxes, and the small windows are covered with clear, foggy plastic to keep out the wind of the high desert winter. Each of Garcia's rooms, one for her and her husband, the other for their four children, two boys and two girls, smells of sweat and dirty clothes. On a step of land above the shack sits a plywood outhouse.

Her little home in the *colonia* of Anapra was purchased for the equivalent of $2,000. She has enclosed her barren yard with a homemade fence of sticks, barbed wire, and burnt-clean wire mattress frames. From a low naked tree hang three wooden cages for songbirds she has captured: the two small red birds are called gurrions, and a bigger one is a chivo. The birds hop nervously back and forth in their shoebox-size confinements. "I like how they sing in the morning," said Garcia.

She works cleaning houses and her husband works day-labor construction. At that time, they had no employment. One of her girls, age eleven, stood nearby as Garcia explained how they survived: "We save food when we have it."

She draws her water from a neighbor's tap. Electricity is pirated from a nearby utility pole. The aging extension cords that feed her home are draped haphazardly over branches and roofs. During rainstorms, jerry-rigged arrangements like these are known to electrocute people who walk too close to them on muddy ground. The average annual rainfall here is minimal—only about eight inches, but parts of Juarez and El Paso are occasionally hit by flash floods. When in August 2006 the skies dumped more than fifteen inches on the region, the pit latrines overflowed, and the slums of Juarez flooded with electrocuting sewage.

Across from the little homestead lies a sandy access road and the metal wall of the US border. Beyond that are the arcing tracks of the Southern

Pacific Railroad, and rising up the slopes of the Franklin Mountains are the middle-class suburbs of El Paso's west side, Coronado Hills and Ridge Crest.

This landscape is so extreme in its social contrasts, so politically didactic, that it could have been invented by revolutionaries, preachers, or lazy journalists had it not already been created by migrants, land speculators, politicians, bureaucrats, and industrial firms in search of cheap labor. This is Juarez: the city NAFTA built and then began to kill. But climate change will finish that task, probably some time around 2050. As climate change pushes people off the land, they come here in search of work and to cross the border. As they wait, the drug economy sucks up their youngsters.

Juarez and the militarized border against which it leans are not the products of climate change, but climate refugees now pass through here, get stuck here, and die here. And the vortex of murder that now defines Juarez is a harbinger of a world in which climate mitigation has been ignored and adaptation takes the form of violent class apartheid.

In the Beginning There Was Murder

The infamous violence of Juarez first attracted attention in 1993, on the eve of the passage of NAFTA. It seemed a serial killer was preying on the young women who toiled in the city's *maquiladora* assembly plants. The women usually turned up dead after having been raped and mutilated. The *maquila* workers were especially vulnerable, it was said, because of their early-morning commutes across desolate stretches of open desert, where they could be kidnapped with ease and anonymity. Juarez has a strangely desolate, patchwork geography that is the result of land speculators leapfrogging one another ever further out into the desert.

The police captured one alleged culprit after another. First, the perpetrator was a known sex offender: an Egyptian chemist who had moved to Juarez from Midland, Texas. He was jailed, but the killing went on. Then police blamed it on a gang of teenage rapists, then on a bus driver. But the killing went on. A superb documentary, *Senorita Extraviada* by Lordes Portillo, presented evidence that linked elements *inside* the police to the rapes and murders.[87] In the last few years, the storyline has shifted way beyond that: from dead women to a whole city dying. The violence now appears, at first glance, to be driven by turf battles and leadership struggles between infinite numbers of *narcoleros*. But it's worse than that.

Charles Bowden, the longtime chronicler of Juarez, described the end-times quality of lawlessness that now obtains: "Imagine living a place where you can kill anyone you wish and nothing happens except that they fall dead. You will not be arrested. Your name will not be in the newspapers. You can continue on with your life. And your killing. You can take a woman and rape her for days and nothing will happen. If you choose, if in some way that woman displeases you, well, you can kill her after raping her. Rest assured, nothing will happen to you because of your actions."[88] Later, he explains it more abstractly: "For years, people have sought a single explanation of violence in Juarez. . . . We insist that power must replace power, that structure replaces an earlier structure. . . . Try for a moment to imagine something else, not a new structure but rather a pattern, and this pattern functionally has no top or bottom, no center or edge, no boss or obedient servant. . . . Violence courses through Juarez like a ceaseless wind. . . . Violence is now woven into the very fabric of the community and has no single cause and no single motive and no off button."[89]

This lawlessness is the context in which climate change is beginning to have effects. It is also part of what makes Mexico highly vulnerable to climate change. So then, what is the history of the narcoviolence that now ravages northern Mexico?

The Pus of Free Trade

By most accounts, the Mexican cartels either had old roots in bootlegging or got their start as auxiliaries of Colombian organizations.[90] During the second half of the 1980s, Mexico became a transshipment point for illicit drug imports to the United States following the US Drug Enforcement Administration (DEA) crackdown on Florida smuggling routes starting in 1982. As Florida closed, Mexico opened.[91] In 1988, cocaine seizures along the California border shot up 700 percent in one year as Colombians moved cocaine through traditional heroin and marijuana routes, known as the "Mexican pipeline." The DEA estimated that 30 to 40 percent of all cocaine entering the United States now arrived via Mexico.[92] That percentage would later rise dramatically.

For years the Mexicans merely facilitated transshipment of cocaine and marijuana on behalf of the more powerful Colombian cartels.[93] In the mid-1990s conditions changed. The Colombian cartels began to fracture. First, the Medellín Cartel's boss, Pablo Escobar, was jailed, then escaped and was killed by DEA commandos. With that, his organization began to splinter and was superseded by the Cali Cartel, which is said to have opened the route through Mexico; soon that cartel's leaders were also rounded up.[94]

A month after Pablo Escobar was killed, the United States and Mexico signed NAFTA. The late Ken Dermota—a great American journalist who interviewed the imprisoned Pablo Escobar and covered the Columbian drug war better than most—reported how the Medellín Cartel awaited free trade with the enthusiasm of children on Christmas Eve. On hearing that NAFTA was coming, a trafficker named Juan Fernando Toro told Dermota, "Soon, I'll be able to ship through Mexico right to the U.S.!"[95]

The Mexican adjuncts of the Colombian organizations soon began to mature, becoming more sophisticated and independent.[96] The year leading up to NAFTA, 1993, was also the year Amado Carrillo Fuentes, aka "Lord of the Skies," founded the Juarez Cartel. A year later, the DEA estimated that 80 percent of cocaine destined for US markets was entering through Mexico, making that country the new center of the Western Hemisphere's narcotics trade.[97] A confidential report called "Drug Trafficking, Commercial Trade and NAFTA on the Southwest Border" produced in 1998 by Operation Alliance, a task force led by the US Customs Service, found traffickers were using "commercial trade-related businesses . . . to exploit the rising tide of cross-border commerce."[98] Phil Jordan, a former DEA official, explained, "For Mexico's drug gangs, the NAFTA was a deal made in narco-heaven. But since both the United States and Mexico are so committed to free trade, no one wants to admit it has helped the drug lords. It's a taboo subject. . . . While I was at DEA, I was under strict orders not to say anything negative about free trade."[99]

Dermota connected the dots: "In the crucial period straddling the inception of NAFTA, Mexico's imports of legal goods from Colombia increased from $17 million in 1990 to $121 million in 1995, while Mexico's trade with the United States doubled." Clearly much of the increased trade was cover for Colombian traffickers, many of whom own and use legitimate companies to move cocaine into Mexico. In 1995, Dermota asked the US ambassador to Colombia if American officials worried that free trade might increase the flow of drugs. The ambassador explained, "It was felt by those who supported NAFTA and by the Clinton Administration that using the argument that any increase in trade could increase drug trafficking and money laundering was not a sufficient argument to overcome the need of the United States for increasing markets for its exports abroad and also to engage in greater trade with countries of the region."[100]

By 1996, the DEA described a Mexican drug federation made up of four major cartels: the Tijuana Organization, the Sonora Cartel, the Juarez Cartel, and the Gulf Group. By the end of the decade, the Tijuana and the Juarez cartels were said to be strongest. Cocaine was still produced in the Andes, but heroin poppies and marijuana were being grown and processed in a few regions of central and northern Mexico, particularly in the states of Michoacán, Sinaloa, and Chihuahua. The cartels' organization and diplomacy allowed the new breed of traffickers to sink deep roots into the political power structure and the fabric of everyday life. Corruption deepened in profound and dangerous ways. The post-NAFTA traffickers became increasingly professional and intertwined with the state.

Robert Collier, then foreign editor of the *San Francisco Chronicle*, painted a grimly humorous picture of the quotidian police corruption that now marked life: "At federal police headquarters . . . virtually all the agents wear heavy gold jewelry and gold watches and drive their own late-model, four-wheel-drive vehicles. Three shoeshine boys permanently work the station's hallways, keeping a sparkle on the agents' alligator-skin boots." When Collier asked a cop how he could afford a new Jeep Cherokee on merely $500 a month, the officer replied, "I save a lot." When Collier asked a Federal Police commander, who was busy busting small marijuana farmers, about Amado Carrillo Fuentes, the commander explained, "I'm not aware of any problems with Mr. Carrillo. . . . There are no major trafficking organizations here in this state."[101]

In the late 1990s and early 2000s, methamphetamine also became part of the industry. Again, it was a crackdown north of the border that pushed the action south. New restrictions in the United States on the sale of the cold medications ephedrine and pseudoephedrine, the primary ingredients for methamphetamine production, pushed much of the industrial scale meth cooking into Mexico, where trade in these legal precursors to the drug was booming.[102]

Destabilization

The relative stability of these new corporate-style cartels was not to last. First, Amado Carrillo Fuentes died during botched plastic surgery. A power struggle among his lieutenants ensued, and rival cartels attempted to move in on the Juarez Cartel.[103] In recent years, the Sinaloa and Juarez cartels and the gangs that work for them, like the Aztecas, have been fighting for control of Ciudad Juarez. After a brief plateau, the violence was again on the rise.

In response to the crisis, rightwing Mexican president Felipe Calderón, who hails from the cowboy culture of Chihuahua, sent in the Mexican army. That might sound like a major step, but it was mere political theater. The deployment came with no real strategy and no additional resources, like extra prosecutors, judges, or development money. Military repression does not set the stage for rebuilding law and order and renovating corrupt civilian institutions. The presence of troops has not changed the fact that very few people are prosecuted for committing murder in Juarez. And the violence only seems to increase.

Already elements of elite Mexican army units have gone over to the drug cartels: the Zetas, ex–special forces, who served the traffickers as muscle, have become their own gang and sometimes get directly involved in trafficking. Some thirty thousand deaths later, President Calderón's crackdown has clearly failed.[104] It pretends to offer a solution, but the situation only gets worse.

Anthony Placido, assistant administrator for intelligence with the DEA, told members of Congress, "The single largest impediment to seriously impacting the drug trafficking problem in Mexico is corruption. . . . In actuality, law enforcement in Mexico is all too often part of the problem rather than part of the solution. This is particularly true at the municipal and state levels of government."[105] Perhaps the most spectacular example of this was the arrest of Noé Ramírez, formerly the head of Mexico's elite antidrug agency. He was charged with accepting a bribe of $450,000 to leak intelligence from his old colleagues to *narcos*.[106] It is now clear: there is rot at the heart of the Mexican state.

Which Way Mexico?

In December 2008, *Forbes* magazine described Mexico as a "failed state." Former Clinton drug czar Barry McCaffrey wrote a memorandum that described Mexico as "fighting for survival against narco-terrorism." In January 2009, planners with the US Special Forces published a threat assessment report that said, "In terms of worst-case scenarios . . . two large and important states bear consideration for a rapid and sudden collapse: Pakistan and Mexico. . . . The Mexican possibility may seem less likely, but the government, its politicians, police, and judicial infrastructure are all under sustained assault and pressure by criminal gangs and drug cartels. How that internal conflict turns out over the next several years will have a major impact on the stability of the Mexican state. Any descent, by Mexico, into chaos would demand an American response based on the serious implications for homeland security alone."[107]

The Mexican government took immediate, and intense, umbrage at this statement; President Calderón called it "absurd."[108] Jorge Castañeda—the man who interprets all things political and Mexican for the North American chattering classes—also rejected the label, reassuring Americans that Mexico "today controls virtually all of its national territory and . . . exercises a quasi monopoly on the use of force within its borders."[109]

A very different assessment appeared in a front-page editorial in the main Juarez paper *El Diario*, after *sicarios* gunned down yet another of its young reporters. An open letter to the city's drug lords, the editorial was titled "¿Qué quieren de nosotros?" or "What do you want from us?" The most chilling lines, in essence, admitted the defeat of reason and law in Juarez: "What are we supposed to publish or not publish, so we know what to abide by," pleaded the editorial. "You are at this time the de facto authorities in this city because the legal authorities have not been able to stop our colleagues from falling."[110]

Mexico is not a failed state, but its formless crisis of violence and lawlessness precludes any rational response, or progressive adaptation, to climate change. It is hard to see how this social structure can survive the next fifty years if emissions of greenhouse gases continue at their current pace along a trajectory of unmitigated fossil fuel consumption. A land of billionaires and hungry masses, of drought and floods, one whose social structure and institutions are infected with the gangrene of narco corruption, is not one that can adapt to rising sea levels, extreme weather, declining crop yields, and the mass migrations these processes will set in motion.

Chapter 15

American Walls and Demagogues

Illegal immigration? Put a fence up and start shooting.

—Sam Wurzelbacher, *aka Joe the Plumber*

José Romero, an agent with the US Customs and Border Protection (CBP), of the Department of Homeland Security (DHS), drove me along the El Paso sector of the frontier with Mexico—260 miles long, with 86 miles of metal fencing. Not far away, on the other side, lay Tanila Garcia's shack. Romero was what you would expect: spit-shined, sporting a crew cut and dark brown uniform, a third-generation Chicano, by the book, ideologically all-American, and a nice host.

"If you have an illegal that crosses here, you can pick them up by their tracks if they cross these breaks. Then the agents can move up to the next section to find where they cross again," Romero said, as he showed me the wide dirt belts, raked bare to catch migrants running north.

Climate change will increase the number of people trying to enter the United States. Recall the estimates that by 2050 as many as 250 million to 1 billion people will be on the move due to climate change.[1] Britain's 2006 Stern Review estimated that by the latter half of this century, climate change will create 10 times the current number of refugees.[2] In this context, the border becomes a text from which to read the future—or a version of it. Here we see how the catastrophic convergence simultaneously creates both state failure in the Global South and authoritarian state hardening in the Global North.

Climate change is an increasingly important driver of immigration. Describing the greenwashing of xenophobia in the US Southwest, Andrew Ross wrote, "An estimated 50 million people have already been displaced by the impact of climate change, and the numbers will escalate in years to come. In northern Mexico, a primary source of migrants to Arizona, soil is eroding rapidly from the decline in precipitation, and studies predict that regional rainfall could decrease by 70 percent by the century's end. Are the emissions pumped into the desert air above central Arizona's sprawl already responsible, however indirectly, for some portion of the 500,000 undocumented migrants in the state?"[3] While the deeper causes of environmental crisis—suburban sprawl and over-consumption—remain unaddressed, repression, surveillance, and violence are emerging as the preferred forms of adaptation. Never mind emissions mitigation as a response to immigration.

Already much of the 1,969-mile US-Mexico border resembles the front lines of a quiet war. One side is defined by the misery of the slums packed along the fence in the great border cities like Tijuana, Mexicali, Nogales, Matamoros, and Juarez. Here, people like Tanila Garcia struggle to feed themselves, while a rising tide of violence swamps and incapacitates society. To the north, 700 miles of steel fencing, military-surplus motion sensors, infrared cameras, and a sky patrolled by unmanned aerial drones and National Guard helicopters characterize the line.[4]

The 1990s were radical growth years for border militarization and all manner of beating up on immigrants. The Department of Justice saw its budget more than double between 1991 and 2002. Since the terrorist attacks of September 11, 2001, and the creation of the DHS, funding for anti-immigrant enforcement has only risen. As border scholar Peter Andres explained, "Law enforcement has been the fastest area of federal government expansion since the end of the Cold War, and its biggest components have been immigration control, drug enforcement, and counterterrorism"—all categories that feed parasitically upon "the border" as political project, militarized space, and xenophobic notion.[5]

Our current style of anti-immigrant policing—of which climate change will surely bring more—is eroding civil liberties and thus fundamentally transforming America, returning the nation to its more primitive condition: a herrenvolk democracy based on segregation and routine violence, in which race and nationality mask raw class power. Border militarization and interior enforcement are the legal gray zone where the US Bill of Rights is most radically curtailed. Immigrants are the canaries in the political coal mine, and immigration is the vehicle by which the logic of the "state of emergency" is smuggled into everyday life, law, and politics.

Spirit of War

The idea of emergency, or the state of exception, is crucial in the political theory of authoritarian states. Carl Schmitt famously theorized the legal basis of dictatorship in Nazi Germany by resort to this notion. In this tradition, emergencies are the means by which democracies smuggle in authoritarian, or absolutist, politics and law enforcement. Political theorist Giorgio Agamben argues that "the voluntary creation of a permanent state of emergency (though perhaps not declared in the technical sense) has become one of the essential practices of contemporary states, including so-called democratic ones."[6] In the United States, the drift toward authoritarianism has so far been driven less by genuine emergencies and more by the crass political theater of posturing candidates and elected officials. Witness, for example, the 2005 declaration of a "border emergency" by then governors Bill Richardson and Janet Napolitano, of New Mexico and Arizona, respectively, both Democrats.[7]

Anti-immigrant policing involves a weird alchemy in which the tools of war and a lack of due process at the border are insinuating themselves into the duties of regular law enforcement and reshaping the everyday practices of state power. Border enforcement involves new equipment, expanded police powers, and unprecedented interagency cooperation. The immigration cops of the Department of Homeland Security—the Immigration and Customs Enforcement (ICE) and CBP—work in joint task forces with the FBI, DEA, local police, and elements of the armed forces. The whole border region now exists in a legal twilight where the US Constitution no longer necessarily applies.

Consider this: "The border" as a legal space is now a 100-mile wide strip that wraps around the entire land and sea boundary of the United States and thus encompasses two-thirds of the US population—or 197.4 million people and 9 of the nation's top 10 largest metropolitan areas.

Normally, the Fourth Amendment prohibits random and arbitrary searches. However, when you cross the international line, different rules apply—even citizens do not have full Fourth Amendment rights. To enter the country, one must show identification and allow one's belongings to be searched. Authorities do not need probable cause or reasonable suspicion. Thanks to post-9/11 administrative changes, similar rules extend to the whole "border region," though in practice these laws are only used regularly in the Southwest.

Yet, even on the Canadian border, the Border Patrol now stops buses, runs checkpoints on highways, and questions drivers on noninternational ferries in Washington State and on Lake Champlain, between Vermont and New York. Legally speaking, these are "administrative stops" in which the Border Patrol is only allowed to ask for proof of citizenship. But the stops frequently go beyond that. A search that begins as administrative can easily escalate as officials find this or that detail suspicious. And when the CBP partners with other police forces, its special border-oriented powers are essentially transferred to their "assisting agencies."

Urban Border

Urban sectors of the border are now locked down with a penal infrastructure of guard towers, 18-foot-high walls topped in some spots with triple coils of razor wire, infrared TV cameras, hypersensitive microphones, thousands of high-tech motion sensors, and scores of new, mobile, stadium-style klieg floodlights. Patrolling the line are 20,000 Border Patrol agents, supported by more than 37,000 civilian staff and customs inspectors. The CBP has more than 500 pilots and 250 aircraft, making it the world's largest nonmilitary law enforcement air force.[8] Varying numbers of DEA and Alcohol, Tobacco, and Firearms agents are in the border region at any given time searching for immigrant lawbreakers. So, too, are 6,000 military personal and their equipment: machine guns, Humvees, Stryker vehicles, and aircraft.[9] Marine and National Guard engineers build access roads and run surveillance operations, while regular National Guard units use border operations as training for overseas deployments to Iraq and Afghanistan.[10] Away from the immediate border—in the barrios of California, Arizona, New Mexico, and Texas—multiagency operations often involve heavily armed tactical raiding parties backed up by helicopters and dogs and result in mass arrests.

In early 2006, ICE ordered all of its seven-member fugitive operation teams (FOTs), which are meant to be investigation driven and precise in their methods, to boost their annual arrest quotas from 125 to 1,000 per year! Overnight, they were expected to become eight times more productive.[11] There soon followed a wave of mass raids. Among other locations, the FOTs hit six meatpacking plants in Texas, Colorado, Minnesota, Iowa, Utah, and Nebraska. During one Nebraska raid, 12,000 workers were herded together at gunpoint and denied access to phones, bathrooms, families, and legal counsel while ICE agents interrogated them one by one. In this operation, ICE had a warrant identifying 133 workers who were using stolen identities. As a report by the United Food and Commercial Workers later explained, "The federal agents could have—as they did a week earlier at a Swift plant in Louisville, Kentucky—gone to the Human Resources office and asked that the identified suspects be pulled from the production line, so they could question and, if necessary, apprehend them. But the ICE warrant on December 12, 2006, was used less as an effective law enforcement tool and more as a way to grab headlines and stir hysteria around immigration and immigrants."[12]

Among those detained was Michael Graves, an African American born in the United States. Graves told the House Judiciary Committee on Immigration, Citizenship, Refugees, Border Security, and International Law, "They just held me there for eight hours. No reason. No probable cause. It was like our plant was transformed into a prison or a detention center. I am a U.S. citizen. I was born and raised in this country. And I was treated as a criminal on a normal day where I just got up and went to work." Another detainee testified, "I was held for six hours. No water, no food."[13]

Latino citizens were told they needed to show either passports or citizenship certificates. Those who could not were transported to a military base 300 miles away in Johnston, Iowa. The new ICE quotas led to a spike in the number of deportations, from 69,226 in fiscal 1996 to almost 400,000 in 2009.[14]

That is what the political theorists' "state of exception" looks like in practice. It has the potential to define everyday life in a world that fails to mitigate greenhouse gas emissions and chooses, late in the game, a form of military adaptation.

Detention

Many people caught at the border are quickly dumped on the other side. However, illegal entry is now a punishable offense, and ICE detains many undocumented immigrants before deporting them. ICE holds about 29,000 detainees on any given day; that is almost 50 percent more than in just 2005.[15] According to the DHS more than 80 percent of these detainees have committed no crime other than illegal entry.[16] As civil—not criminal—prisoners, they have no right to government-funded attorneys, and most are too poor to hire private ones. When the Associated Press analyzed an official ICE database, obtained under the Freedom of Information Act, it found a detainee population of 32,000 on the evening of January 25, 2009. A shocking 18,690 of those detainees had absolutely *no criminal conviction*—not even for previous illegal entry. Over 400 of those totally innocent prisoners had been locked up for a year or more.[17]

ICE operates a network of more than five hundred detention facilities that cost $1.7 billion and are scattered across the country. Many of these are run-down but fortified motels or converted suburban office parks; all are infamous for their wretched conditions, overcrowding, and violence.[18] The majority of these facilities are managed by state and local governments and specialized private firms, like Corrections Corporation of America, which runs sixty lockups of various types. Abuse in these prisons and detention centers is widespread, though the inmates, all poor and headed for deportation, have a difficult time bringing complaints or lawsuits against their jailers. So, it is hard to know what is really happening inside the ICE gulag.

Yet, there are hints. We know of two dim-witted Mexican men who languished in detention for years for no reason except their mental disabilities. Their deportation cases were completed in 2005 and 2006, respectively, yet both—having only the mental abilities of little children—did not know when they were due for release, did not pester their jailers, and thus got lost, "shuttled through a network of jails, psychiatric hospitals and detention centers."[19]

Women in Maricopa County, Arizona, describe physical abuse, including being shackled during childbirth.[20] In March 2008, Jarrod Hankins, a bailiff for the Washington County Sheriff's Department, locked an undocumented immigrant from Mexico, named Adriana Torres-Flores, in a small courthouse holding cell. Hankins then forgot about his prisoner as she suffered without food or water for four days. Sleeping on the floor, she drank her own urine to survive.[21] Until at least 2008, ICE officers would regularly inject deportees with psychotropic sedatives before their deportation flights. The "preflight cocktail" was sometimes so heavy that ICE agents had to use wheelchairs to get the slumped deportees on board.[22]

Desperation among detainees sometimes boils over. On December 12, 2008, a riot broke out at a private facility in Pecos, Texas, run by the GEO Group. The immigrant detainees were protesting the death of Jesus Manuel Galindo due to lack of medical care. Billed as the world's "largest detention/correctional facility under private management," the sprawling complex is ringed by razor wire and has cells for thirty-seven hundred undocumented immigrants but no infirmary or clinic. On February 2, 2010, journalist Tom Barry went to investigate, and by chance the detainees rioted a second time, burning a whole housing unit.[23] Barry described the immigration detention network as "the new face of imprisonment in America. . . . Because they rely on project revenue instead of tax revenue, these prisons do not need voter approval. Instead they are marketed by prison consultants to municipal and county governments as economic-development tools promising job creation and new revenue without new taxes."[24]

Another feature of the ICE detention network is the constant transfer of prisoners. Though usually detained at the border or near their homes, in the cities of the Northeast and California, captured immigrants are routinely transferred to remote, rural detention facilities in Arizona, Louisiana, or Texas, hundreds or thousands of miles away from families and sympathetic lawyers. Human Rights Watch found that from 1999 to 2008, at least 1.4 million detainee transfers occurred.[25] Whether by political design or bureaucratic habit, the transfer policy is a sadistic mechanism of control and demoralization.

This is the face of climate change. Drought and flood in Mexico and Central America are expressed, later and elsewhere, as the ICE detention gulag. As the planet warms, the political tumors of American authoritarianism, our current repression of immigrants, will metastasize. A similar illness infects Europe, and climate change will intensify even if necessary mitigation finally begins. Already we see the forms that adaptation in the developed world will take. The de facto authoritarian, cryptoracist state hardening, encapsulated by the war on immigrants, will accelerate as climate-change-driven migration become an ever more pressing issue.

Land of Violent Talk

Border militarization, the paramilitary immigrant roundups, the largely privatized ICE detention network—it is all a human rights abomination. But it is also policy as ideological spectacle. When the government treats innocent brown people as criminals, it lends respectability to racism. Native-born people, particularly white people, get the message and feel invited to catharsis via tribal solidarity, especially during hard times.

The flow of people from south to north—people deracinated by the structural violence of neoliberal economics, Cold War militarism, and now climate change—is met not only with walls, armed patrols, and cells but also with the calumny, hatred, and ideological spittle of rightwing demagogues. Nowhere is this more evident than on American talk radio. All day and night, up and down the dial, one can hear raw, uncut hate speech. Glenn Beck, Rush Limbaugh, and Mike Savage are only the most well-known of those who talk hate for a living. Every day tens of millions of people listen to the hard-right messages that vomit out across the airwaves. While they drive, work, tinker in the basement, or lie awake at night rehearsing personal worries, Americans are kept company by talk radio's constant rhythm of fear, resentment, exaggeration, and free market fundamentalism.

A central trope in this embittered carnival is the specter of immigration. Xenophobia and smug nationalism are old American traditions. Tocqueville found it back in 1835: "Nothing is more annoying in the ordinary intercourse of life than this irritable patriotism of the Americans. A foreigner will gladly agree to praise much in their country, but he would like to be allowed to criticize something, and that he is absolutely refused."[26] Today's version of this irritable patriotism takes place in a warming world where populations are increasingly on the move. The rate, intensity, and desperation of migration is guaranteed to increase precipitously throughout this century. Thus, the hate in American politics is becoming an expression of the catastrophic convergence. It is sobering to listen to talk radio with an eye toward the future and an understanding of climate science. It is also important to remember that the rightist xenophobes, though repulsive, nonetheless play upon real issues: The political economy of the world *is* unfair, and immigration *is* an increasingly challenging social issue that requires new policy—that is to say, climate adaptation based on social justice.

Consider again the words of the former intelligence officers, military men, and politicians who wrote that Pentagon-oriented report on climate change, *Age of Consequences*. Here is James Woolsey, former head of the CIA, writing in a chapter addressing the worst-case scenario of unmitigated growth of greenhouse gas emissions:

If Americans have difficulty reaching a reasonable compromise on immigration legislation today, consider what such a debate would be like if we were struggling to resettle millions of our own citizens—driven by high water from the Gulf of Mexico, South Florida, and much of the East Coast reaching nearly to New England—even as we witnessed the northward migration of large populations from Latin America and the Caribbean. Such migration will likely be one of the Western Hemisphere's early social consequences of climate change and sea level rise of these orders of magnitude. Issues deriving from inundation of a large amount of our own territory, together with migration toward our borders by millions of our hungry and thirsty southern neighbors, are likely to dominate U.S. security and humanitarian concerns. Globally as well, populations will migrate from increasingly hot and dry climates to more temperate ones.[27]

Adaptation as the armed lifeboat is only possible if Americans think in certain ways, and not in others. This raises the question, How are the media educating adult Americans? It is instructive to survey the messages that spill forth across the nation, for this is the political context in which immigration and climate change are being understood. When immigration reform came up for debate in 2006, much of the American media worked itself into a hate-filled lather. In 2010, immigration again came up, and the controversy erupted anew. Those episodes offer a glimpse of how opinion makers will frame a future immigration crisis.

Ideological Parapets

You can hear the bad future of the armed lifeboat in the words of self-described Northern Californian, environmentalist, and feminist Brenda Walker. A radical Malthusian, Walker is a green racist who was inspired to politics after reading Paul Erlich's *The Population Bomb*. Speaking on the *Peter Boyles Show*, a Denver-based talk radio program, Walker said, "If there's one thing that the Mexicans are good at, it's establishing smuggling infrastructures. They can get through, you know, obviously, millions of illegal aliens and WMDs as well."[28]

Or consider the comments of William Gheen, president of Americans for Legal Immigration on the same program: "Oh, look, I'll take it further than that, Peter. Let me say something about these brown Nazis. . . . Get out of my country—now. Take a hint. Vamoose. I don't got to say, 'Don't let the border gate hit you on the backside on the way out.' And I mean it. I'm very serious about it. Americans are the Jews."[29]

Here is another canard from radio host Jay Severin (formerly Jay Severino): "So now, in addition to venereal disease and the other leading exports of Mexico—women with mustaches and VD—now we have swine flu." On another occasion, he put it this way: "When we are the magnet for primitives around the world—and it's not the primitives' fault by the way, I'm not blaming them for being primitives—I'm merely observing they're primitive. . . . It's millions of leeches from a primitive country come here to leech off you and, with it, they are ruining the schools, the hospitals, and a lot of life in America."[30] Always the position of the nativist is aggrieved, put-upon, outnumbered, abandoned, almost overrun. Increasingly the nativists see themselves as nature's staunch defender, its last bulwark against the human locusts.

Consider the ravings of another nationally syndicated DJ, Michael Alan Weiner, now known by the rather more Teutonic sounding name Mike Savage: "Burn a Mexican flag for America, burn a Mexican flag for those who died that you should have a nationality and a sovereignty, go out in the street and show you're a man, burn 10 Mexican flags, if I could recommend it. Put one in the window upside down and tell them to go back where they came from!"[31] This self-appointed tribune of real Americans traffics under the website tagline "borders, language, culture." In a different context, that slippery triptych could pass for a postmodern academic subtitle, but here it recalls fin de siècle Anglo-Saxonism in the style of Madison Grant's *Passing of the Great Race*.[32] Savage describes himself as "an ardent conservationist" and claims to have 100 million listeners per week. More objective sources, like *Talkers* magazine, put his audience at 8 million—still very large.

What do the xenophobes suggest be done? Here is Neal Boortz, one of the top talk radio hosts in the country: "They are not going to be shipped back. I mean, Royal [his off-air producer], think about it—Mexico doesn't want 'em back, first of all. Think what happens if we round—first of all, where do we store 11 million Hispanics just waiting to ship 'em back to Nicaragua, Colombia, Costa Rica, Mexico. Where do we store 'em? . . . The Superdome! Exactly. And the Astrodome in Houston. That's where we'll put 'em."[33] During a 2006 broadcast, he addressed the same theme: "When we defeat this illegal alien amnesty bill and when we yank out the welcome mat and they all start going back to Mexico, as a going-away gift let's all give them a box of nuclear waste. Give 'em all a little nuclear waste and let 'em take it on down there to Mexico. Tell 'em it can—it'll heat tortillas. Or something like that."[34]

More mainstream characters are almost as bad. Here is Lou Dobbs, formerly of CNN, now a Fox business news host: "There are some Mexican citizens and some Mexican-Americans who want to see California, New Mexico and other parts of the Southwestern United States given over to Mexico. These groups call it the *reconquista*, Spanish for reconquest. And they view the millions of Mexican illegal aliens in particular entering the United States as potentially an army of invaders to achieve that takeover."[35] Dobbs—echoing nineteenth-century concerns about hookworm among Chinese immigrants on the West Coast—likes to equate immigration with infectious disease: "The invasion of illegal aliens is threatening the health of many Americans. Highly-contagious diseases are now crossing our borders decades after those diseases had been eradicated in this country."[36]

Glenn Beck is another respectable mainstream fanatic. Here he is on Muslims: "All right. Here it is. Tonight's exclusive: In 10 years, Muslims and Arabs will be looking through a razor wire fence at the West. . . . The Muslim community better find a spokesman who isn't a 'yes, but' Muslim. They shouldn't even understand the word 'but,' because if they don't, when things heat up, the profiling will only get worse, and the razor wire will be coming."[37]

Like Dobbs, Bill O'Reilly—who is more respectable than the baby-faced, conspiracy-theorizing, ranting, dry-drunk Beck—dabbles in *reconquista* paranoia. On May 1, 2006, while Latinos were marching for their rights in California, O'Reilly warned some of his 3.25 million weekly viewers, "And then there's the hardcore militant agenda of 'You stole our land, you bad gringos.' This is the organizers of these demonstrations: 'The border—we didn't cross the border, the border crossed us.' That is their slogan. That you stole our land, and now, we're going to take it back by massive, massive migration into the Southwest. And we're going to control those places, because you stole it from us, and that's the agenda underneath."[38] At times his war rhetoric gets more explicit: "You have no policy unless you have border security. . . . So now, it's becoming a race war. That's what it's becoming—a race war. You see half a million people show up in L.A. and they were waving Mexican flags. And they're saying, 'Hey, we have a right to be here.' No, you don't. If you're illegal, you don't have a right to be here."[39]

Season of Hate, Again

In 2010, immigration politics heated up again with the passage of Arizona's Senate Bill 1070, which ordered all police officers to stop and interrogate anyone they suspected of being undocumented. Furthermore, it allowed citizens to sue if they felt an officer was negligent in these anti-immigrant efforts.[40] SB 1070 embodied the lifeboat politics of armed adaptation. Internationally, the face of the bill was Governor Jan Brewer, whose bleached-blonde hair, spray-on tan, and perpetual, unblinking, grimace-like smile gave her a robotic affect. The backdrop to all this was Arizona's economic crisis: it had the third-highest foreclosure rate in the United States and an unemployment rate that reached 10 percent in July 2010.

With the new law, thousands of terrified undocumented Latinos fled the state. Critics said the bill would, among others things, make Arizona less safe as it would be harder for police to solve crimes if Latinos began avoiding cops. Brewer defended the crackdown by claiming that immigrants were beheading innocent victims. But no such crimes were occurring. Neither she nor anyone else could find *any evidence* to back her claim. Next, Governor Brewer banned ethnic studies in Arizona schools on the grounds, as her spokesperson put it, that "public school students should be taught to treat and value each other as individuals and not be taught to resent or hate other races or classes of people."[41]

Bill O'Reilly defended anti-immigrant repression by repeating myths about immigrant violence: "Arizona had to do something. In the capital city Phoenix, crime is totally out of control. . . . The recent murder of an Arizona rancher by a suspected illegal alien and the shooting of a deputy sheriff by alleged alien drug dealers have made the situation almost desperate."[42] Later, the story of the wounded deputy, like Brewer's decapitation claims, started to fall apart. Forensic pathologists noted powder burns on the sheriff's skin, indicating that the muzzle of the gun was in contact with his body when it fired and not twenty-five yards away as he claimed.[43]

Even Chris Mathews, while debating Amy Goodman, suggested, "Cultural change is not something any society accepts easily, or even with any kind of positive feelings about."[44] Mathews also promoted Pat Buchanan's *State of Emergency: The Third World Invasion and Conquest of America*. Fittingly, this book's title refers, however cryptically, to the Nazi-justifying legal theory of Carl Schmitt. As the title implies, the book posits that immigration is destroying America.[45] Here, trimming only slightly, is the broad scope of history as seen through the narrow confines of Buchanan's mind:

From the fifteenth to the twentieth century, the West wrote the history of the world. Out of the Christian countries of Europe came the explorers, the missionaries, the conquerors, the colonizers, who, by the twentieth century, ruled virtually the entire world. But the passing of the West had begun.

Spain's empire was the first to fall. . . . By 1918 the German Austro-Hungarian and Russian empires collapsed. World War II bled and broke the British and French. One by one, after war's end, the strategic outposts of empire—Suez, the Canal Zone, Rhodesia, South Africa, Hong Kong—began to fall. Within three decades, Europe's headlong retreat from Asia and Africa was complete.

From 1989–1991, the Soviet Union Empire fell and the Soviet Union split into fifteen pieces, half a dozen of them Muslim nations that have never before existed. Now, the African, Asian, Islamic and Hispanic peoples that the West once ruled are coming to repopulate the mother countries. . . . The crisis of Western civilization consists of three imminent and mortal perils: dying populations, disintegrating cultures and invasions unresisted . . . as Rome passed away, so, the West is passing away, from the same causes in much the same way. What the Danube and Rhine were to Rome, the Rio Grande and Mediterranean are to America and Europe, the frontiers of a civilization no longer defended.[46]

Elsewhere, the book oozes with more of the same: "We are witnessing how nations perish. We are entered upon the final act of our civilization. The last scene is the deconstruction of the nations. The penultimate scene, now well underway, is the invasion unresisted." And, "Chicano chauvinists and Mexican agents have made clear their intent to take back through demography and culture what their ancestors lost through war. . . . We are in the midst of a savage culture war in which traditionalist values have been losing ground for two generations."[47]

Buchanan is not of the lunatic fringe. Rather, he is a major figure in American life, aide to presidents, force in the Republican Party, and political analyst for MSNBC. His politics are mainstream.

The Paranoid Style and Its Rational Uses

Welcome to the new American *Volksstaat*. Here, hate wears a smile and operates in the name of fairness and freedom. The war on immigrants is very much a war of ideas. Richard Hofstadter dissected the elements of this worldview a generation ago in *Anti-Intellectualism in American History*, then in the famous article that followed from the book, "The Paranoid Style in American Politics." Here is Hofstadter in 1964—note how current the critique sounds:

The paranoid spokesman sees the fate of conspiracy in apocalyptic terms—he traffics in the birth and death of whole worlds, whole political orders, whole systems of human values. He is always manning the barricades of civilization. He constantly lives at a turning point. Like religious millennialists he expresses the anxiety of those who are living through the last days and he is sometimes disposed to set a date for the apocalypse. . . . America has been largely taken away from them and their kind, though they are determined to try to repossess it and to prevent the final destructive act of subversion. The old American virtues have already been eaten away by cosmopolitans and intellectuals; the old competitive capitalism has been gradually undermined by socialistic and communistic schemers; the old national security and independence have been destroyed by treasonous plots, having as their most powerful agents not merely outsiders and foreigners as of old but major statesmen who are at the very centers of American power. Their predecessors had discovered conspiracies; the modern radical right finds conspiracy to be betrayal from on high.[48]

This mentality underwrites the current xenophobia. In 2010, Pew pollsters found that 67 percent of Americans said they "approved of allowing police to detain anyone who cannot verify their legal status," while 62 percent approved of "allowing police to question people they think may be in the country illegally." And 59 percent said they approved of Arizona's profile and arrest law.[49]

Nor is it a coincidence that some of the biggest financial supporters of the xenophobic and "paranoid style" are oil magnates, most famously, the Koch brothers. These two mild-mannered and quiet billionaires started Americans for Prosperity, a free market advocacy shop that passed on at least $5 million in start-up money to the Tea Party. The Koch family has long followed Hayek's ultra-antistatist theories and more recently has promoted climate-change denial. The two positions are naturally aligned: to venerate the market and despise the state is to oppose legal limits on greenhouse gas emissions. During the 1980s and 1990s, the Koch brothers spent more than $100 million to assist a network of thirty-four Far Right political and policy organizations. Among these were the Cato Institute, the Heritage Foundation, the Independent Women's Forum, and the American Enterprise Institute.[50] The noise from this network is a mash-up of free market fanaticism, climate-change denial, and xenophobia. Talk radio and cable TV are the amplifiers.

Fortress Europe

In Europe, the xenophobic Right is also alive and well. The older crypto-fascist leaders, like Jean-Marie Le Pen, founder of France's *Front National,* and Jörg Haider, long-time leader of Austria's Freedom Party, are now fading.[51] But a new generation of leaders is taking the old message mainstream; among them are Dutch politician Geert Wilders and Danish People's Party leader Pia Kjærsgaard.[52] Perhaps more worrying is the adoption of overtly racist policies by center-right governments: witness, for example, President Nicolas Sarkozy's expulsion of eight thousand Roma from France, Chancellor Angela Merkel's statement that Germany's multiculturalism had "utterly failed," and the walling off of Roma communities in the Czech Republic.[53]

Romancing the End Times

Even among good liberals, one finds the temptation to embrace the armed lifeboat. Consider environmental writer and activist Bill McKibben, who has done stellar work bringing the reality of climate science to a mass audience and started the international climate activist group 350.org. In his latest book, when he addressed the question of climate security, his politics faltered:

> If you think about the cramped future long enough, for instance, you can end up convinced you'll be standing over your vegetable patch with your shotgun, warding off the marauding gang that's after your carrots. . . . The marines aren't going to be much help there—they're not geared for Mad Max—but your neighbors might be. Imagining local life in a difficult world means imagining taking more responsibility not only for your food but for your defense. (Consider Switzerland, for example, where every adult male is a soldier.) *Militia* is an ugly word to many of us, but

it's worth remembering, at least for those of us with tricorne hats in the closet, that a local militia fought the fight on Lexington Green.[54]

That is an image of America as a failed state. There really must be a better option. Civilization, for all its faults, has much to recommend it, much within it that is worth defending. World civilization, this largely capitalist global economy, for all its exploitation and inequity, has produced phenomenal wealth and technology. Can we really not imagine a way to redeploy and redistribute these assets and capacities?

CHAPTER 16

Implications and Possibilities

In fact, the artist's design seemed this: a final theory of my own, partly based upon the aggregated opinions of many aged persons with whom I conversed upon the subject. The picture represents a Cape-Horner in a great hurricane; the half-foundered ship weltering there with its three dismantled masts alone visible; and an exasperated whale, purposing to spring clean over the craft, is in the enormous act of impaling himself upon the three mast-heads.

—HERMAN MELVILLE, *Moby Dick*

CIVILIZATION IS IN CRISIS, though the effects are not yet fully felt. The metabolism of the world economy is fundamentally out of sync with that of nature. And that is a mortal threat to both. In the preceding pages, I have shown how the social impacts of climate change are already upon us, articulating themselves through the preexisting crises of poverty and violence, which are the legacies of Cold War militarism and neoliberal economics. The combination of these factors, their imbrications and mutual acceleration, is the catastrophic convergence. As part of the catastrophic convergence, we see forms of violent adaptation emerging.

In the Global South these take the form of: ethnic irredentism, religious fanaticism, rebellion, banditry, narcotics trafficking, and the small-scale resource wars like the desperate skirmishing over water and cattle in which the Turkana herder Ekaru Loruman was killed. In the North, the multilayered crisis appears as the politics of the armed lifeboat: the preparations for open-ended counterinsurgency, militarized borders, aggressive anti-immigrant policing, and a mainstream proliferation of rightwing xenophobia.

And keep in mind this key fact: even if all greenhouse gas emissions stopped immediately—that is, if the world economy collapsed today, and not a single light bulb was switched on nor a single gasoline-powered motor started ever again—there is already enough carbon dioxide in the atmosphere to cause *significant* warming and disruptive climate change, and with that considerably more poverty, violence, social dislocation, forced migration, and political upheaval. Thus we must find humane and just means of adaptation, or we face barbaric prospects.

I will not offer a program of green development, nor one of grassroots peace building and disarmament, nor a list of NGOs that point the way forward with their good deeds. Such efforts must be generated in their appropriate contexts by the protagonists of specific local dramas. Our crisis is not a matter of the reading public lacking the names and addresses of groups to work with. Likewise, there are almost endless examples of small-scale, grassroots forms of socially just adaptation that use appropriate technology and are embedded in participatory democracy. But these will remain Lilliputian until they become central to *state policies* and a formal agenda of economic redistribution on an international scale.

Furthermore, to dwell on noble grassroots groups and ingenious new, appropriate technologies can easily miss the point. The climate crisis is not a *technical* problem, nor even an *economic* problem: it is, fundamentally, a *political* problem.

Consider these factors in tandem.

Technology

Is there enough technology for mitigation or making the transition to a carbon-neutral economy? Yes, technologies to create large amounts of carbon-neutral energy already exist. You know what they are: wind, solar, geothermal, and tidal kinetic power all feeding an efficient smart grid that, in turn, feeds electric vehicles and radically more energy-efficient build-ings. Clean tech is not without its problems, but it is here now, already available, and it works at an industrial scale. Can citizens of the Global North, particularly Americans, be as wasteful as they are currently? No. We will have to use energy and resources carefully.

Some see mitigation as hinging on a high-technology breakthrough. Bil-lionaire software mogul Bill Gates, environmental scientist James Lovelock, and even NASA's James Hansen pin their hopes on pie-in-the-sky fourth-generation nukes (known as IV Gen in the industry). Such technology would surely be safer than today's rickety old plants and could be feasible given several decades and hundreds of billions of dollars of investment. But industrial-scale application of IV Gen nukes would arrive too late to stave off climate tipping points. The US Department of Energy, a major booster of all things atomic, gives 2021 as the earliest possible date for a IV Gen nuclear plant to open.[1] And keep in mind no atomic plant has yet been built on time or within budget, so the DOE's forecast is very optimistic.

Science tells us that aggressive emissions reductions need to start *im-mediately*. Emissions need to peak by 2015, then decline precipitously, if we are to avoid dangerous climate change. Such a time frame means we must scale up actually existing clean technology. That will take massive invest-ments and serious planning—but that project has already begun. The United States remains as a laggard, but other leading economies are be-ginning the transformation.

What about the technological aspects of adaptation? All over the world, one can find small-scale, often grassroots projects that point the way for-ward. My colleague, environmental journalist Mark Hertsgaard, has reported on the "quiet green miracle" of a tree-based approach to farming that is transforming the western Sahel. The farm communities he visited in Burk-ina Faso had been in slow-motion crisis since "the terrible drought of 1972–84, when a 20 percent decline in average annual rainfall slashed food production throughout the Sahel, turned vast stretches of savanna into desert and caused hundreds of thousands of deaths from hunger." But widespread adaptation of the new "agroforestry" or "farmer-managed natural regenera-tion"(FMNR)—essentially the same sort of methods we saw in Brazil's

Nordeste but developed for an African context—have led to the mass regeneration of tree coverage across parts of Mali, Niger, and Burkina Faso. And with that, despite a locally growing population, water tables have actually *risen* between five and seventeen meters.[2] That is truly amazing.

Other examples of positive change are found in the portfolio of the UN Development Program's Global Environmental Facility, which distributes small grants to community-proposed adaptation and mitigation projects. The UNDP GEF has work going in 29 countries. Its projects include community-based forestry projects and energy-efficiency projects in Kenya; wind- and solar-based electrification and solar-power electricity generation to displace charcoal and diesel; improved watershed management, fighting desertification, protecting biodiversity. In Bolivia this UN program is establishing 22 rural clean-tech electrification projects, providing power to 200,000 rural households and, in so doing, it will prevent 21,000 million tons of CO_2 emissions over the next 25 years.[3]

But, as with the agroforestry projects we saw in Brazil, all these remain small scale, operating at the periphery of state policy. That needs to change. Brazil under Lula made great strides in addressing poverty, in large part by repudiating the moralistic, planning-phobic nostrums of new classical economic orthodoxy.[4] But the light pink, semisocialist reforms in the style of Brazil will only work as socially just adaptation if reconciliation with nature is at the center of the agenda.

Economics

Is there enough money for mitigation and adaptation? Actually, yes: there are enormous pools of capital sloshing around the international financial system looking for profitable outlets and in the process creating dangerous destabilizing speculative bubbles.

In May 2010, the *Washington Post* reported that "Nonfinancial companies are sitting on $1.8 trillion in cash, roughly one-quarter more than at the beginning of the recession."[5] But, as the article went on to point out, they were not investing in creating new jobs. According to Federal Reserve data from late 2010, American companies had not sat on so much uninvested cash since 1956.[6] Many of the large banks spent the first years of the great recession engaged in an international "carry trade," borrowing money from the US Federal Reserve at very low interest rates, then lending it back to the US government—that is, buying Treasury Bonds. This largely passive and parasitic style of speculation, rather than investment in real capital stock, was the basis for two years of record bonuses on Wall Street. In 2010, the top twenty-five Wall Street firms paid out $135 billion in compensation to their traders and analysts.[7] Meanwhile, the real economy stagnated. Coal and natural gas remain the dominant fuel sources, and there was no government policy in place to help structure, guide, encourage, mandate, or in anyway bring about a new wave of private investment in clean-technology-based industrialization.

As I write, those pools of liquidity are bidding up a speculative bubble in primary commodities like grains and metal ores. "Between 2003 and 2008, the amount of speculative money in commodities grew from $13 billion to $317 billion, an increase of 2,300 percent."[8] The Commodity Food Price Index rose by almost 75 percent between 2006 and the end of 2010.[9] Wheat prices surged 56 percent in just the second half of 2010. This was also due in part to climate crises—floods in Pakistan and Australia and forest fires in Russia—led to a decrease in supply and a spike in demand. Once the price was moving up, speculators awash in cash and cheap credit started driving it up further.[10]

Not only is government failing to push private capital to invest in clean technology, but it is itself failing to invest. We suffer an appalling dearth of public money being directly invested in clean technology; nor is there a robust program of subsidies. At the same time, federal tax policy did almost *nothing* to penalize or prohibit speculation. The US government has resources available for the transition, even without raising taxes on speculators. Consider the military budget. When the 2010 federal budget was signed into law on October 28, 2009, the final size of the Department of Defense's budget was $680 billion. Defense-related expenditures by other parts of the federal government—such as weapons testing and storage by the DOE, security for the State Department in combat zones, health care for wounded veterans, the antiterrorism functions of the Department of

Homeland Security, military aspects of NASA's work, etc.—constitute between $300 and $600 billion more, according to various estimates, which
would bring the total for defense spending to between $1 and $1.3 trillion
in fiscal year 2010. To play it safe, we can say that direct military spending,
plus supplemental war-fighting costs, plus the DOE's atomic weapons program totaled $722 billion in 2010.[11] In short, there's money to be found—
if we want to find it.

Nor should we allow the issue of government debt to trick us into
thinking the economy lacks the wealth to invest in both mitigation and
adaptation. For most of the twentieth century, the top marginal tax rate in
the United States was above 50 percent and frequently as high as 90 percent. From 1933, at the start of the New Deal, until 1980, the top rate
never dipped below 70 percent. In 1993, Clinton raised the top marginal
tax rate from 31 to 39.6 percent; in so doing, he paid down the debt, and
by 1998 the federal government was *running a surplus*.[12] If taxes on the superrich were increased, the US government could lower the national debt
and have money to invest in clean tech.

Politics

Is there political will to make the transition? Alas, no.

Established corporate interests—the fossil fuel companies and the
pampered large banks, for example—do not wish to see downward redistribution of wealth and power, nor the economic annihilation of all the
sunk capital that is the fossil fuel economy. Few issues encapsulate this
political problem better than the story of the fossil fuel industry's promotion of climate denialism.

For twenty years the fossil fuel lobby has funded and organized attacks
on climate science. Most prominently, between 1998 and 2008, Exxon do-
nated $23 million in support of the climate denial movement.[13] In 2006,
the Royal Society, the United Kingdom's most prestigious scientific body,
demanded that Exxon stop funding misinformation. The company promised it would, but it continues to do so anyway. In 2009, Greenpeace reported that Exxon gave $1.3 million to organizations with histories of

climate change denial, including the Heritage Foundation, the American Enterprise Institute, and the Washington Legal Foundation.[14]

Another source of climate skepticism is the wealth of the Koch brothers, owners of a huge, privately held conglomerate involved in manufacturing, refining, and distributing petroleum and chemicals, as well as energy, plastics, minerals, and fertilizers. Koch Industries is ranked as the second-largest privately held company in the United States after Cargill, and, not surprisingly, it is ranked among the top ten air polluters in the United States.[15] In keeping with the pattern of their investments, the Koch brothers are philanthropists of a hard-right variety, followers of Hayek, and they fund groups that push climate change denial.[16] A Greenpeace report found that between 2005 and 2008, Koch-controlled foundations contributed $24.9 million to organizations promoting climate denial. This campaign seems to have borne fruit. Pew research polls have found that in 2006, 77 percent of those questioned agreed that there was evidence that the Earth was warming; by 2009, that number had dropped to 57 percent.[17]

Resistance North

Where is the countervailing force? Climate-justice movements in the United States are largely moribund and under attack. In Europe, they are somewhat stronger, though they are under pressure there and have been infiltrated by the police. A recent scandal in Britain revealed that at least fifteen police officers had infiltrated and sabotaged that country's green movement.[18] Nonetheless, grassroots greens in the United Kingdom and Europe have a relatively robust climate-justice movement.

In the United States, there is also a movement for climate justice, though it is small, and after an upsurge, has suffered setbacks. As Brian Tokar points out, "[a] marked shift in perception began in 2005–6 when Hurricane Katrina flooded New Orleans." Then came Al Gore's widely viewed documentary *An Inconvenient Truth* that was followed in 2007 by the IPCC's dire and authoritative fourth assessment report "on climate science and its consequences." The combination of all this momentarily forced climate change to the center of our national discussion.[19]

In this context, efforts to create a successor agreement to the Kyoto Protocol were gaining momentum. Barack Obama was elected, in part, by promising to invest $150 billion over ten years to jump-start a clean-technology industrial revival. And by 2009, a comprehensive international treaty looked possible. Domestically, Democrats began pushing national climate legislation, so-called cap and trade, but these efforts were badly flawed and compromised by corporate lobbies. Beltway-oriented "Big Green" groups tended to see the legislative language as a glass half full, while the more left-leaning "Little Green" groups saw the bills as dangerously inadequate.

Much of big business—embodied in the Chamber of Commerce, the National Association of Manufacturers, the Western Fuels Association, the International Petroleum Institute—pushes back hard against climate legislation. As London's *Guardian* reported, by the summer of 2009 America's oil, gas, and coal industries had increased their antigreen lobbying budgets by 50 percent, "with key players spending $44.5m in the first three months" of that year.[20] Comprehensive climate legislation in the United States indeed failed. And that helped undermine the UNFCCC talks in Copenhagen in 2009 and in Cancún the following year.

In the face of these setbacks some US greens refocused on more local and confrontational strategies. Exemplary in this was the fight against coal during the first decade of this century led by the Sierra Club, Rainforest Action Network, numerous local outfits, and, more recently, Greenpeace. These anticoal campaigns have used mass protest and direct action, like mountaintop occupations, as well as financial and political pressure to halt construction of 130 proposed new coal plants.[21]

Other, more media-oriented organizations also exist, like 350.org—the name refers to 350 ppm of CO_2 in the atmosphere, beyond which dangerous climate change is likely. That group, started by environmental writer Bill McKibben and some of his students at Middlebury College, has done amazing work in educating the global public about the scientific realities of climate change and the idea of thresholds and tipping points. But as Henry Miller says toward the end of *Tropic of Capricorn*, "It is the essence of symbols to be symbolic."[22] Political power, like economic power, is ultimately made of thicker stuff—bodies, labor, nature, the things and places that bodies have built, and the physical violence that controls bodies.

Resistance South

Act One

It was late May 2005, and Bolivia was in the grip of massive multi-week-long protests—the people, most of them Quechan and Aymaran Indians, wanted Bolivia's natural gas industry to be nationalized. A general strike had been called. And now, a huge march was descending from El Alto to La Paz. The protesters were trade unionists, miners, teachers, and landless peasants. Their destination was the Congress and Presidential Palace, in front of which stood serried ranks of riot police.

As they approached, the marchers smashed out the windows of the few minibuses that had ignored the movement's strike order. When they met the police lines, some miners tossed small charges of dynamite. Windows shattered up and down the block; police fell back and blocked the blasts with their Plexiglas shields, then answered with volleys of tear gas and rubber bullets. Back and forth the battle went continued for three weeks. With La Paz and most of Bolivia's other major cities blockaded, food and fuel ran low; buses and taxis sat stranded. Protesters occupied several gas fields and a pipeline station. It had been five hundred years of theft and abuse, the indigenous people of Bolivia wanted justice.

Act Two

Six months later I was back in Bolivia. Awakening in a shabby La Paz hotel after a long night flight, I turned on the TV. To my surprise, onscreen sat Raul Prada, a short, thickset Marxist intellectual with permanently bent eyeglasses. The last time I'd seen Prada he was in the streets dodging tear gas with the masses. Now an adviser to President Evo Morales—yes, president, what a difference a year makes—Prada was explaining why the government had nationalized a big part of Bolivia's natural gas industry.

There were other changes as well. Morales had promised to go beyond gas, announcing plans to renationalize mining and forestry and to confiscate and redistribute unused ranch lands, boost the minimum wage, and increase spending on health care. And after decades of IMF-imposed austerity, one of the new government's earliest acts was to allow the expiration of a three-year financing deal with the Fund—effectively kicking it out of Bolivia.

In a chilly drawing room of the presidential palace, I met with Vice President Álvaro García Linera. Only forty-two years old, he had a résumé that included stints as a guerrilla fighter, prisoner, powerhouse author, and intellectual. "Transnational corporations are welcome in Bolivia," explained the boyish VP. "But they will not dominate the economy. They should expect to pay taxes and submit to reasonable environmental and social regulations. But they will still make profits." As García Linera explained, all that the state could do was impose equilibrium and a minimal humanity on the savageness and chaos of Bolivian capitalism and grow the economy with a progressive and greenish version of Keynesianism. Many industrialists in La Paz—the owners of construction-supply companies, potato chip factories, and small foundries, the "national bourgeoisie," if you will—came to see the virtues of this strategy. And within the confines of this realism, Bolivia gropes toward a new model of a mixed economy.[23]

Act Three

By 2010 Bolivia was again in the news, this time because it was hosting the World People's Conference on Climate Change in anticipation of the COP 16 meeting to be held in Cancún that December. The year before, Bolivia's delegation had worked tirelessly with the G77—the main group of seventy-seven poor and developing countries from the Global South—to achieve deep emissions reductions and a robust transfer of capital and technology to the Global South as part of a binding treaty. Instead, COP 15 was marked by what John Vidal called "fantastically pompous speeches about being green" and produced a merely nonbinding, elite-negotiated "accord." The accord recognized, as one report put it, "the scientific case for keeping temperature rises to no more than 2°C" but did not mandate emissions reductions or North-to-South aid to assist with adaptation.[24]

As COP 16 wrapped up in Cancún, the quest for a binding agreement had collapsed. Instead, the world was now wrangling over the voluntary "accord" rather than a binding treaty. When added up, all the voluntary (thus unlikely) emissions reductions pledged by the largest economies still allowed the average global temperature to rise by 3.2°C, even though the IPCC sees a 2°C increase as the outer limit of safety. Even a 2°C increase could be too much and cause runaway climate change.

The only country that refused to go along with this charade was Bolivia. Their lead negotiator—the stern and intense Bolivian ambassador to the United Nations, Pablo Solon—laid out his country's position in the *Guardian*. In explaining his "obligation to set aside diplomacy and tell the truth," Solon wrote:

> Many commentators have called the Cancún accord a "step in the right direction." We disagree: it is a giant step backward. The text replaces binding mechanisms for reducing greenhouse gas emissions with voluntary pledges that are wholly insufficient. These pledges contradict the stated goal of capping the rise in temperature at 2°C, instead guiding us to 4°C or more. The text is full of loopholes for polluters, opportunities for expanding carbon markets and similar mechanisms. . . . We feel a deep responsibility not to sign off on any paper that threatens millions of lives.[25]

And so it was that in five years, protest on the streets of La Paz had become protest on the world stage. Had the democratic revolution in Bolivia translated into substantial forward movement in the international arena? No. But Bolivia's commitment to a progressive politics of climate mitigation provides bold and vital leadership that would otherwise be lacking. Even the once plucky Maldives, having entered into secret negotiations with the United States for aid money, essentially retired from the field and endorsed the lame Cancún agreement. At the same time, the United States cut $3 million in aid to Bolivia because of the Andean nation's efforts to oppose the voluntary and inadequate accord. The US government pressured European countries to do the same.[26]

In essence, Bolivia is attempting to confront the catastrophic convergence by addressing the problems through which climate change articulates itself.

If there is to be more progress on an international agreement that mitigates emissions and funds adaptation, it will be in large part by thanks to the brave example of impoverished and landlocked little Bolivia. That a country so poor, so underdeveloped, economically marginalized, fettered by widespread illiteracy, disease, and hunger, its politics for so long stunted by racism, exploitation, and dictatorship, could organize itself, avoid civil war, proceed toward a new path of mixed economic development, begin to take environmental issues seriously, and then to bring all of this to the international stage with dignity, is a feat of absolutely heroic and epic proportions.

Mitigation Now

A burdensome, if obvious, realization hit me while writing this book. Peaceful, progressive adaptation versus bad, violent adaptation is a difficult choice, but it is a struggle that is itself predicated on *robust mitigation*. Without mitigation, we run the very real risk of unleashing a process of self-fueling, runaway climate change to which there can be little successful adaptation.

As discussed earlier, scientists believe that stabilizing the climate system requires that we return to an atmospheric carbon dioxide concentration of less than 350 parts per million. The extremely bad news—we are now at 390 parts per million. The World Meteorological Organization has determined 2010 to have been one of the hottest ever recorded. And all year, extreme weather battered the Northern Hemisphere. Add to this the steady drip of new scientific reports on the degraded state of the world's oceans, ice packs, and forests. The IPCC says rich countries like the United States must cut emissions 25 to 40 percent below 1990 levels by 2020 and thereafter make precipitous cuts to almost zero emissions.

If we don't act now, average global temperatures will likely increase by much more than 2 degrees Celsius and that will likely trigger a set of dangerous positive-feedback loops that will unleash self-compounding, runaway climate change. For example, if the permafrost of the arctic keeps melting, and the massive stores of methane (CH_4) contained beneath it are released, global warming will accelerate radically because methane "is over 20 times more effective in trapping heat in the atmosphere than carbon dioxide."[27] At the moment, these vast stores of methane remain locked up under ice, beneath the tundra and ocean floor. But this frozen lid of mud is melting, threatening a rapid warming with attendant rises in sea levels, devastated agriculture, and social chaos.

As this book goes to press in 2011, very little mitigation is under way. The core problem in the international effort to cut emissions is fundamentally the intransigence of the United States: it failed to ratify the Kyoto Protocol and has played an obstructionist role at subsequent negotiations. Domestically, progress has been just as frustratingly slow despite wide public support for environmental protections. As of this writing, no climate legislation has been passed in the United States. We have no price on carbon, nor any program of robust investment in clean technology. Even the minimal production tax credit for clean energy generated by solar, wind, and hydro power has not been locked in as a long-term commitment. As a result, private investment in clean tech moves forward only in fits and starts.

China, on the other hand, now the world's second-largest economy and largest greenhouse gas polluter, is moving ahead with a robust and fast-growing clean-tech industry—that is to say, with mitigation. The Chinese wind sector has grown steadily since 2001. In 2009, the sector grew by 113 percent, according to the World Wind Energy Report. This growth is the result, in part, of robust government support: China has invested $200.8 billion in stimulus funding for clean tech. Estimates of US stimulus funding for clean technology range from $50 to $80 billion.[28]

The EU is also moving forward to create a regional supergrid and plans to spend 1 trillion euros in doing so.[29] Germany and Portugal, in particular, are moving aggressively to expand their already quite large clean-tech sectors. Action in the core industrial economies is essential because only they have the infrastructure that can propel the clean-tech revolution and transform the world economy.

Pathways Forward

Despite US political sclerosis and fossil fuel fundamentalism, there are paths forward. First and foremost, there is the Environmental Protection

Agency. Thanks to the pressure and lawsuits of green activists, the EPA is now obliged to regulate greenhouse gas emissions. If the EPA were to act robustly, it could achieve significant and immediate emissions reductions using nothing more than existing laws and current technologies.

According to Kassie Siegel at the Center for Biological Diversity, "The Clean Air Act can achieve everything we need: a 40 percent reduction of greenhouse gas emissions over 1990 levels by 2020."[30] The two most important things the EPA could do are to halt any permitting of new coal-fired power plants—about fifty new plants are seeking approval as this book goes to press—and to force all existing coal-fired facilities to switch to natural gas. This "fuel switching" requires little to no retrofitting of most existing power plants. If that happened, total non-vehicle US emissions would be reduced by 13 percent or more in a matter of a year or two, say various experts. As a fuel, natural gas is generally half as polluting as coal. But in the case of old, inefficient coal-fired plants, switching to gas can reduce emissions by as much as two-thirds.

Though natural gas drilling is highly problematic, with regulation it could become less polluting. And there is plenty of natural gas: discoveries have glutted the market, and prices are down more than 60 percent from their peak. Gas is not a solution; it is not clean. Gas merely offers a cleaner, realistic "bridging fuel" as we move toward power generated from wind, solar, geothermal, and hydro sources.

Big Green Buy

Another tool of transformation readily at hand is direct government procurement of clean technology. Currently, leading clean technology remains slightly more expensive than the old dirty-tech alternatives. This so-called "price gap" is holding back clean technology's mass application. The simple fact is that capitalist economies will not switch to clean energy until it is cheaper than fossil fuels.

The price gap results partly from dirty tech's history of subsidies ($72.5 billion between 2002 and 2008) and partly from the massive economies of scale that the fossil fuel industry enjoys. The fastest way to close the price gap is to build large clean-tech markets that allow for similar economies of scale. And the fastest way to do that is to reorient government procurement away from fossil fuel energy toward clean energy and technology—to use the government's vast spending power to create a market for clean energy.

After all, the government didn't just fund the invention of the microprocessor, it was also the first major consumer of the device. It not only created the technology, it created its market. Throughout the 1950s, *more than half* of IBM's revenue came from government contracts. Along with money, these contracts provided a guaranteed market, as well as stability for IBM and its suppliers, and thus helped coax in private investment—all of which helped make IBM the market leader.[31]

Now consider the scale of the problem: our asphalt transportation arteries are clogged with 250 million gasoline-powered vehicles sucking down an annual $200 to $300 billion worth of fuel from more than 121,000 filling stations. Add to that the cost of heating and cooling buildings, jet travel, shipping, powering industry, and the energy-gobbling servers and mainframes that are the Internet, and the US energy economy reaches a spectacular annual tab of $2 to $3 trillion.

Those are enormous sums, but federal, state, and local government constitutes more than 38 percent of our GDP. The federal government spent about $3.6 trillion in 2010. In more concrete terms, the federal government is the world's largest consumer of energy and vehicles—it owns or leases more than 430,000 buildings, mostly large office buildings, and 650,000 vehicles. As a result, it is the nation's largest greenhouse gas emitter. Add in state and local government activity, and those numbers grow again by about a third.

A redirection of government purchasing would create massive markets for clean power, electric vehicles, and efficient buildings, as well as for more sustainably produced furniture, paper, cleaning supplies, uniforms, food, and services. If government bought green, that would drive down the price of clean technology, and then the momentum toward green tech would become self-reinforcing and spread to the private sector.

Government has tremendous latitude to leverage green procurement because it requires no new taxes, programs, or spending, nor is it hostage to

the holy grail of sixty votes in the Senate. It is simply a matter of changing how the government buys its energy, vehicles, and services

Capitalism versus Nature?

There is one last imperative question. Several strands of green thinking
maintain that capitalism is incapable of arriving at a sustainable relationship
with nature because, as an economic system, capitalism must grow expo-
nentially, while the earth is finite.[32] You will find this argument in the literature of ecosocialism, deep ecology, and ecoanarchism. The same argument
is often cast by liberal greens in deeply ahistorical and antitheoretical terms
that, while critical of the economic system, often decline to name it. Back in
the early 1970s, the Club of Rome's book *Limits to Growth* fixated on the
dangers of "growth" but largely avoided explaining why capitalism needs
growth or how growth is linked to private ownership, profits, and interfirm
competition. Whether these literatures describe the problem as "modern industrial society," "the growth cult," or the profit system, they often have a
similar takeaway: we need a totally different economic system if we are to live
in balance with nature.

Some of the first to make such an argument were Marx and Engels.
They came to their ecology through examining the local problem of relations between town and country—which was expressed simultaneously as
urban pollution and rural soil depletion. In exploring this question they
relied on the pioneering work of soil chemist Justus von Liebig. And from
this small-scale problem, they developed the idea of capitalism's overall
"metabolic rift" with nature.[33] Here is how Marx explained the dilemma:

> Capitalist production collects the population together in great centres, and
> causes the urban population to achieve an ever-growing preponderance.
> This has two results. On the one hand it concentrates the historical mo-
> tive force of society; on the other hand, it disturbs the metabolic interac-
> tion between man and the earth, i.e. it prevents the return to the soil of its
> constituent elements consumed by man in the form of food and clothing;
> hence it hinders the operation of the eternal natural condition for the last-

ing fertility of the soil. . . . All progress in capitalist agriculture is a progress in the art, not only of robbing the worker, but of robbing the soil.[34]

From that grew the Marxist belief that capitalism, as a whole, is irreconcilably in contradiction with nature; that the economic system creates a rift in the balance of exchanges, or metabolism, connecting human society and natural systems. As with "soil robbing," so too with forests, fish stocks, water supplies, genetic inheritance, biodiversity, and atmospheric CO_2 concentrations. The natural systems are out of sync; their elements are being rearranged and redistributed, ending up as garbage and pollution.

As Mary Douglas, paraphrasing William James, put it, "Uncleanliness is matter out of place."[35] At a large enough scale, that disruption of elements threatens environmental catastrophe.

It may be true: capitalism may be, ultimately, incapable of accommodating itself to the limits of the natural world.

However, that is *not* the same question as whether capitalism can solve the climate crisis. Because of its magnitude, the climate crisis can appear as if it is the combination of all environmental crises—overexploitation of the seas, deforestation, overexploitation of freshwater, soil erosion, species and habitat loss, chemical contamination, and genetic contamination due to transgenic bioengineering. But halting greenhouse gas emissions is a much more specific problem; it is only one piece of the apocalyptic panorama. Though all these problems are connected, the most urgent and all encompassing of them is anthropogenic climate change.

The fact of the matter is time has run out on the climate issue. Either capitalism solves the crisis, or it destroys civilization. Capitalism begins to deal with the crisis now, or we face civilizational collapse beginning this century. We cannot wait for a socialist, or communist, or anarchist, or deep-ecology, neoprimitive revolution; nor for a nostalgia-based *localista* conversion back to the mythical small-town economy of preindustrial America as some advocate.

In short, we cannot wait to transform *everything*—including how we create energy. Instead, we must begin immediately transforming the energy economy. Other necessary changes can and will flow from that.

Hopeless? No. If we put aside the question of capitalism's limits and deal only with greenhouse gas emissions, the problem looks less daunting. While capitalism has not solved *the* environmental crisis—meaning the fundamental conflict between the infinite growth potential of the market and the finite parameters of the planet—it has, in the past, solved *specific* environmental crises. The sanitation movement of the Progressive Era is an example.

By the 1830s, industrial cities had become perfect incubators of epidemic disease, particularly cholera and yellow fever. Like climate change today, these diseases hit the poor hardest, but they also sickened and killed the wealthy. Class privilege offered some protection, but it was not a guarantee of safety. And so it was that middle-class do-gooder goo-goos and mugwumps began a series of reforms that contained and eventually defeated the urban epidemics.

First, the filthy garbage-eating hogs were banned from city streets, then public sanitation programs of refuse collection began, sewers were built, safe public water provided, housing codes were developed and enforced. And, eventually, the epidemics of cholera stopped. So, too, were other infectious diseases, like pulmonary tuberculosis, typhus, and typhoid, largely eliminated.[36]

Thus, at the scale of the urban, capitalist society solved an environmental crisis through planning and public investment. Climate change is a problem on an entirely different order of magnitude, but past solutions to smaller environmental crises offer lessons.

Ultimately, solving the climate crisis—like the nineteenth-century victory over urban squalor and epidemic contagions—will require a relegitimation of the state's role in the economy. We will need planning and downward redistribution of wealth. And, as I have sketched out above, there are readily available ways to address the crisis immediately—if we make the effort to force our political leaders to act. We owe such an effort to people like Ekaru Loruman, who are already suffering and dying on the front lines of the catastrophic convergence, and to the next generation, who will inherit the mess. And, we owe it to ourselves.

ACKNOWLEDGMENTS

Foremost thanks go to my dear friend and colleague Ruth Baldwin, who championed this book and kept all the moving pieces from crashing. My agent Howard Yoon, a true gentleman and scholar, guided the contract patiently and superbly. He secured the advance upon which all of this was possible. Neil Smith, David Harvey, and Padmini Biswas at the Center for Place Culture and Politics at the CUNY Graduate Center, provided crucial institutional and intellectual support without which research for this book would have been impossible. The Rockefeller Brothers Foundation facilitated work with a substantial grant. Also, the Nation Institute supported me over the course of many trips, some of which are discussed in these pages, many of which are not, but all of which shaped my thinking. And thanks more recently to The Puffin Foundation for their support.

Deepest thanks to Betsy Reed, my editor at *The Nation* for her patience, diligence, clarity, and friendship. Josh W. Mason also gave me a much needed, very helpful edit. Thanks to Carl Bromley of Nation books, Taya Kitman, and Katrina vanden Heuvel for all their hard work at the Nation Institute and *The Nation* magazine. For careful copyediting, thanks to Jen Kelland. Marissa Colón-Margolies and Chantal Flores helped with some key research and fact checking. And thanks to all the good people at Perseus Books, like John Sherer, with whom it is a pleasure to work again. Thanks also to David Callahan and Lew Daily at Demos for offering to support the promotion of this book.

Some of the travels that appear in or inform this work happened variously in the company of Ian Olds, Ryan Grim, Jessica Dimmock, Christopher Anderson, and Teru Kuwayama. In traveling for this book I worked with Casper Waithaka, Ananthkumar Chintalapalli, Michel Mbula, Tshibasu Dieudonné, Pedro Stillner, Julian Cardona, my friend Lina Britto, and my very close friend Naqeeb Sherzad. I also worked with Ajmal Nakshbandi. Ajmal was murdered by the Taliban in 2007. He is missed and his death is still a bitter lesson.

Tala Hadid, Rob Eshelman, and Forrest Hylton were essential intellectual comrades in this process. Sadia Abbas assisted with important good ideas. In India I was the guest of the inspiring and gracious Biju Mathews. Chris Cook, John Marshall, Tina Gerhardt, Jeff Burt, and Sara Kazemi; Ted Hamm, Bill Cole, Chris Reilly, Jeremy Freeman, Jan Chelminski, and Jay Stewart; Ed and Sekeena Gavagan; and Eyal Press were all good comrades.

Very importantly, Doug Henwood and Liza Featherstone fed me, informed me, shared ideas, and indulged my late-night excesses. On occasions Adolph Reed was there to make it all better. Last but not least, deep appreciation goes to Rebecca Lossin, who gave me support, comfort, company, and love.

I am lucky to say there are many other excellent friends, old and new, who were kind to me during this project and I feel deep appreciation for all of them. The more I travel, read, and learn, the more I value friendships. I see in friendship the rudimentary components—generosity, loyalty, solidarity, patience—that are the building blocks of a better society.

Christian Parenti
Brooklyn, New York

NOTES

Chapter 1

1. On Africa the Intergovernmental Panel on Climate Change writes, "Warming is *very likely* to be larger than the global annual mean warming throughout the continent and in all seasons, with drier subtropical regions warming more than the moister tropics. Annual rainfall is *likely* to decrease in much of Mediterranean Africa and the northern Sahara, with a greater likelihood of decreasing rainfall as the Mediterranean coast is approached. Rainfall in southern Africa is *likely* to decrease in much of the winter rainfall region and western margins. There is *likely* to be an increase in annual mean rainfall in East Africa. It is unclear how rainfall in the Sahel, the Guinean Coast and the southern Sahara will evolve." Susan Solomon, Dahe Qin, Martin Manning, and Intergovernmental Panel on Climate Change Working Group I, *Climate Change 2007: The Physical Science Basis: Contribution of Working Group I to the Fourth Assessment Report of the Intergovernmental Panel on Climate Change* (Cambridge: Cambridge University Press, 2007), 850.

2. James Hansen, *Storms of My Grandchildren: The Truth About the Coming Climate Catastrophe and Our Last Chance to Save Humanity* (New York: Bloomsbury Press, 2009).

3. See "About Science and Impacts," Pew Center on Global Climate Change, www.pewclimate.org/science-impacts/about.

4. The IPCC has rather famously lowered its projected sea level rises between its third and fourth assessment reports. But the fourth assessment's lower range of projected rises has been roundly attacked as optimistic because they do not take into account new evidence of very rapid melting in Greenland and Antarctica. *New Scientist* summed up the dilemma of projecting sea level rises as follows: "Because modeling how the Greenland and Antarctic ice sheets will react to rising temperatures is fiendishly complicated, the IPCC did not include either in its estimate. It's no small omission: the Greenland ice cap, the smaller and so far less stable of the two, holds enough water that if it all melted, it would raise sea levels by 6 metres on average across the globe." The same piece then goes on to quote Eric Rignot of the University of California, Irvine, and NASA's Jet Propulsion Laboratory, saying, "As a result of the acceleration of outlet glaciers over large regions, the ice sheets in Greenland and Antarctica are already contributing more and faster to sea level rise than anticipated. . . . If this trend continues, we are likely to witness sea level rise 1 metre or more by year

2100." See Catherine Brahic, "Sea Level Rise Could Bust IPCC Estimate," *New Scientist* (March 2009).

5. John Vidal, "Global Warming Causes 300,000 Deaths a Year," *Guardian*, May 29, 2009.

6. Jianjun Yin et al. "Model Projections of Rapid Sea-Level Rise on the Northeast Coast of the United States," *Nature Geoscience* 2 (March 15, 2009): 262–266. In 2007 the IPCC Fourth Assessment Report, based on data that was already several years dated upon publication, projected that neither Greenland nor Antarctica would lose significant mass by 2100. In fact, both are losing mass very quickly. From the new data come the new projections.

7. Koko Warner et al., "In Search of Shelter: Mapping the Effects of Climate Change on Human Migration and Displacement," Earth Institute of Columbia University, May 2009, http://ciesin.columbia.edu/documents/clim-migr-report-june09 _media.pdf.

8. Kristina Stefanova, "Rising Sea Levels in Pacific Create Wave of Migrants," *Washington Times*, April 19, 2009.

9. Quoted in Susan George, "Globalisation and War" (paper presented at the International Congress of the International Physicians for the Prevention of Nuclear War, New Delhi, March 10 2008); "Climate Change and Conflict," International Crisis Group Report, November 2007, www.crisisgroup.org/en/key-issues/climate-change-and-conflict.aspx.

10. Dan Smith and Janani Vivekananda, *A Climate of Conflict: The Links Between Climate Change, Peace and War* (Stockholm: Swedish International Development Cooperation Agency, Febuary 2008), 7. This publication can be downloaded/ordered from www.sida.se/publications.

11. Statistically, "battle-related deaths" worldwide have declined since World War II and especially since the end of the Cold War—which in the frontline states of the Global South was often quite hot. But other amorphous types of violence linked to social breakdown are spreading. Take the case of El Salvador: twelve years of civil war ended in 1993, but "deaths by homicide in the post war era at one point surpassed the death rate during the war." And they remain almost as high today. Or consider Caracas. In the 1970s Venezuela suffered a series of small guerrilla insurgencies; in fact, the young paratrooper Hugo Chavez fought Maoist guerillas around Lake Maricaibo. Today, Venezuela is "at peace," but the hillside barrios of Caracas are hyperviolent with crime; Caracas is far more violent than during the era of civil war. The Caracas murder rate is about 130 per 100,000. In 2008 a total of 2,415 people were killed and 5,098 others were injured. See, for example, Sara Miller Llana, "Will Venezuela's Murder Rate Hurt Chávez?" *Christian Science Monitor*, December 3, 2008; "Highlights: Venezuela Crime, Narcotics Issues 29 Jun–5 Jul 09," *World News Connection* (US Department of Commerce), July 5, 2009.

Chapter 2

1. "Statement for the Record of Dr. Thomas Fingar," Office of the Director of National Intelligence, June 25, 2008, www.dni.gov/testimonies/20080625_testimony.pdf (accessed on June 25, 2008); Kevin Whitelaw, "Climate Change Will Have Destabilizing Conse-

quences, Intelligence Agencies Warn," *US News & World Report*, June 25, 2008. The report was called "The National Security Implications of Global Climate Change to 2030."

2. Laura Sullivan, "Prison Economics Help Drive Ariz. Immigration Law," *All Things Considered* (NPR Radio), October 28, 2010.

3. This report is widely available on the Web—for example, on the Global Business Network website at www.gbn.com/GBNDocumentDisplayServlet.srv?aid=26231 &url=/UploadDocumentDisplayServlet.srv?id=28566.

4. On bombing and Paris negotiations, see Gabriel Kolko, *Anatomy of a War: Vietnam, the United States and the Modern Historical Experience* (New York: New Press, 1985), 440–444; Stanley Karrnow, *Vietnam: A History* (New York: Penguin, 1997).

5. Jeff Goodell, *How to Cool the Planet: Geoengineering and the Audacious Quest to Fix Earth's Climate* (New York: Houghton Mifflin Harcourt, 2010).

6. For a thorough discussion of the ocean's thermaline circulation system, see the following: Tim Flannery, *The Weather Makers: How Man Is Changing the Climate and What It Means for Life on Earth* (New York: HarperCollins, 2006); Elizabeth Kolbert, *Field Notes from a Catastrophe: Man, Nature and Climate Change* (New York: Bloomsbury Press, 2006); Eugene Linden, *The Winds of Change: Climate, Weather, and the Destruction of Civilizations* (New York: Simon & Schuster, 2006); Al Gore, *Earth in the Balance* (New York: Plume, 1993); Al Gore, *An Inconvenient Truth* (New York: Rodale Books, 2006); George Monbiot, *Heat: How to Stop the Planet from Burning* (New York: Doubleday, 2006).

7. Peter Schwartz and Doug Randall, "Report on Abrupt Climate Change and Its Implications for the United States National Security" (report prepared for the Pentagon Office of Net Assessment, Global Business Network, February 2003), 2.

8. CNA Corporation, *National Security and the Threat of Climate Change* (Alexandria, VA: CNA Corporation, 2007), 44.

9. CNA Corporation, *National Security and the Threat of Climate Change*, 16.

10. CNA Corporation, *National Security and the Threat of Climate Change*, 60.

11. Kurt M. Campbell et al., *The Age of Consequences: The Foreign-Policy National Security Implications of Global Climate Change* (Washington DC: Center for Strategic and International Studies and the Center for New American Security, 2007), 35.

12. Campbell et al., *Age of Consequences*, 9.

13. Campbell et al., *Age of Consequences*, 85–86.

14. Jonathan Pearlman and Ben Cubby, "Defense Warns of Climate Conflict," *Sydney Morning Herald*, January 7, 2009; the Australian Defense Forces analysis, titled *Climate Change: The Environment, Resources and Conflict*, was completed in November 2007.

15. "Climate Change and International Security" (paper from the High Representative and the European Commission to the European Council, S113/08, March 14, 2008), 1–2. This report is available online at www.consilium.europa.eu/ueDocs/cms_Data/docs/pressData/en/reports/99387.pdf.

16. "Climate Change and International Security," 3–5.

17. Thomas Barnett, "The Pentagon's New Map," *Esquire*, March 2003. It is tempting to give American foreign policy an intellectual coherence that it doesn't necessarily have. Although general goals are agreed on, namely projecting American power for the sake of American business, policy circles are divided into different schools of thought, cliques, and networks that compete for the influence of opposing visions.

18. Immanuel Wallerstein, *The Modern World-System I: Capitalist Agriculture and the Origins of the European World-Economy in the Sixteenth Century* (New York: Academic Press, 1974).

19. John Stuart Mill, *Principles of Political Economy* (New York: Longman, Green and Co., 1909), 685.

20. Larry Elliott and Mark Tran, "UN Report Warns of Threat to Human Progress from Climate Change," *Guardian*, November 4, 2010.

Chapter 3

1. Interview with Colonel Gary Anderson, USMC, March 1999; Frank L. Jones, "Marine Corps Civil Affairs and the Three Block War," *Marine Corps Gazette* 86, no. 3 (March 1, 2002). Derek Summerfield, "The Psychosocial Effects of Conflict in the Third World," *Development in Practice* 1, no. 3 (autumn 1991): 159–173: 2.

2. CNA Corporation, *National Security and the Threat of Climate Change* (Alexandria, VA: CNA Corporation, 2007), 44. Emphasis added. That was Gen. Anthony Zini (Ret.) reflecting on the military implications of climate change, but Woolsey, Panetta, and the others all make similar statements.

3. *Tactics in Counterinsurgency* (FM 3–24.2). US Military Counterinsurgency Field Manual (Washington, DC: Department of the Army, 2009), p. viii.

4. John A. Nagl, *Learning to Eat Soup with a Knife: Counterinsurgency Lessons from Malaya and Vietnam* (Chicago: University of Chicago Press, 2005); David Kilcullen, *The Accidental Guerrilla: Fighting Small Wars in the Midst of a Big One* (Oxford: Oxford University Press, 2009); Thomas Ricks, *The Gamble: General David Patraeus and the American Military Adventure in Iraq, 2006–2008* (New York: Penguin Press, 2009). For an excellent and critical history of counterinsurgency in Colombia see, Forrest Hylton, "Plan Colombia: The Measure of Success," *Brown Journal of World Affairs* Vol. XVII, no. I (Fall/Winter 2010): 99115.

5. For the classic discussion of anomie, see Robert K. Merton, "Social Structure and Anomie," *American Sociological Review* 3, no. 5 (October 1938): 672–682.

6. Jose Harris, "War and Social History: Britain and the Home Front During the Second World War," *Contemporary European History* 1, no. 1 (March 1992): 17–35: 18.

7. Indeed, that is what unlucky "guests" of the Taliban, like Jerey van Dyke, describe. By his account, the Taliban give the impression that drone strikes build unity on the ground, even if they fray and wear upon the Taliban leadership networks. Jerey Van Dyke, *Captive: My Time As a Prisoner of the Taliban* (New York: Times Books, 2010).

8. Summerfield, "The Psychosocial Effects of Conflict," 159–173: 2.

9. I am thinking here most specifically of political Islam. See Oliver Roy, *The Failures of Political Islam* (Cambridge, MA: Harvard University Press, 1994), in which French scholar Roy argues that political Islam, once in power, necessarily tempers its radicalism, for there is no "Islamic" way to run a modern economy or state because Islam is not a social theory but a moral theory.

10. Robert J. Bunker, "Epochal Change: War over Social and Political Organization," *Parameters* 27 (summer 1997): 15–25.

11. As often happens in colonial situations, there were both resistance and creative adaptation on the part of the colonized people. As explained in Theda Perdue and Michael Green's excellent *The Cherokee Nation and the Trail of Tears*, the Cherokees used the "civilizing" process, turning it to their own national ends. They adopted modern farming methods and tools, as well as created a Cherokee script, newspapers, a constitution, and a modern sovereign state. They engaged in long-distance trade and the cash economy, even buying and owning slaves, and brought in white indentured servants to work their lands. But they resisted efforts to privatize their land holdings and hung on to their language and customs and thereby, through partial acculturation, thwarted conquest. Interestingly, the Kikuyu of Kenya and the Chagga of Tanzania also both resisted and adapted to colonialism in a similar fashion to the Cherokee. On the Cherokee, see Theda Perdue and Michael Green, *The Cherokee Nation and the Trail of Tears* (New York: Viking, 2007).

12. Erving Goffman, *Asylums: Essays on the Social Situation of Mental Patients and Other Inmates* (New York: Anchor, 1961). General George Crook quoted in John A. Nagl, *Counterinsurgency Lessons from Malaya and Vietnam: Learning to Eat Soup with a Knife* (Chicago: University of Chicago Press, 2005).

13. If this sounds a lot like Judeo-Christian eschatology, that is because there was significant influence from the Mormon Church and, strangely, the Shakers on the founding leaders of the Ghost Dance Cult, like the Paiute prophet Wovoka. See Frank D. McCann Jr., "The Ghost Dance, Last Hope of Western Tribes, Unleashed the Final Tragedy," *Montana: The Magazine of Western History* 16, no. 1 (winter 1966): 25–34. For a historiographical survey of the literature on the Lakota ghost dance, see Michael A. Sievers, "The Historiography of 'The Bloody Field . . . That Kept the Secret of the Everlasting Word': Wounded Knee," *South Dakota History* 6, no. 1 (1975): 33–54; Raymond J. DeMallie, "The Lakota Ghost Dance: An Ethnohistorical Account," *The Pacific Historical Review* 51, no. 4 (November 1982): 385–405.

14. Captain E. D. Swinton, D.S.O., R.E., *The Defense of Duffer's Drift* (Washington, DC: US Infantry Association, 1916), 9.

15. Swinton, *The Defense of Duffer's Drift*, 36.

16. Hans Schmidt, *Maverick Marine: General Smedley D. Butler and the Contradictions of American Military History* (Lexington: University Press of Kentucky, 1998).

17. For more on this, see Dunbar Ortiz, "Indigenous Rights and Regional Autonomy in Revolutionary Nicaragua," *Latin American Perspectives* 14, no. 1 (winter 1987): 43–66; Jane Freeland, "Nationalist Revolution and Ethnic Rights: The Miskitu Indians of Nicaragua's Atlantic Coast," *Third World Quarterly* 11, no. 4 (October 1989): 166–190. A famous innovator of small-war tactics and doctrine was Maj. Gen. Merritt A. Edson (USMC), who led, and later wrote about, a 1928 campaign to pacify Nicaragua's Rio Coco.

18. On the last example, see the excellent article by Shane Bauer, "Iraq's New Death Squad," *The Nation*, June 22, 2009.

19. United States Marine Corps, *Small Wars Manual* (Washington, DC: Government Printing Office, 1940), 2.

20. This is from a report from the Brady brigade commander dated October 1919, quoted in Hans Schmidt, *The United States Occupation of Haiti, 1915–1934* (New Brunswick, NJ: Rutgers University Press, 1995), 105.

21. Like the cavalry, the marines, emphasizing small mobile units, adopted local methods of transportation—on rivers, mountain trails, or country roads. Resupply was limited, and marines tended to live off the land—which is to say, the local population. Discussing marine suppression of rebellion in Haiti during America's intermittent fourteen-year occupation there, Lester Langley gives this description of tactics: "Marine commanders in the guard had to adapt to rebel tactics. A patrol could travel twenty to thirty miles in a day, moving single file along trails flanked by dense growth, stopping usually at midafternoon to rest. Since pack mules ordinarily moved slower than men, animals were limited to the minimum necessary for carrying blanket, rolls, food, and ammunition. . . . Everything was sacrificed to speed on the trail, to having men in condition to fight. . . . What could not be scavenged was flown in by the air squadron." Lester D. Langley, *The Banana Wars: United States Intervention in the Caribbean, 1898–1934* (Wilmington, DE: SR Books, 2002), 207. This was the age of gun boat diplomacy, and the manual refers explicitly to the imperial nature of such engagements: "Small wars, generally being the execution of the responsibilities of the President in protecting American interests, life and property abroad, are therefore conducted in a manner different from major warfare. In small wars, diplomacy has not ceased to function and the State Department exercises a constant and controlling influence over the military operations. The very inception of small wars, as a rule, is an official act of the Chief Executive who personally gives instructions without action of Congress."

22. Louis Gannett, "In Haiti," *The Nation*, September 28, 1927.

23. Schmidt, *Maverick Marine*, 2.

24. Ernesto Che Guevara, *Guerrilla Warfare* (Lincoln, NE: Bison Books, 1998), 19.

25. Guevara, *Guerrilla Warfare*, 10.

26. Guevara, *Guerrilla Warfare*, 10–11.

27. Danilo Valladares, "Youth Gangs—Reserve Army for Organized Crime," Inter Press Service, September 21, 2010.

28. Dennis Rodgers, "Living in the Shadow of Death: Gangs, Violence and Social Order in Urban Nicaragua, 1996–2002," *Journal of Latin American Studies* 38, no. 2 (2006): 267–292: 267.

29. Here is a random sampling of stories on the postwar violence: "Gunmen Slaughter 14 Football Players," *Independent* (UK), November 1, 2010; Valladares, "Youth Gangs"; Nick Miroff and William Booth, "Violence Accompanies Mexican Drug Cartels As They Move South," *Washington Post*, July 27, 2010. And here are academic articles analyzing the crisis: Sonja Wolf, "Subverting Democracy: Elite Rule and the Limits to Political Participation in Post-War El Salvador," *Journal of Latin American Studies* 41, no. 3 (2009): 429–465; Rodgers, "Living in the Shadow of Death."

30. Tim Rogers, "The Spiral of Violence in Central America," *Z Magazine*, September 2000.

31. Mark Bowden, *Black Hawk Down: A Story of Modern War* (Berkeley, CA: Atlantic Monthly Press, 1999).

32. Mike Davis, "The Pentagon As Global Slumlord," TomDispatch.com, April 19, 2004, www.alternet.org/story/18457.

33. See Greg Grandin's excellent *Empire's Workshop: Latin America, the United States, and the Rise of the New Imperialism* (New York: Metropolitan, 2005), 87–88.

34. Peter Maas, "The Salvadorization of Iraq?" *New York Times Magazine*, May 1, 2005.

Chapter 4

1. On Africa, the IPCC writes, "Warming is *very likely* to be larger than the global annual mean warming throughout the continent and in all seasons, with drier subtropical regions warming more than the moister tropics. Annual rainfall is *likely* to decrease in much of Mediterranean Africa and the northern Sahara, with a greater likelihood of decreasing rainfall as the Mediterranean coast is approached. Rainfall in southern Africa is *likely* to decrease in much of the winter rainfall region and western margins. There is *likely* to be an increase in annual mean rainfall in East Africa. It is unclear how rainfall in the Sahel, the Guinean Coast and the southern Sahara will evolve." Susan Solomon, Dahe Qin, Martin Manning, and Intergovernmental Panel on Climate Change Working Group I, *Climate Change 2007: The Physical Science Basis: Contribution of Working Group I to the Fourth Assessment Report of the Intergovernmental Panel on Climate Change* (Cambridge: Cambridge University Press, 2007), 850.

2. Mwangi Ndirangu, "The Vanishing Snow of Mount Kenya," *Daily Nation* (Nairobi), December 17, 2009.

3. M. Boko et al. "Africa," in *Climate Change 2007: Impacts, Adaptation and Vulnerability. Contribution of Working Group II to the Fourth Assessment Report of the Intergovernmental Panel on Climate Change*, ed. M. L. Parry et al. (Cambridge: Cambridge University Press, 2007), 440.

4. John Vidal, "Climate Change Is Here, It Is a Reality," *Guardian*, September 3, 2009.

5. The Kalenjin are made up of the Kipsigis, Nandi, Tugen, Keiyo, Marakwet, Pokot (in the past called the Suk), Sabaot, and Terik. Many of these tribes live in the Mount Elgon region, overlapping the Kenya-Uganda border. They were the political base of Daniel Arap Moi. Kalenjin political identity had first begun to take shape in the 1940s, among independent but culturally and linguistically similar tribes. Kalenjin translates roughly as "I tell you," and it seems to have emerged among servicemen who were shipped off to fight for Britain in World War II. These men addressed each other as *kale* (which referred to one who had killed an enemy in battle). Wartime radio broadcasts hailed them with the plural *kalenjok*. After the war a Kalenjin political club formed at Alliance High School and at Makerere College. From the beginning the Kalenjin united to counterbalance the power of the Kikuyu, who had lost most of their land to the British, then led the Mau Mau rebellion and were soon to dominate postindependence political and economic life in Kenya. By 1948 there was a Kalenjin Union in Eldoret and a monthly magazine called *Kalenjin* in the 1950s. See Benjamin E. Kipkorir, *The Marakwet of Kenya* (Nairobi: East African Educational Publishers, 1982).

6. "Clashes in North Kenya over Cattle Raiding Kill 26," Associated Press Worldstream, August 1, 2008.

7. On the population and geography of this culture, see Elliot Fratkin, "East African Pastoralism in Transition: Maasai, Boran, and Rendille Cases," *African Studies Review* 44, no. 3 (December 2001): 1–25. Fratkin writes, "Pastoralists occupy 70 percent

of the total land of Kenya, 50 percent of Tanzania, and 40 percent of Uganda. But their populations are numerically small (fewer than 1.5 million of Kenya's 30 million, Tanzania's 35 million, and Uganda's 23 million people), and they find themselves politically disempowered and economically marginalized in national polities that are dominated by people from agricultural communities. Pastoralist groups of East Africa include cattle-keeping Maasai (300,000 in southern Kenya and 150,000 in northern Tanzania), Samburu (75,000), Turkana (200,000), Boran and Orma (75,000), and Karimojong, Dodoth, Teso, and Jie peoples in Uganda (total about 200,000). Camel-keeping pastoralists occupy the drier regions of northeastern Kenya, southern Ethiopia, and Somalia and include Afro-Asiatic-speaking Gabra (25,000), Rendille (25,000), and pastoral Somali (about 1 million of Somalia's 6.5 million people). In addition, many agricultural groups in East Africa raise large herds of cattle, including Kalenjin speakers (Nandi, Kipsigi, Pokot) in western Kenya and Bantu-speaking Ba Ankole in western Uganda and Tutsi in Rwanda and Burundi" (3–4).

8. Fratkin, "East African Pastoralism," 8.

9. Eleanor J. Burke, Simon J. Brown, and Nikolaos Christidis, "Modeling the Recent Evolution of Global Drought and Projections for the Twenty-First Century with the Hadley Centre Climate Model," *Journal of Hydrometeorology* 7, no. 5 (October 2006): 1113–1125.

10. Dr. David Kimenye, "Life on the Edge of Climate Change: The Plight of the Pastoralists in Northern Kenya," Christian Aid, November 13, 2006, p. 2.

11. Mwaniki Wahome, "For Agriculture, Larger Budget Allocation Vital," *The Nation,* June 12, 2008; see also the introduction of Victor A. Orindi, Anthony Nyong, and Mario Herrero, "Pastoral Livelihood Adaptation to Drought and Institutional Interventions in Kenya," in *Fighting Climate Change: Human Solidarity in a Divided World* (occasional paper, Human Development Report Office, United Nations Development Program, 2007/2008).

12. USAID FEWS NET, Weather Hazards Impacts Assessment for Africa, December 13–20, 2007.

13. Jeffrey Gettleman, "Ripples of Dispute Surround Tiny Island in East Africa," *New York Times,* August 17, 2009.

14. Barnabas Bii and Kennedy Masibo, "Banditry Death Toll Rises Now to 74," *The Nation* (Kenya), August 5, 2008; "Kenya to Forcefully Disarm Pastoralists in Rift Valley," World News Connection, August 3, 2008; Lucas Ng'asike, "Raiders Shoot Dead 30 Herders," *The Nation* (Kenya), August 12, 2008; "11 Killed As They Pursue Raiders," *The Nation* (Kenya), August 20, 2008; Peter Ng'etich, "Ten Herders Die in Bomb Raid," *The Nation* (Kenya), August 22, 2008; "'Sudanese Raiders' Kill Eight in Northwestern Kenya" (text of report by Kenyan privately owned TV station KTN on 30 August), BBC International Reports, Monitoring Service, August 30, 2008; Peter Ng'etich and Oliver Mathenge, "Two Reservists Killed in Raid," *The Nation* (Kenya), September 2, 2008; Peter Ng'etich, "Two Killed As Raiders Steal Cattle," *The Nation* (Kenya), September 4, 2008.

15. Claire McEvoy and Ryan Murray, "Gauging Fear and Insecurity: Perspectives on Armed Violence in Eastern Equatoria and Turkana North," *Sudan Issue Briefs* 14 (July 2008): 10: 14.

Chapter 5

1. J. K. Muhindi et al., *Rainfall Atlas for Kenya* (Nairobi: Drought Monitoring Center, 2001), 5.

2. Where the trade winds collide and the air rises, we find an area of strange calm, known to sailors as the doldrums.

3. Muhindi et al., *Rainfall Atlas for Kenya*, 7. John E. Oliver, *Encyclopedia of World Climatology* (New York: Springer), p. 430.

4. Recall the basics: as the Earth, tipped on its axis, revolves around the sun during the course of a year, the sun focuses more forcefully on one, then the other, hemisphere. In the process, it slowly transits north and south across the equator. During its summer, the Northern Hemisphere is tipped toward the sun, and the ITCZ is pulled north toward the Tropic of Capricorn. As the season changes, the Southern Hemisphere receives a greater portion of sunlight, and the ITCZ is pulled south across the equator toward the Tropic of Cancer.

5. On Africa the IPCC writes, "Warming is *very likely* to be larger than the global annual mean warming throughout the continent and in all seasons, with drier subtropical regions warming more than the moister tropics. Annual rainfall is *likely* to decrease in much of Mediterranean Africa and the northern Sahara, with a greater likelihood of decreasing rainfall as the Mediterranean coast is approached. Rainfall in southern Africa is *likely* to decrease in much of the winter rainfall region and western margins. There is *likely* to be an increase in annual mean rainfall in East Africa. It is unclear how rainfall in the Sahel, the Guinean Coast and the southern Sahara will evolve." Susan Solomon, Dahe Qin, Martin Manning, and Intergovernmental Panel on Climate Change Working Group I, *Climate Change 2007: The Physical Science Basis: Contribution of Working Group I to the Fourth Assessment Report of the Intergovernmental Panel on Climate Change* (Cambridge: Cambridge University Press, 2007), 850.

6. Katharine Houreld, "Kenya: 10 Million Risk Hunger After Harvests Fail," Associated Press, January 9, 2009.

7. "Heavy Rains to Affect Hundreds of Thousands," *IRIN*, November 14, 2008.

8. The preceding section is based on James Hansen, *Storms of My Grandchildren: The Truth About the Coming Climate Catastrophe and Our Last Chance to Save Humanity* (New York: Bloomsbury Press, 2009); Bill McKibben, *Earth: Making a Life on a Tough New Planet* (New York: Henry Holt & Co., 2010); Tim Flannery, *The Weather Makers: How Man Is Changing the Climate and What It Means for Life on Earth* (New York: HarperCollins, 2006); Elizabeth Kolbert, *Field Notes from a Catastrophe: Man, Nature and Climate Change* (New York: Bloomsbury Press, 2006); Eugene Linden, *The Winds of Change: Climate, Weather, and the Destruction of Civilizations* (New York: Simon & Schuster, 2006); Al Gore, *Earth in the Balance* (New York: Plume, 1993); Al Gore, *An Inconvenient Truth* (New York: Rodale Books, 2006); George Monbiot, *Heat: How to Stop the Planet from Burning* (New York: Doubleday, 2006). Climate Change 2007: *Working Group I: The Physical Science Basis: Human and Natural Drivers of Climate Change, IPCC Fourth Assessment Report* (2007): http://www.ipcc.ch/publications _and_data/ar4/wg1/en/spmsspm-human-and.html. For latest atmospheric CO_2 concentrations see http://www.esrl.noaa.gov/gmd/ccgg/trends/

9. "Towards a Goal for Climate Change Stabilisation," ch. 13 (13.5) in *Stern Review on the Economics of Climate Change* (Treasury of the Government of the UK, 2006).

10. Clive Hamilton, Charles Stuart Professor of Public Ethics, Centre for Applied Philosophy and Public Ethics at the Australian National University, "Is It Too Late to Prevent Catastrophic Climate Change?" (lecture to a meeting of the Royal Society of the Arts, Sydney, Australia, October 21, 2009), 11. Available at www.clivehamilton .net.au (accessed January 19, 2011).

11. Kevin Anderson et al, "From Long-Term Targets to Cumulative Emission Pathways: Reframing UK Climate Policy," *Energy Policy* 36, no. 10 (2008): 3714–3722.

12. For details on this activism, see the 350.org website (www.350.org). Hassen's paper can be found at J. Hansen et al., "Target Atmospheric CO_2: Where Should Humanity Aim?" Cornell University Library, October 15, 2008, http://arxiv.org/ abs/0804.1126.

13. For a review of the literature and its research methods, see Nils Petter Gleditsch, "Armed Conflict and the Environment: A Critique of the Literature," *Journal of Peace Research* 35, no. 3 (May 1998): 381–400.

14. "Thousands Flee amid Fears of Fighting Along Border," *IRIN*, November 29, 2008.

15. This debate is covered very well in Adanoo Wario Roba and Karen M. Witsenburg, *Surviving Pastoral Decline: Pastoral Sedentarization, Natural Resource Management and Livelihood Diversification in Marsabit District, Northern Kenya* (Lampeter, PA: Edwin Mellen Press, 2008), 735.

16. Val Percival and Thomas Homer-Dixon, "Environmental Scarcity and Violent Conflict: The Case of South Africa," *Journal of Peace Research* 35, no. 3 (May 1998): 279–298: 281.

17. Kennedy Agade Mkutu, *Guns and Governance in the Rift Valley: Pastoral Conflict and Small Arms* (Bloomington: Indiana University Press, 2008), 7.

18. David Anderson, "Stock Theft and Moral Economy in Colonial Kenya," *Africa: Journal of the International African Institute* 56, no. 4 (1986): 399–416: 406.

19. Anderson, "Stock Theft," 408; for discussion of a similar process in Tanzania, see Michael L. Fleisher, "Kuria Cattle Raiding: Capitalist Transformation, Commoditization, and Crime Formation Among an East African Agro-Pastoral People," *Comparative Studies in Society and History* 42, no. 4 (October 2000): 745–769.

Chapter 6

1. J. Forbes Munro, "Shipping Subsidies and Railway Guarantees: William Mackinnon, Eastern Africa and the Indian Ocean, 1860–93," *Journal of African History* 28, no. 2 (1987): 209–230: 210. Munro forcefully argues against the lame, very typical apologias that would have Mackinnon going to Africa out of noneconomic interests. In fact, the company was run by shipowners and merchants who stood to gain from expanded trade due to opening East Africa, even if the company itself were bankrupted.

2. Quoted in G. H. Mungeam, "Masai and Kikuyu Responses to the Establishment of British Administration in the East Africa Protectorate," *Journal of African History* 11, no. 1 (1970): 127–143: 136.

3. R. B. Buckley, "Colonization and Irrigation in the East Africa Protectorate," *The Geographical Journal* 21, no. 4 (April 1903): 349–371: 350, 355–356.

4. John Lonsdale and Bruce Berman, "Coping with the Contradictions: The Development of the Colonial State in Kenya, 1895–1914," *Journal of African History* 20, no. 4 (1979): 487–505.

5. J. M. Lonsdale, "The Politics of Conquest: The British in Western Kenya, 1894–1908," *The Historical Journal* 20, no. 4 (December 1977): 841–870: 851.

6. As Lonsdale and Berman put it in "Coping with the Contradictions," "Late-nineteenth-century imperialism in Africa was the final sortie by which the world capitalist system captured the last continent to remain partially beyond its pale. The system was comprised, then as now, of a hierarchy of many differing modes of production linked at the level of exchange and all under the domination of the most advanced forms of capital, whether that was based in the formally responsible imperial power or in one of its industrial rivals" (486).

7. Lonsdale, "The Politics of Conquest."

8. Lonsdale and Berman, "Coping with the Contradictions."

9. Colin Leys, *Underdevelopment in Kenya: The Political Economy of Neo-Colonialism* (Berkeley: University of California Press, 1975).

10. Frank Corfield, *The Origins and Growth of Mau Mau: An Historical Survey* (Nairobi: Government of Kenya, 1960).

11. Caroline Elkins, *Imperial Reckoning: The Untold Story of Britain's Gulag in Kenya* (New York: Owl Books, 2005).

12. David Anderson, "Stock Theft and Moral Economy in Colonial Kenya," *Africa: Journal of the International African Institute* 56, no. 4 (1986): 399–416: 405.

13. On colonial and postindependence efforts to create law and order in development among pastoralists, see Fratkin, "East African Pastoralism"; for clear argument that raiding has increased since 1980, see Dr. Paul Goldsmith, *Conceptualizing the Costs of Pastoralist Conflicts in Northern Kenya* (Cemiride, Kenya: The Center for Minority Rights Development, March 2005). Attempts to turn nomadic pastoralists into more sedentary ranchers and agriculturalists are, unfortunately, associated with rapid soil degradation.

14. "Obote Is Ousted by Ugandan Army," *New York Times*, January 26, 1971.

15. "Uganda's New Military Ruler," *New York Times*, January 28, 1971.

16. "Amin, Uganda's New Leader, Charges Tanzania Plans an Attack," *New York Times*, January 28, 1971.

17. Patrick Chabal and Jean-Pascal Daloz, *Africa Works: Disorder As a Political Instrument* (Oxford: University of Indiana Press/International African Institute, 1999), 15.

18. "Fall of Idi Amin," *Economic and Political Weekly* 14, no. 21 (May 26, 1979): 907–910: 907.

19. "US Senate Votes to Lift Economic Sanctions That Had Been Applied Against Uganda During Former Pres Idi Amin's Reign," *New York Times*, May 8, 1979; "Conflict Between Uganda Pres Amin and US over Amin's Order Forbidding Americans to Leave," *New York Times*, March 6, 1977.

20. "When a State Goes Insane," *New York Times*, May 2, 1979; "Fall of Idi Amin"; John Darton, "Invaders in Uganda Close In on Capital," *New York Times*, April 5, 1979.

21. Gregory Jayne, "African Apocalypse," *New York Times*, November 16, 1980.

22. Mustafa Mirzeler and Crawford Young, "Pastoral Politics in the Northeast Periphery in Uganda: AK-47 As Change Agent," *Journal of Modern African Studies* 38, no. 3 (September 2000): 407–429: 416.

23. Barry Shilachter, "Ugandan Warriors Becoming Dirt Farmers in Settlement Scheme," Associated Press, August 4, 1985.

24. Jayne, "African Apocalypse."

25. David Crary, "Well-Armed Cattle Raiders Terrorize East African Villages," *AP Online*, November 17, 1986.

26. Conan Businge, "400,000 Illegal Guns in Circulation," *New Vision* (Uganda), December 19, 2008.

27. "Where Natural and Man-Made Disaster Go Together," *The Economist*, June 14, 1980.

28. On guns, see Mirzeler and Young, "Pastoral Politics in the Northeast Periphery"; on drought, see Elliot Fratkin, "East African Pastoralism in Transition: Maasai, Boran, and Rendille Cases," *African Studies Review* 44, no. 3 (December 2001): 1–25: 8.

29. Jayne, "African Apocalypse."

30. Jayne, "African Apocalypse," 417.

31. *The Economist,* "Where Natural and Man-Made Disaster Go Together."

Chapter 7

1. I. M. Lewis, *Blood and Bones: The Call of Kinship in Somali Society* (Trenton, NJ: Red Sea Press, 1994), 150; I. M. Lewis, "Somalia Nationalism Turned Inside Out," *MERIP Reports*, no. 106 (June 1982); I. M. Lewis, *A Pastoral Democracy: A Study of Pastoralism and Politics Among the Northern Somali of the Horn of Africa* (London: Oxford University Press, 1962); I. M. Lewis, *The Modern History of Somaliland: From Nation to State* (New York: F. A. Praeger, 1965); David D. Laitin and Said S. Samatar, *Somalia: A Nation in Search of a State* (Boulder, CO: Westview Press, 1987); Abdi Ismail Samatar, "Destruction of State and Society in Somalia: Beyond the Tribal Convention," *The Journal of Modern African Studies* 30, no. 4 (December 1992): 625–641.

2. John Markakis, "Garrison Socialism: The Case of Ethiopia," *MERIP Reports*, no. 79 (June 1979): 5.

3. Robert G. Patman, *The Soviet Union in the Horn of Africa: The Diplomacy of Intervention and Disengagement* (Cambridge: Cambridge University Press, 1990), 49.

4. Gian Carlo Pajetta, "Interview on Ethiopia and Somalia," *New Left Review* 1, no. 107 (January–February 1978): 43–45; Emilio Sarzi Amade, "Ethiopia's Troubled Road," *New Left Review* 1, no. 107 (January–February 1978): 40–43.

5. "The Soviet Flight from Egypt," *Time*, July 31, 1972.

6. "The Model Socialist State That Prays Five Times a Day," *The Economist*, May 14, 1977.

7. Piero Gleijeses, *Conflicting Missions: Havana, Washington, and Africa, 1959–1976* (Chapel Hill: University of North Carolina Press, 2002). This book is a truly impressive accomplishment, based on ten years of research using declassified US intelligence, interviews with principal players, and, most importantly, vaults of never before re-

vealed Cuban documents from the Communist Party Central Committee, armed forces, and foreign ministry.

8. "The Cubans in Africa," *Newsweek*, March 13, 1978.

9. David B. Ottaway, "Soviets Said to Press Somalia for Cease-Fire in Ethiopia," *Washington Post*, August 4, 1977; Gebru Tareke, "The Ethiopia-Somalia War of 1977 Revisited," *The International Journal of African Historical Studies* 33, no. 3 (2000): 635–667: 642.

10. Pamela S. Falk, "Cuba in Africa," *Foreign Affairs* 65, no. 5 (summer 1987): 1077–1096.

11. David Ottoway, "Soviet Wooing of Ethiopia May Push Somalia Toward U.S.," *Washington Post*, February 28, 1977; Murrey Marder, "Soviets: Carter Distorted Role in Somalia," *Washington Post*, January 14, 1978; "Cuba, Somalia to Resume Diplomatic Relations," Xinhua General News Service, August 1, 1989.

12. Harry Ododa, "Somalia's Domestic Politics and Foreign Relations Since the Ogaden War of 1977–78," *Middle Eastern Studies* 21, no. 3 (July 1985): 285–297: 285.

13. For details on the war, see Tareke, "The Ethiopia-Somalia War of 1977 Revisited"; David D. Laitin, "The War in the Ogaden: Implications for Siyaad's Role in Somali History," *Journal of Modern African Studies* 17, no. 1 (March 1979): 95–115; Mohamud H. Khalif, "The Politics of Famine in the Ogaden," *Review of African Political Economy* 27, no. 84 (June 2000): 333–337; I. M. Lewis, "The Ogaden and the Fragility of Somali Segmentary Nationalism," *African Affairs* 88, no. 353 (October 1989): 573–579; Jeffrey Clark, "Debacle in Somalia," *Foreign Affairs* 72, no. 1 (1992–1993): 109–123; Ododa, "Somalia's Domestic Politics and Foreign Relations."

14. "Somalia Says Two Towns Hit by Ethiopian Planes," *Washington Post*, December 29, 1977.

15. David B. Ottaway, "Castro Seen Mediator in Africa Talks," *Washington Post*, March 18, 1977; "Red Hands Off the Red Sea," *The Economist*, March 26, 1977; Arnaud de Borchgrave, "Trouble on the Horn," *Newsweek*, June 27, 1977.

16. Clark, "Debacle in Somalia."

17. Abdi Ismail Samatar, "Structural Adjustment As Development Strategy? Bananas, Boom, and Poverty in Somalia," *Economic Geography* 69, no. 1 (January 1993): 25–43: 27.

18. Charles Mitchell, "Ethiopia Bombs Somali Towns," United Press International, May 25, 1984.

19. Clark, "Debacle in Somalia," 111.

20. World Bank figures are cited in Samatar, "Structural Adjustment As Development Strategy?"

21. Ismail I. Ahmed and Reginald Herbold Green, "The Heritage of War and State Collapse in Somalia and Somaliland: Local-Level Effects, External Interventions and Reconstruction," *Third World Quarterly* 20, no. 1 (February 1999): 113–127: 115–116.

22. Terrence Lyons and Ahmed Ismail Samatar, *State Collapse, Multilateral Intervention, and Strategies for Political Reconstruction* (Washington DC: Brookings Institution, 1995), 1. For a discussion of the state, state officials, and the politics of their discourse, see Stefano Harney, *State Work: Public Administration and Mass Intellectuality* (Durham, NC: Duke University Press, 2002).

Chapter 8

1. Martin Dugard, *Into Africa: The Epic Adventures of Stanley and Livingstone* (New York: Broadway, 2004).

2. Failed states: this phrase appears to be the property of the pro-war, national security intellectuals and the Pentagon planners who see a future of open-ended counterinsurgency. As it can carry a whiff of racism, a hint victim blaming, some on the Left oppose the idea. See Nome Chomsky, *Failed States: The Abuse of Power and the Assault on Democracy* (New York: Metropolitan Books, 2006).

3. Max Weber, *The Theory of Social and Economic Organization* (New York: Free Press, 1964), 154,

4. Stephen Harney, *State Work Public Administration and Mass Intellectuality* (New York: Monthly Review, 2002). Harney makes the point that the state is an idea that is produced as an institution only by the labor of its officialdom.

5. Max Weber, "Politics As a Vocation," in *From Max Weber: Essays in Sociology*, ed. H. H. Gerth and C. Wright Mills (New York: Oxford University Press, 1959), 77–128.

6. Norman F. Cantor, *In the Wake of the Plague* (New York: Harper Perennial, 2002); Barbara W. Tuchman, *A Distant Mirror: The Calamitous 14th Century* (New York: Ballantine Books, 1987). It is worth noting that Rome fell slowly, weakened by corruption, hierarchy, imperial overreact, and bloat well before its sacking. The Visigoths first crossed the Danube not as an invading army but as armed refugees fleeing the Huns, who were pressing in from the east. They tricked into Rome, violated the terms of their amnesty, and kept their arms, then slowly started making war again. See, for examples, chapter 2 in Frederic Austin Ogg, *A Source Book of Medieval History: Documents Illustrative of European Life and Institutions from the German Invasions to the Renaissance* (New York: American Book Company, 1908).

7. Walt W. Rostow, *The Stages of Economic Growth: A Non-Communist Manifesto* (Cambridge: Cambridge University Press, 1990).

8. Charles Tilly, "War Making and State Making As Organized Crime," in *Bringing the State Back In*, ed. Peter Evans, Dietrich Rueschemeyer, and Theda Skocpol (Cambridge: Cambridge University Press, 1985), 169–191.

9. Tilly, "War Making and State Making," 170.

10. Tilly, "War Making and State Making," 183.

11. Anthony Giddens, *The Nation-State and Violence*, vol. 2 of *A Contemporary Critique of Historical Materialism* (Berkeley: University of California Press, 1987).

Chapter 9

1. We were in the little village of Tutu in Sherzad District. Khogyani is made up of a cluster of districts: Bihsud, Khogyani, Sherzad, Shinwar, Bati Kot, Pachir Wa Agam, and, depending on who is explaining the region, parts of Chaparhar and Surkh Rod.

2. Matthew Savage et al., "Socio-Economic Impacts of Climate Change in Afghanistan," Department of International Development and Stockholm Environment Institute DFID CNTR 08 8507, executive summary, 2.

3. "Floods in Pakistan" (publication of the Humanitarian Communication Group, United Nations, October 4, 2010).

4. Tage R. Sivall, "Synoptic-Climatological Study of the Asian Summer Monsoon in Afghanistan," *Geografiska Annaler: Series A, Physical Geography* 59, no. 1/2 (1977): 67–87; chart on 76.

5. Savage et al., "Socio-Economic Impacts of Climate Change in Afghanistan," 5.

6. Raja Anwar, *The Tragedy of Afghanistan* (London: Verso, 1988), 69.

7. Louis Dupree, *Afghanistan* (New York: Oxford University Press, 2002).

8. James P. Sterba, "Starving Afghan Children Await Death Along Roads," *New York Times*, June 16, 1972, 1; Sterba e-mail to author, April 9, 2009.

9. Henry Kamm, "Afghans Striving to Aid Famine Areas," *New York Times*, November 19, 1972, 28.

10. "Upheaval in Kabul," *New York Times*, July 20, 1973, 30.

11. "Afghan Parliament, in Session for a Year, Has Voted No Legislation," *New York Times*, November 22, 1970.

12. James P. Sterba, "Afghans Begin Inquiry on Distribution of Food for Famine Relief," *New York Times*, July 11, 1972, 6.

13. "Leftist Protest Mars Agnew's Arrival in Kabul: Students in Afghan Capital Fail to Halt Motorcade Crowds Welcome Visitor," *New York Times*, January 7, 1970.

14. *An Afghan Village*, produced by Norman Miller with the co-operation of Toryali Shafaq Afghan Films and the Government of Afghanistan, 1974.

15. "Afghan King Overthrown: A Republic Is Proclaimed," *New York Times*, July 18, 1973.

16. Kamm, "Afghans Striving to Aid Famine Areas."

17. "Afghanistan Coup Topples Monarchy," *MERIP Reports*, no. 19 (August 1973): 18.

18. "Afghans Seem Happy That King Is Gone," *New York Times*, July 24, 1973.

19. Amaury de Riencourt, "India and Pakistan in the Shadow of Afghanistan," *Foreign Affairs* 61, no. 2 (winter 1982): 416–437.

20. Anwar, *The Tragedy of Afghanistan*, 78–81.

21. The story of Murtaza Bhutto is laid out in historical and personal detail in Raja Anwar, *The Terrorist Prince: The Life and Death of Murtaza Bhutto* (Verso: London, 1997), and also in Fatima Bhutto's *Songs of Blood and Sword* (New York: Nation Books, 2010).

22. S. R. Sonyel, "Enver Pasha and the Basmaji Movement in Central Asia," *Middle Eastern Studies* 26, no. 1 (January 1990): 52–64; Martha B. Olcott, "The Basmachi or Freemen's Revolt in Turkestan, 1918–24," *Soviet Studies* 33, no. 3 (July 1981): 352–369; William S. Ritter, "The Final Phase in the Liquidation of Anti-Soviet Resistance in Tadzhikistan: Ibrahim Bek and the Basmachi, 1924–31," *Soviet Studies* 37, no. 4 (October 1985): 484–493.

23. For more on this history, see Steve Coll, *Ghost Wars: The Secret History of the CIA, Afghanistan and Bin Laden, from the Soviet Invasion to September 10, 2001* (New York: Penguin, 2004).

24. Savage et al., "Socio-Economic Impacts of Climate Change in Afghanistan," 5.

25. Matthew King and Benjamin Sturtewagen, *Making the Most of Afghanistan's River Basins: Opportunities for Regional Cooperation* (New York: East West Institute, 2010), 17.

26. Savage et al., "Socio-Economic Impacts of Climate Change in Afghanistan," 21.

27. Emma Graham-Harrison and Sue Pleming, "Spectre of Afghan Drought Brings Hunger, Poppy Fears," Reuters, January 14, 2010.

28. "Floods Destroy 3,000 Houses in Takhar Abdul Matin Sarfaraz," *Pajhwok Afghan News*, May 7, 2010; "Floods Inflict Heavy Damage on Four Districts," *Pajhwok Afghan News*, May 9, 2010.

29. Steff Gaulter, "Flood of Misery: Pakistan's Uneasy Relationship," Al Jazeeria.net, August 9, 2010.

30. Graham-Harrison and Pleming, "Spectre of Afghan Drought"; Sediqullah Bader, "Afghanistan: Drought, Poppy Profits Cause Wheat Shortage," Inter Press Service, August 7, 2006.

31. Graham-Harrison and Pleming, "Spectre of Afghan Drought."

32. Quoted in Johann Hari, "Legalize It; Why Destroy Poppies and Afghan Farmers When the World Needs Legal Opiates?" *Los Angeles Times*, November 6, 2006.

33. Ahmed Rashid, *Descent into Chaos: The United States and the Failure of Nation Building in Pakistan, Afghanistan, and Central Asia* (New York: Viking, 2008), 401.

34. Michael Renner, "Water Challenges in Central-South Asia," Noref Policy Brief No. 4 (Oslo: Norwegian Peacebuilding Centre, December 2009).

Chapter 10

1. Quoted in Timur Toktonaliev and Izomiddin Ahmedjanov, "Why Anger Finally Boiled Over in Kyrgyzstan," *Bradenton Herald* (Florida), April 20, 2010.

2. Luke Harding, "Kyrgyzstan Opposition Seizes Power After Day of Protests," *Guardian*, April 9, 2010. Numerous reports noted the utility price hikes, but few explored their history and causes. See Michael Schwritz, "Kyrgyzstan, Facing Continuing Violence, Reaches Out to Russia for Help," *New York Times*, June 13, 2010; see also "Kyrgyzstan: A Hollow Regime Collapses," Asia Briefing No. 102, International Crisis Group, April 27, 2010, www.crisisgroup.org/en/regions/asia/central-asia/kyrgyzstan/B102-kyrgyzstan-a-hollow-regime-collapses.aspx.

3. Michael Schwirtz, "Fierce Fighting in Kyrgyzstan Poses Challenge to Government," *New York Times*, June 12, 2010.

4. "Kyrgyz Govt Calls for Increasing Utilities Prices," Russia & CIS Business and Financial Daily (newswire), April 2, 2008.

5. Andrew E. Kramer, "Government Buildings Retaken in Kyrgyzstan," *New York Times*, May 14, 2010; "Uzbekistan: Concern at Ethnic Trouble in Kyrgyzstan," Institute for War and Peace Reporting, May 25, 2010, http://iwpr.net/report-news/uzbekistan-concern-ethnic-trouble-kyrgyzstan; Jonibek Kadamjayov, "Fergana Valley: Relations Cooling, Uzbek-Kyrgyz Border Growing Increasingly Violent," EurasiaNet.org, March 9, 2010, www.eurasianet.org/departments/civilsociety/articles/eav030910a.shtml.

6. Luke Harding, "Kyrgyzstan Calls for Russian Help to End Ethnic Riots," *Guardian* (UK), June 12, 2010.

7. "Where Is the Justice? Interethnic Violence in Southern Kyrgyzstan and Its Aftermath," Human Right Watch, August 16, 2010, www.hrw.org/en/reports/2010/08/16/where-justice-0.

8. Kramer, "Government Buildings Retaken in Kyrgyzstan"; "Uzbekistan: Concern at Ethnic Trouble in Kyrgyzstan."

9. "Electricity Cut at Night in Kyrgyzstan for Six Months: Minister," Agence France-Presse, April 14, 2008; "Bakiyev Calls for an End to Rolling Blackouts in Kyrgyzstan," Central Asia General Newswire/Interfax, January 12, 2010.

10. Peter Leonard, "Uzbeks Rebut Critics of Pullout from Power Grid," Associated Press, December 3, 2009.

11. Gulnara Mambetalieva, "Energy Fears As Kyrgyz Winter Approaches: Threat of More Blackouts Despite Efforts to Hoard Water for Hydropower Ahead of Cold Season," RCA Issue 557, Institute for War and Peace Reporting, December 3, 2008, http://iwpr.net/report-news/energy-fears-kyrgyz-winter-approaches.

12. Mambetalieva, "Energy Fears."

13. Quoted in Mambetalieva, "Energy Fears."

14. Quoted in Mambetalieva, "Energy Fears."

15. "Kyrgyz Protest Electricity Price Hike," Radio Free Europe/Radio Liberty, February 25, 2010, www.rferl.org/content/Kyrgyz_Protest_Electricity_Price_Hike_/1968192.html.

16. "Bishkek Mayor Believes Rise of Electricity, Heating Tariffs to Bring Poor Population to Abject Poverty," AKIpress News Agency, November 13, 2009.

17. Ahmed Rashid, "The Fires of Faith in Central Asia," *World Policy Journal* 18, no. 1 (spring 2001): 45–55.

18. Martin C. Spechler, "The Economies of Central Asia: A Survey," *Comparative Economic Studies* 50, no. 1 (March 1, 2008): 30–50.

19. Ahmed Rashid, "The New Struggle in Central Asia: A Primer for the Baffled," *World Policy Journal* 17, no. 4 (winter 2000–2001): 33–45: 42.

20. "Millions of People in Central Asia Live Below the Poverty Line," *Times of Central Asia* (Kyrgyzstan), August 10, 2010.

21. Spechler, "The Economies of Central Asia."

22. Gareth Evans, "Force Is Not the Way to Meet Central Asia's Islamist Threat," *International Herald Tribune*, March 10, 2001.

23. S. R. Sonyel, "Enver Pasha and the Basmaji Movement in Central Asia," *Middle Eastern Studies* 26, no. 1 (January 1990): 52–64; Martha B. Olcott, "The Basmachi or Freemen's Revolt in Turkestan, 1918–24," *Soviet Studies* 33, no. 3 (July 1981): 352–369; William S. Ritter, "The Final Phase in the Liquidation of Anti-Soviet Resistance in Tadzhikistan: Ibrahim Bek and the Basmachi, 1924–31," *Soviet Studies* 37, no. 4 (October 1985): 484–493; Louis Dupree, Afghanistan (New York: Oxford, 2002).

24. Ahmed Rashid, *Jihad: The Rise of Militant Islam in Central Asia* (New York: Penguin, 2002), 44.

25. Rashid, *Jihad*, 96.

26. "KGB Chief Visits Soviet Border Areas Attacked by Afghan Rebels," Associated Press, April 30, 1987.

27. "Pakistan's 'Fanatical' Uzbek Militants," *BBC News*, October 29, 2009, http://news.bbc.co.uk/2/hi/south_asia/8331860.stm.

28. "Volume of Water in Toktogul Exceeds 19.472 Billion Cubic Meters," zprtssrg.com, August 2, 2010.

Chapter 11

1. Stephan Faris, "The Last Straw," *Foreign Policy* (July 1, 2009).

2. Phillips Talbot, "Kashmir and Hyderabad," *World Politics* 1, no. 3 (April 1949): 321–332: 323.

3. Talbot, "Kashmir and Hyderabad," 327. Both parties were said to have secretly accepted an agreement to fix the Pakistan-Indian border along the Line of Control in 1971. But when Pakistan finally won the release of its ninety thousand prisoners of war captured in East Pakistan and Bangladesh, it reneged.

4. Alice Thorner, "The Kashmir Conflict," *Middle East Journal* 3, no. 1 (January 1949): 17–30: 18.

5. Thorner, "The Kashmir Conflict," 19.

6. Thorner, "The Kashmir Conflict," 25.

7. Thorner, "The Kashmir Conflict," 25.

8. Robert Trumblull, "Use of Regulars Laid to Pakistan," *New York Times*, July 18, 1948.

9. Quoted in Undala Z. Alam, "Questioning the Water Wars Rationale: A Case Study of the Indus Waters Treaty," *The Geographical Journal* 168, no. 4 (December 2002): 341–353.

10. Sumit Ganguly, *Conflict Unending: India-Pakistan Tensions Since 1947* (New York: Columbia University Press, 2002); J. V. Deshpande, "Talking with Pakistan," *Economic and Political Weekly* 36, no. 16 (April 21–27, 2001): 1303–1306.

11. Alam, "Questioning the Water Wars Rationale."

12. Alam, "Questioning the Water Wars Rationale."

13. Alam, "Questioning the Water Wars Rationale."

14. Alam, "Questioning the Water Wars Rationale."

15. From June to mid-August 2010, fifty-seven protesters had been killed. Aijaz Hussain, "Officer Lauded in Indian Kashmir for Hurling Shoe," Associated Press, August 16, 2010; Tariq Ali, "Not Crushed, Merely Ignored," *London Review of Books* 32, no. 14 (July 22, 2010).

16. Jessica Stern, "Pakistan's Jihad Culture," *Foreign Affairs* 79, no. 6 (November–December 2000): 115–126: 117.

17. Stern, "Pakistan's Jihad Culture," 118.

18. Ben Arnoldy, "The Other Kashmir Problem: India and Pakistan Tussle over Water," *Christian Science Monitor*, August 11, 2010.

19. Shripad Dharmadhikary, "Mountains of Concrete: Dam Building in the Himalayas," Table 3, International Rivers Network, December 2008, www.international rivers.org/files/IR_Himalayas.pdf.

20. "India Constructing 52 Dams on Pak Water," *The Nation*, April 9, 2010.

21. Andrew Buncombe and Omar Waraich, "India Is Stealing Water of Life, Says Pakistan," *The Independent* (UK), March 26, 2009.

22. Athar Parvaiz, "Indus Water Treaty Agitates Kashmiris," Inter Press Service, October 15, 2008.

23. Ifrah Kazmi and Maria Fatima, "Water—Save the Last Drop!" *Business Recorder*, May 29, 2010.

24. Manipadma Jena, "Not a Single Drop to Drink," *The Telegraph* (Kolkata, India), May 6, 2010.

25. Karin Brulliard, "Rhetoric Heated in Water Dispute Between India, Pakistan," *Washington Post*, May 28, 2010.

26. M. Zulqernain, "Pak Must Keep Option of Force over Water Row with India: JuD," Press Trust of India, May 10, 2010.

27. "Pak Radical Outfit Issues Warning to India over Water Dispute," Press Trust of India, May 30, 2010.

28. Ahmed Rashid, *Descent into Chaos: The United States and the Failure of Nation Building in Pakistan, Afghanistan, and Central Asia* (New York: Viking, 2008), 221.

29. Christian Parenti, "Afghanistan: The Other War," *The Nation*, March 27, 2006.

30. Parenti, "Afghanistan"; see also the documentary *Fixer: The Taking of Ajmal Naqshbandi*, directed by Ian Olds (HBO, 2009).

31. Matt Waldman, "The Sun in the Sky: The Relationship Between Pakistan's ISI and Afghan Insurgents" (Discussion Paper 18, Carr Center for Human Rights Policy and Kennedy School of Government, Harvard University, June 2010), 1; also see Declan Walsh, "Clandestine Aid for Taliban Bears Pakistan's Fingerprints," *Guardian*, July 5, 2010.

32. Dennis C. Blair, "Annual Threat Assessment of the US Intelligence Community" (testimony before the Senate Select Committee on Intelligence, February 2, 2010).

33. "U.S. Seeks to Balance India's Afghanistan Stake," Reuters, May 31, 2010; Abdul Waheed Wafa and Alan Cowell, "Bomber Strikes Afghan Capital; At Least 41 Die," *New York Times*, July 8, 2008; Anand Gopal, "Indian Embassy in Kabul Is Bombed," *Wall Street Journal*, October 9, 2009; Aman Sharma, "Indians Easy Target in Kabul," *Mail Today* (India), February 28, 2010.

Chapter 12

1. R. D. Oldham, "The Evolution of Indian Geography," *The Geographical Journal* 3, no. 3 (March 1894): 169–192: 180.

2. The Western press has announced the decline of the Maoists ever since the date of their birth. For example, see Kasturi Rangan, "Maoist Movement Declining in India," *New York Times*, August 5, 1972. Then, three years later the same author in the same paper reported, "Maoist extremists in India, after being quiet for nearly 3 years, have become active again." Kasturi Rangan, "Maoists Resume Violence in India," *New York Times*, June 9, 1975.

3. See Figure 2.5 in *Main Report*, vol. 1 of *Drought in Andhra Pradesh: Long-Term Impacts and Adaptation Strategies, Final Report* (Washington, DC: South Asia Environment and Social Development Department, World Bank, September 2005), 28.

4. "Hyderabad: Silver Jubilee Durbar," *Time*, February 22, 1937, www.time.com/time/magazine/article/0,9171,770599,00.html. Despite the nizam's decadence, he occasionally showed concern for public welfare. When *adivasis* rebelled in the 1930s, he sent out a German anthropologist, Christoph von Fürer-Haimendorf, to better understand the tribal people's grievances. Haimendorf came back recommending investment in education and health care as a means to counteract the social and economic

exclusion of the tribals. To his credit, the nizam followed the suggestions, and the Gond people of Adilabad District saw conditions improve considerably. To this day the Gonds remember Haimendorf fondly, even as one of their own.

5. N. S. Jodha, "Role of Credit in Farmers' Adjustment Against Risk in Arid and Semi-Arid Tropical Areas of India," *Economic and Political Weekly* 16, no. 42/43 (October 17–24, 1981): 1696–1709; J. G. Ryan et al., "Socio-Economic Aspects of Agricultural Development in the Semi-Arid Tropics" (paper presented at the International Workshop on Farming Systems, ICRISAT, Hyderabad, India, November 18–21, 1974).

6. Edward Duyker, *Tribal Guerrillas: The Santals of West Bengal and the Naxalite Movement* (New York: Oxford University Press, 1987).

7. "Chaos in West Bengal," *New York Times*, March 18, 1970. On the reluctance of the Communist Party of India (Marxist-Leninist) to actually rule, see "The Reluctant Rulers," *Economic and Political Weekly* 2, no. 10 (March 11, 1967): 510–511. Williams Borders, "Once-Volatile Indian State Peaceful Under Red Rule," *New York Times*, January 28, 1978; Kasturi Rangan, "Five-Party Marxist Coalition Takes Over West Bengal," *New York Times*, June 22, 1977.

8. Joseph Lelyveld, "Left Communists in West Bengal Are Deeply Split," *New York Times*, July 5, 1967. Naxalite methods were a hybrid of modern ideological zeal and the bloody-minded pragmatism of West Bengal social banditry: Pulan Devi plus *The Little Red Book*. To their credit, the Naxalites also organized nonviolent mass movements that used direct actions to occupy land, confront landlords, and set up road blockades to demand justice, an end to repression, and economic concessions from the state.

Throughout India, Marxist parties have played crucial roles in coalition governments or even dominated them. Very often their progressive reforms have led to real development. Not only were these reforms progressive in content, but they were often radical in form: policy was not just delivered from the top down, but grassroots mobilization was also facilitated. Under the first United Front government in West Bengal in the early 1970s, four Marxist parties held the balance of power; the same rough coalition was later elected as the Left Front. In those heady days, Jyoti Basu, of the Communist Party (Marxist), was given the Home Ministry portfolio and thus had control of the state police. He used these forces to help peasants facilitate land seizures and played referee during the sometimes violent confrontations with the employer class. But the developmentalist thrust of most Indian communists was never enough for the Naxalite fanatics. In their eyes the mainstream communist parties were a Soviet-style capitulation to imperialism. The Naxals preferred the righteous path of Chairman Mao. In those days, West Bengal was a crazy Red maelstrom of center-left versus left, versus ultraleft, versus underground left.

9. S. Harpal Singh, "Gonds on the Path of Progress," *Hindu*, April 20, 2009; N. S. Saksena, *India, Towards Anarchy, 1967–1992* (New Delhi: Abhinav Publications, 1993), 76.

10. "Maoists Target Jawans Again," *Hindustan Times*, April 5, 2010.

11. "Andhra Pradesh Receives 27% Excess Rain During Monsoon," *Hindu Business Line*, July 27, 2010.

12. Orville Schell, "The Message from the Glaciers," *New York Review of Books*, May 27, 2010.

13. Z. W. Kundzewicz et al., "Freshwater Resources and Their Management," *Climate Change 2007: Impacts, Adaptation and Vulnerability. Contribution of Working Group II to the Fourth Assessment Report of the Intergovernmental Panel on Climate Change*, ed. M. L. Parry et al. (Cambridge: Cambridge University Press, 2007), 187, available at www.ipcc.ch/pdf/assessment-report/ar4/wg2/ar4-wg2-chapter3.pdf. Estimates are that 120 million to 1.2 billion people in Asia will face increased water stresses by the mid-2020s.

14. James Lamont et al., "India Widens Climate Rift with West," *Financial Times*, July 23, 2009.

15. Some scientists predict that by the end of the century, India will experience a three- to five-degree Celsius temperature increase and with it a 20 percent rise in summer monsoon rainfall.

16. Dennis C. Blair, "Annual Threat Assessment of the US Intelligence Community" (testimony before the Senate Select Committee on Intelligence, February 2, 2010).

17. Schell, "The Message from the Glaciers."

18. Kundzewicz et al., "Freshwater Resources and Their Management, 493.

19. Emily Wax, "Global Warming Threatens to Dry Up Ganges," *Washington Post*, June 24, 2007.

20. That characterization came from Charles Kennel, senior strategist at the University of California, San Diego, Sustainability Solutions Institute and former director of Scripps Institution of Oceanography. Cited in Stephen Leahy, "Climate Change: Snow Cover Turning to Lake in the Himalayas," Inter Press Service, May 7, 2009.

21. Aiguo Dai, Taotao Qian, and Kevin E. Trenberth, "Changes in Continental Freshwater Discharge from 1948–2004," National Center for Atmospheric Research, Boulder, Colorado, November 18, 2008; also personal communication from Dr. Aiguo Dai of the National Center for Atmospheric Research.

22. "Water Levels Dropping in Some Major Rivers As Global Climate Changes," University Corporation for Atmospheric Research, April 21, 2009, www.ucar.edu/news/releases/2009/flow.jsp (cited on May 5, 2009). National Center for Atmospheric Research scientists "examined stream flow from 1948 to 2004 [and] found significant changes in about one-third of the world's largest rivers. Of those, rivers with decreased flow outnumbered those with increased flow by a ratio of about 2.5 to 1. Several of the rivers channeling less water serve large populations, including the Yellow River in northern China, the Ganges in India, the Niger in West Africa, and the Colorado in the southwestern United States. In contrast, the scientists reported greater stream flow over sparsely populated areas near the Arctic Ocean, where snow and ice are rapidly melting."

23. "Water Levels Dropping in Some Major Rivers As Global Climate Changes," University Corporation for Atmospheric Research, April 21, 2009, www.ucar.edu/news/releases/2009/flow.jsp (cited on May 5, 2009). National Center for Atmospheric Research scientists "examined stream flow from 1948 to 2004, found significant

changes in about one-third of the world's largest rivers. Of those, rivers with decreased flow outnumbered those with increased flow by a ratio of about 2.5 to 1. Several of the rivers channeling less water serve large populations, including the Yellow River in northern China, the Ganges in India, the Niger in West Africa, and the Colorado in the southwestern United States. In contrast, the scientists reported greater stream flow over sparsely populated areas near the Arctic Ocean, where snow and ice are rapidly melting."

24. David Mosse, "Rule and Representation: Transformations in the Governance of the Water Commons in British South India," *Journal of Asian Studies* 65, no. 1 (2006): 61–90: 63.

25. Karl Wittfogel, *Oriental Despotism: A Comparative Study of Total Power* (New Haven, CT: Yale University Press, 1957), 15. Wittfogel's hydraulic despotism is an extension of Marx's conception of an "Asiatic mode of production."

26. Murray J. Leaf, "Irrigation and Authority in Rajasthan," *Ethnology* 31, no. 2 (April 1992): 115–132.

27. Kathleen Gough, "Modes of Production in Southern India," *Economic and Political Weekly* 15, no. 5/7 (February 1980): 337–364; M. J. K. Thavaraj, "The Concept of Asiatic Mode of Production: Its Relevance to Indian History," *Social Scientist* 12, no. 7 (July 1984): 26–34.

28. Mosse, "Rule and Representation," 65.

29. Amy Waldman, "Debts and Drought Drive India's Farmers to Despair," *New York Times*, June 6, 2004.

30. Anuradha Mittal, "Harvest of Suicides: How Global Trade Rules Are Driving Indian Farmers to Despair," *Earth Island Journal* (March 22, 2008); also see Somini Sengupta, "On India's Despairing Farms, a Plague of Suicide," *New York Times*, September 19, 2006.

31. Sengupta, "On India's Despairing Farms."

32. E. Revathi, "Farmers' Suicide," *Economic and Political Weekly* 33, no. 20 (May 16–22, 1998): 1207. These amounts are calculated at thirty-six rupees to the dollar, which was the rate of exchange when the article quoted was written.

33. "Climate Change Impacts in Drought and Flood Affected Areas: Case Studies in India South Asia Region" (India Country Management Unit, Sustainable Development Department, Social, Environment and Water Resources Management Unit, Document of the World Bank, Report No. 43946-IN, June 1, 2008), 40.

34. W. W. Rostow, *The Stages of Economic Growth: A Non-Communist Manifesto*, 3rd ed. (Cambridge: Cambridge University Press, 2008).

35. Bernhard Glaeser, ed. *The Green Revolution Revisited: Critique and Alternatives* (London: Allen and Unwin, 1987).

36. K. N. Ninan and H. Chandrashekar, "Green Revolution, Dryland Agriculture and Sustainability: Insights from India," *Economic and Political Weekly* 28, no. 12/13 (March 20–27, 1993): A2–A7.

37. Ernest Feder, "McNamara's Little Green Revolution: World Bank Scheme for Self-Liquidation of Third World Peasantry,'" *Economic and Political Weekly* 11, no. 14 (April 3, 1976).

38. A. K. Chakravarti, "Green Revolution in India," *Annals of the Association of American Geographers* 63, no. 3 (September 1973): 319–330. For critiques of the Green Revolution, see France Moore Lappe, *Aid As Obstacle* (Oakland, CA: Food First Books, 1980).

39. Vamsi Vakulabharanam, "Immiserizing Growth: Globalization and Agrarian Change in Telangana Between 1985 and 2000" (PhD diss., University of Massachusetts, Amherst, Economics Department, 2004).

40. Vakulabharanam, "Immiserizing Growth."

41. Vakulabharanam, "Immiserizing Growth," iv–vii. Or, to quote Vakulabharanam: "First, even as the prices of market-oriented crops have declined between 1991 and 2000 (during the phase of globalization), the planted area in the output of these crops has been rising rapidly. Second, between 1985 and 2000 the annual exponential growth rate of real agricultural output in the telethon region of South India has been more than 4%, higher than much of the developing world during the same period, even as a majority of the farming population has undergone significant income/consumption losses, tragically manifested in the suicides of more than a thousand farmers."

42. Vakulabharanam, "Immiserizing Growth," 107.

43. Lakshman Yapa, "What Are Improved Seeds? An Epistemology of the Green Revolution," *Economic Geography* 69, no. 3, Environment and Development, Part 1 (July 1993): 254–273.

44. Ramachandra Guha, "A War in the Heart of India," *The Nation*, June 27, 2007; "Naxalites Abandon Train, Passengers Unharmed," *Hindu*, March 15, 2006; Sonali Das, "Naxals Release Passengers on Train," *Times of India*, April 22, 2009; Mehul Srivastava, "Maoists in India Blow Up Pipelines, Putting $78 Billion at Risk," Bloomberg, July 29, 2010.

45. For example, see Air Commander Arjun Subramaniam, "Air Power to Fight Guerrilla War," *Sify News*, February 13, 2009. This piece ran in Indian papers and can be found online at www.bloomberg.com/news/2010-07-29/Maoists-in-india-blow-up-pipelines-as-78-billion-in-resources-threatened.html.

46. On the early days of the Greyhounds, see K. Balagopal, "Herald the Hunting Dogs That Are Grey in Colour," *Economic and Political Weekly* 23, no. 28 (July 9, 1988); M. Shatrugna, "NTR and the Naxalites," *Economic and Political Weekly* 24, no. 28 (July 15, 1989).

47. Jason Motlagh, "India's Maoists Shift to Attacks on Police," *Washington Times*, November 22, 2007; Jason Motlagh, "The Maoists in the Forest: Tracking India's Separatist Rebels," *Virginia Quarterly Review* 84, no. 3 (July 1, 2008): 102–129.

48. "Guns Are Again Booming in Andhra Pradesh," Indo-Asian News Service, April 3, 2005.

49. Sumanta Banerjee, "Naxalites: Time for Introspection," *Economic and Political Weekly* 38, no. 44 (November 1–7, 2003): 4635–4636: 4635.

50. Omer Farooq, "India's Andhra Pradesh State Announces Cease-Fire Against Communist Rebels," Associated Press, June 16, 2004.

51. Rakesh K. Singh, "New Centre Plan to Solve Naxal Issue," World News Connection, August 6, 2006; "On the development front, the centre has decided to allocate

Rs 500 crores [\$116 million] during the 11th Five-Year Plan for development of infrastructure in Naxal-hit areas. Emphasis will be laid on upgrading existing roads and tracks in inaccessible areas and securing camping grounds at strategic locations." Devyani Srivastava, "Terrorism in India (Jan–Mar 2008)," IPCS (Indian Government) Special Report No. 54, June 2008.

52. "Guns Are Again Booming in Andhra Pradesh." Two other poets, Gaddar and Kalyan Rao, were also on political murder charges.

53. "Salva-Judum Men Go After Maoist Sympathizers," *Hindu*, March 13, 2006.

54. Anshuman G. Dutta, "Holding State to Ransom India: 'Spread' of Left-Wing Extremism Prompts States to Raise Commando Outfits," World News Connection, May 21, 2006.

55. "Salva Judum 'Massacred' Chhattisgarh Tribals: Panel," *Hindu*, January 28, 2009.

56. "Salva Judum 'Massacred' Chhattisgarh Tribals."

57. Farhan Bokhari and James Lamont, "An Altered Reality," *Financial Times*, May 12, 2009.

58. Admittedly, this class, or clique, of superrich took a serious hit in 2009 as the Indian economy finally caught the cold of economic decline that had started in the West. Naazneen Karmali, "India's Billionaire Drop-Offs," Forbes.com, March 11, 2009, www.forbes .com/2009/03/11/india-financial-loss-billionaires-2009-billionaires-india.html.

Chapter 13

1. For an overview of that literature, see Joan Neff Gurney and Kathleen J. Tierney, "Relative Deprivation and Social Movements: A Critical Look at Twenty Years of Theory and Research," *The Sociological Quarterly* 23, no. 1 (winter 1982): 33–47. On violence in cities, see Saskia Sassen, "When the City Itself Becomes a Technology of War," *Theory, Culture & Society* 27, no. 6 (December 17, 2010).

2. Celia Landmann Szwarcwald et al. "Income Inequality and Homicide Rates in Rio de Janeiro, Brazil," *American Journal of Public Health* 89, no. 6 (June 1999): 849.

3. "Rio Drug Gangs Battle Police, 13 People Killed," Reuters, November 24, 2010.

4. "Rains, Floods in São Paulo Kill 64," Agence France-Presse, January 29, 2010.

5. "Lula Skips G20 Summit due to Deadly Brazil Floods," *Times of Oman* (Reuters) June 27, 2010; Felipe Dana, "Brazil: Population of Small Village Survived Massive Flooding by Clinging to Jack Fruit Trees," *Canadian Press*, June 24, 2010.

6. G. Magrin et al., "Latin America," in *Climate Change 2007: Impacts, Adaptation and Vulnerability. Contribution of Working Group II to the Fourth Assessment Report of the Intergovernmental Panel on Climate Change*, ed. M. L. Parry et al. (Cambridge: Cambridge University Press, 2007), Section 13.2.2, "Weather and Climate Stresses."

7. Anthony Pereira, "Brazil's Agrarian Reform: Democratic Innovation or Oligarchic Exclusion Redux?" *Latin American Politics and Society* 45, no. 2 (summer 2003): 41–65: 42.

8. Gary Duffy, "Changing Times for Brazil's Landless," *BBC News*, January 23, 2009, http://news.bbc.co.uk/2/hi/7845611.stm.

9. F. E. Wagner and John O. Ward, "Urbanization and Migration in Brazil," *American Journal of Economics and Sociology* 39, no. 3 (July 1980): 249–259: 256.

10. Wagner and Ward, "Urbanization and Migration in Brazil," 249.

11. Anthony W. Pereira, "The Dialectics of the Brazilian Military Regime's Political Trials," *Luso-Brazilian Review* 41, no. 2 (2005): 162–183.

12. In English, see Brazil Archdiocese of São Paulo, *A Shocking Report on the Pervasive Use of Torture by Brazilian Military Governments, 1964–1979, Secretly Prepared by the Archdiocese of São Paulo*, ed. Joan Dassin, trans. Jaime Wright (Austin: University of Texas Press, 1998).

13. Ben Penglase, "The Bastard Child of the Dictatorship: The Comando Vermelho and the Birth of 'Narco-Culture' in Rio de Janeiro," *Luso-Brazilian Review* 45, no. 1 (2008): 118–145: 125.

14. Penglase, "The Bastard Child."

15. Penglase, "The Bastard Child"; Luke Dowdney, *Children of the Drug Trade: A Case Study of Children in Organized Armed Violence in Rio de Janeiro* (Rio de Janeiro: 7 Letras, 2003); Louis Kontos and David C. Brotherton, eds., *Encyclopedia of Gangs* (Santa Barbara, CA: Greenwood, 2007), 16–18.

16. Enrique "Desmond" Arias, *Drugs and Democracy in Rio de Janeiro: Trafficking, Social Networks, and Public Security* (Chapel Hill: University of North Carolina Press, 2006); also see Carlos Amorim, *Comando Vermelho, a história secreta do crime organizado* (Rio de Janeiro: Editora Record, 1993); William da Silva, *Quatrocentos contra um* (Rio de Janeiro: Vozes, 1991); Dowdney, *Children of the Drug Trade*; Aziz Filho and Francisco Alves Filho, *Paraíso armado inter-pretações da violência no Rio de Janeiro* (São Paulo: Editora Garçoni, 2003); Michel Misse, *Crime e violência no Brazil contemporâneo* (Rio de Janeiro: Editora Lumen Juris, 2006).

17. James Brooke, "Brazil Writhes Under Debt Burden," *Miami Herald*, February 7, 1983. An excellent critic of neolibralism in Brazil is offered by James F. Petras and Henry Veltmeyer, *Cardoso's Brazil: A Land for Sale* (Lanham, MD: Rowman & Littlefield, 2003). "March by São Paulo Jobless Turns to Looting Riot; One Dead," *Miami Herald*, April 6, 1983.

18. Renato P. Colistete, "Revisiting Import-Substituting Industrialization in Brazil: Productivity Growth and Technological Learning in the Post-War Years" (draft paper prepared for the Conference "Latin America, Globalization, and Economic History," University of California, Los Angeles, April 24–25, 2009), 7, available online at www.international.ucla.edu/economichistory/Summerhill/Colistete.pdf.

19. Colistete, "Revisiting Import-Substituting Industrialization in Brazil," 32.

20. David Harvey, "Neo-Liberalism As Creative Destruction," *Geografiska Annaler* 88, no. 52 (June 1, 2006): 145–158: 148.

21. Philip Armstrong, Andrew Glyn, and John Harrison, *Capitalism Since 1945* (Oxford: Basil Blackwell, 1991), 155. For the quintessential story of successful state-led capitalist development, see Alice Amsden, *Asia's Next Giant: South Korea and Late Industrialization* (Oxford: Oxford University Press, 1992).

22. Juliet B. Schor, *The Overworked America: The Unexpected Decline of Leisure* (New York: Basic Books, 1992), 111.

23. Charles Sable quoted in Bennett Harrison and Barry Bluestone, *The Great U-Turn: Corporate Restructuring and the Polarizing of America* (Boulder, CO: Basic Books, 1990), 10.

24. On excess capacity or overaccumulation, see Armstrong, Glyn, and Harrison, *Capitalism Since 1945*, esp. ch. 11.

25. Brooke, "Brazil Writhes Under Debt Burden."

26. Harrison and Bluestone, *The Great U-Turn*, 7; see also Norman Glickman, "Cities and the International Division of Labor," in *The Capitalist City*, ed. Peter Michael Smith (Oxford: Blackwell, 1987), 71.

27. Samuel Bowles, David M Gordon, and Thomas E. Weisskopf, *After the Waste Land: A Democratic Economics for the Year 2000* (Armonk, NY: M. E. Sharpe, 1990), 45. See Figure 4.4, "Declining Profitability After the Mid Sixties"; Andrew Glyn et al., "The Rise and Fall of the Golden age," in *The Golden Age of Capitalism: Reinterpreting the Post-War Experience*, ed. Stephen A. Marglin and Juliet B. Schor (Oxford: Clarendon Press, 1990), 77, figure 2.10.

28. John Morris, "Markets Recover from Losses, but Outlook Is Grim," *American Banker*, December 6, 1982.

29. Paul Volker is quoted by Steven Rattner, "Volker Asserts U.S. Must Trim Living Standards," *New York Times*, October 18, 1979, A1.

30. George Hanc, *An Examination of the Banking Crises of the 1980s and Early 1990s*, vol. 1 of *History of the 80s* (Arlington, VA: FDIC Public Information Center, 1999), 199.

31. Andres Oppenheimer, "Recession, Debt Batter Americas," *Miami Herald*, April 18, 1983.

32. "Brazil Inflation Sets a Record," *New York Times*, December 29, 1989.

33. James Brooke, "Growth of Southern Giants Stifled by Austerity Plans," *Miami Herald*, April 18, 1983.

34. Oppenheimer, "Recession, Debt."

35. Juan de Onis, "Brazil Wants New Loans, Not Outside Pressures," *Los Angeles Times*, June 23, 1986.

36. Mark Weisbrot, "Quem será capaz de levar o país adiante?" *Folha de São Paulo* (Brazil), August 27, 2010.

37. Enrique "Desmond" Arias, "The Dynamics of Criminal Governance: Networks and Social Order in Rio de Janeiro," *Journal of Latin American Studies* 38, no. 2 (May 2006): 293–325.

38. For details, see Mike Davis, *Late Victorian Holocausts: El Niño Famines and the Making of the Third World* (London: Verso, 2002).

39. Timothy Finan, "Drought and Demagoguery: A Political Ecology of Climate Variability in Northeast Brazil" (paper presented at the workshop "Public Philosophy, Environment, and Social Justice," Carnegie Council on Ethics and International Affairs, October 21–22, 1999), 3.

40. Liqiang Sun et al., "Climate Variability and Corn Yields in Semiarid Ceara, Brazil," *Journal of Applied Meteorology* 46, no. 2 (February 1, 2007), 226–239.

41. Sun et al., "Climate Variability," 227.

42. Rob Wilby, "Review of Climate Scenarios in Northeast Brazil" (a technical brief for Tearfund, Teddington, UK, June 2008), 2; Saulo Araujo, "Lessons from Northeast Brazil: 'You Can't Fight the Environment,'" Grassroots International, March 2, 2009, www.grassrootsonline.org/news/blog/lessons-northeast-brazil-you-can't-fight-environment.

43. Joseph A. Page, *The Brazilians* (New York: Da Capo Press, 1996), 186.

44. Section 13.5.1.1, "Natural Ecosystems," in Magrin et al., *Climate Change 2007*.

45. Edmund Conway, "Economics IMF Warns That It May Soon Be Broke," *Daily Telegraph,* May 5, 2006. The heading for this section comes from the excellent book by Theda Skocpol, Peter B. Evans, and Dietrich Rueschemeyer, eds., *Bringing the State Back In* (Cambridge: Cambridge University Press, 1985).

46. Christian Parenti, "Retaking Rio," *The Nation*, May 31, 2010.

47. Donald R. Nelson and Timothy J. Finan, "Praying for Drought: Persistent Vulnerability and the Politics of Patronage in Ceara, Northeast Brazil," *American Anthropologist* 111, no. 3 (September 2009): 302–316: 305.

Chapter 14

1. Darlene Superville, "Michelle Obama Launches Solo Agenda on Mexico Tour," Associated Press, April 14, 2010.

2. Charles Bowden on *Democracy Now*, April 14 2010.

3. Kevin Johnson, "Violence Drops in U.S. Cities Neighboring Mexico," *USA Today,* December 28, 2009.

4. "Juarez Massacres: Where Will Cartels Attack Next?" *El Paso Times,* February 2, 2010.

5. Elisabeth Malkin, "Gunmen in Mexico Kill 13 at Party," *New York Times,* January 31, 2010.

6. William Booth, "Mexico's Drug Gangs Go on the Offensive Against Authorities," *Washington Post*, May 2, 2010.

7. Shuaizhang Feng, Alan B. Krueger, and Michael Oppenheimer, "Linkages Among Climate Change, Crop Yields and Mexico-US Cross-Border Migration," *Proceedings of the National Academy of Sciences* 107, no. 32 (August 10, 2010): 14257–14262.

8. Nacha Cattan, "Climate Change Set to Boost Mexican Immigration to the US, Says Study," *Christian Science Monitor,* July 27, 2010.

9. Oli Brown, *Migration and Climate Change* (Geneva: International Organization for Migration, 2008), 10.

10. Sam Knight, "Human Tsunami," *Financial Times,* June 19, 2009.

11. Quoted in Amy Kazmin, "Rising Sea Levels Hit Bangladesh Livelihoods," *Financial Times*, September 22, 2009.

12. William Lacy Swing, "Let's Invest Now for Tomorrow's Migration," *Migration* (Magazine of the International Organization for Migration), winter 2010.

13. Kazmin, "Rising Sea Levels Hit Bangladesh Livelihoods."

14. A similar, but different, story could be told about Africans and Middle Easterners moving to Europe. The best book on these dynamics is still Saskia Sassen, *The Mobility of Labor and Capital* (New York: Cambridge University Press, 1990).

15. A 2007 longitudinal country profile plotting Mexico's loss of mangroves, titled "Mangroves of North and Central America, 1980–2005: Country Reports," can be found on the Food and Agriculture Organization website at ftp://ftp.fao.org/docrep/fao/010/ai446t/ai446t00.pdf; for more on the crisis, see "President Felipe Calderon

Signs Legislation to Protect Coastal Wetlands; Governors Threatened to Define New Law," Mex Economic News & Analysis on Mexico, February 14, 2007.

16. The Food and Agricultural Organization of the United Nations keeps data on fisheries. Its country profile of Mexico notes, "The current status of the decreasing production trend in fisheries yield is due to overexploitation, poor management, an increase of fishing effort, lack of surveillance, naturally occurring changes in each reservoir and the poor quality of broodstock and fingerlings produced at government fish culture centers that have resulted in smaller fish size and hybridization." This is found at "Fishery and Aquaculture Country Profiles: Mexico," FAO, Fisheries and Aquaculture Department, www.fao.org/fishery/countrysector/FI-CP_MX/en. For a graph of total catch over time, see www.fao.org/fishery/countrysector/FI-CP_MX/3/en.

17. Alonso Aguilar Ibarra, Chris Reid, and Andy Thorpe, "The Political Economy of Marine Fisheries Development in Peru, Chile and Mexico," *Journal of Latin American Studies* 32, no. 2 (May 2000): 503–527: 521.

18. For a full discussion of Mexican corporatism and fisheries policy, see Emily Young, "State Intervention and Abuse of the Commons: Fisheries Development in Baja California Sur, Mexico," *Annals of the Association of American Geographers* 91, no. 2 (June 2001): 283–306: 242.

19. Ibarra, Reid, and Thorpe, "The Political Economy of Marine Fisheries," 526.

20. John Wright, "Mexico Announces Liberalization of Foreign Investment Rules," AP Online, May 15, 1989.

21. Young, "State Intervention and Abuse of the Commons," 288.

22. Young, "State Intervention and Abuse of the Commons," 300.

23. Tim Weiner, "In Mexico, Greed Kills Fish by the Seaful," *New York Times*, April 10, 2002.

24. Tim L. Merrill and Ramón Miró, eds., *Mexico: A Country Study* (Washington, DC: Government Printing Office, 1996).

25. Richard Grant, *God's Middle Finger: Into the Lawless Heart of the Sierra Madre* (New York: Simon & Schuster, 2008), 242.

26. Mexico lost 6.9 percent from FAO 2005 assessment. "A lingering question in economic geography is the degree to which there is a link between neoliberal policies and environmental degradation. Research is needed to relate such policies empirically to local-level decision making, both to evaluate their consequences and to contribute to an understanding of how cross-scalar dynamics drive processes of land-use change" (Martín Ricker, "The Role of Mexican Forests in the Storage of Carbon to Mitigate Climate Change" ["El papel de los bosques mexicanos en el almacenamiento de carbono para mitigar el cambio climático"], Sociedad Mexicana de Física, April 2008, www.smf.mx/C-Global/webElpapelbosquesmex2.htm); COSYDDAC, *The Forest Industry and Forest Resources in the Sierra Madre de Chihuahua: Social, Economic, and Ecological Impacts* (*La industria forestal y los recursos forestales en la Sierra Madre de Chihuahua: Impactos sociales, económicos y ecológicos*), Texas Center for Policy Studies, December 1999, www.texascenter.org/publications/forestal.pdf.

27. Rene Dumont, "Mexico: The 'Sabotage' of the Agrarian Reform," *New Left Review* I/17 (winter 1962): 46–63.

28. Elisabeth Malkin, "Mexico Now Enduring Worst Drought in Years," *New York Times*, September 12, 2009.

29. "Mexico Says Corn Supply Not Threatened by Drought," EFE World News Service, January 5, 2010.

30. Koko Warner et al., "In Search of Shelter: Mapping the Effects of Climate Change on Human Migration" (report by CARE International and UN University, 2009), http://ciesin.columbia.edu/documents/ClimMigr-rpt-june09.pdf.

31. Herbert Ingram Priestley, "The Contemporary Program of Nationalization in Mexico," *The Pacific Historical Review* 8, no. 1 (March 1939): 59–74: 60. Under Diaz, however, Mexico was hardly a banana republic; in fact he began as something of a progressive, nineteenth-century liberal and presided over some meaningful development—encouraging railroads, telegraphs, and basic factories—but declined into sclerotic corruption.

32. Carleton Beals, *Porfirio Diaz, Dictator of Mexico* (Philadelphia: J. P. Lippincott, 1932), 307.

33. Paul Garner, *Porfirio Diaz* (London: Longman, 2001).

34. Beals, *Porfirio Diaz*, 334.

35. Adolfo Gilly, *The Mexican Revolution* (New York: New Press, 2005); John Womack Jr., *Zapata and the Mexican Revolution* (New York: Vintage, 1970); there was, in fact, quite a bit of behind-the-scenes jockeying and rivalry between foreign capitalists to support either the Diaz government or the revolution. Even among American firms, which generally supported President Francisco Madera, there was subterfuge and division. John Skirius, "Railroad, Oil and Other Foreign Interests in the Mexican Revolution, 1911–1914," *Journal of Latin American Studies* 35, no. 1 (February 2003): 25–51.

36. Frank Tannenbaum, *Peace by Revolution: An Interpretation of Mexico* (New York: Columbia University Press, 1933), 115.

37. COSYDDAC, *The Forest Industry and Forest Resources*.

38. This translation of Mexico's 1917 constitution can be found at www.latin americanstudies.org/mexico/1917-Constitution.htm.

39. Gilly, *The Mexican Revolution*, 338.

40. Dumont, "Mexico."

41. Remonda Bensabat Kleinberg, "Strategic Alliances: State-Business Relations in Mexico Under Neo-Liberalism and Crisis," *Bulletin of Latin American Research* 18, no. 1 (January 1999): 71–87: 72.

42. Kleinberg, "Strategic Alliances."

43. Terry McKinley and Diana Alarcon, "Mexican Bank Nationalization," *Latin American Perspectives* 20, no. 3 (summer 1993): 80–82: 80.

44. Priestley, "The Contemporary Program of Nationalization in Mexico," 66.

45. Priestley, "The Contemporary Program," 62.

46. Of course, as one academic reminds us, the postrevolutionary Mexico "never operated along purely corporatist lines, and some sectors of society were tied to these arrangements much more closely than others." James G. Samstad, "Corporatism and Democratic Transition: State and Labor During the Salinas and Zedillo Administrations," *Latin American Politics and Society* 44, no. 4 (winter 2002): 1–28: 3. See Gilly's classic radical history *The Mexican Revolution*.

47. For a good overview of the changing relationship between the state and capital in Mexico, see Kleinberg, "Strategic Alliances," 72.

48. As Leo Panitch described it in a classic essay, corporatism is "a political structure within advanced capitalism which integrates organized socioeconomic producer groups through a system of representation and cooperative mutual interaction at the leadership level and mobilization and social control at the mass level." Leo Panitch, "Recent Theorizations of Corporatism: Reflections on a Growth Industry," *British Journal of Sociology* 31 (1980): 159–187: 173. For more on the subject and its links to authoritarian states, see David Collier, ed., *The New Authoritarianism in Latin America* (Princeton, NJ: Princeton University Press, 1980).

49. George Philip, *Oil and Politics in Latin America: Nationalist Movements and State Companies* (Cambridge: Cambridge University Press, 1982); George W. Grayson, *Oil and Mexican Foreign Policy* (Pittsburgh, PA: University of Pittsburgh Press, 1988). It was during this crisis of nationalization that the current ruling party, the Partido Accion Nacional (PAN), was formed from a coalition of right-wing groups, including bankers, industrial capitalists, landowners, religious elements, and even members of the Union Nacional Sinarquista, a Catholic and cryptofascist party on the model of the Falange. Michelle Dion, "The Political Origins of Social Security in Mexico During the Cárdenas and Ávila Camacho Administrations," *Mexican Studies/Estudios Mexicanos* 21, no. 1 (winter 2005): 59–95.

50. Kleinberg, "Strategic Alliances," 72.

51. George W. Grayson, "Oil and U.S.-Mexican Relations," *Journal of Interamerican Studies and World Affairs* 21, no. 4 (November 1979): 427–456: 428; Arthur Howe, "OPEC'S Grip on Oil Markets Slipping Away," *Philadelphia Inquirer*, December 7, 1983.

52. On the guerilla movements of Mexico, see O'Neill Blacker, "Cold War in the Countryside: Conflict in Guerrero, Mexico," *The Americas* 66, no. 2 (October 2009): 181–210; on labor, see Dale A. Hathaway, *Allies Across the Border: Mexico's "Authentic Labor Front" and Global Solidarity* (Boston: South End Press, 2000).

53. Adam David Morton, "Structural Change and Neoliberalism in Mexico: 'Passive Revolution' in the Global Political Economy," *Third World Quarterly* 24, no. 4 (August 2003): 631–653.

54. William Chislett, "Black Gold Fuels Economic Turnaround," *Globe and Mail*, May 26, 1980. In 1978, it looked as though the shah of Iran's regime might collapse, and if Iran tipped into chaos, oil would spike. Just as prices were rising, Pemex Mexico found another enormous petroleum patch. By the end of 1976, Mexico was producing eight hundred thousand barrels daily and exporting about ninety-four thousand barrels each day. By 1980 production was approaching 2.2 million barrels a day, and exports had increased ninefold, to 850,000 barrels a day. This was the fastest increase in oil production in world history.

55. John Crewdson and Vincent J. Schodolski, "Price of Reform Cripples Mexico," *Chicago Tribune*, November 23, 1986.

56. Chislett, "Black Gold Fuels Economic Turnaround."

57. Alan Ridding, "Taming Mexico's Passion for More," *New York Times*, September 12, 1982.

58. Michael Kevane, "Commodities in Crisis: The Commodity Crisis of the 1980s and the Political Economy of International Commodity Policies, by Alfred Maizels," *Economic Development and Cultural Change* 45, no. 1 (October 1996): 205–208.

59. James Thompson and Sean O'Grady, "Commodity Crisis Sparks Fear of Food Inflation on High Street," *The Independent* (UK), August 10, 2010. For a historical chart of commodity prices, see the Index Mundi website (www.indexmundi.com). The IMF's Commodity Price Index is found at www.indexmundi.com/commodities/?commodity=commodity-price-index&months=300.

60. Walden Below, *Dark Victory: The United States and Global Poverty* (Oakland, CA: Food First Books, 1999).

61. Oakland Ross, "Dropping Oil Prices Leave Mexico in Economic Limbo," *Globe and Mail*, August 6, 1982.

62. Michael Vaply, "Today's Catastrophe," *Globe and Mail*, August 20, 1982.

63. Marlise Simons, "Mexican Peso Devalued for Second Time in 6 Months," *New York Times*, August 7, 1982.

64. Alan Riding, "Mexico Devalues Peso 30%," *New York Times*, February 19, 1982; Alan Riding, "Worry Spreads After Peso Curbs," *New York Times*, August 14, 1982.

65. Robert A. Bennett, "Mexico Seeking Postponement of Part of Debt," *New York Times*, August 20, 1982.

66. Richard J. Meislin, "Mexico Is Selling Stock Held by Seized Banks," *New York Times*, May 22, 1984.

67. "Mexican Peso Plunges in Value," *Globe and Mail*, August 20, 1982; Robert Bennett, "Bankers Pressured to Assist Mexico," *New York Times*, August 21, 1982.

68. "Mexico Plans 106 Closings," *New York Times*, November 17, 1982; on Ocean Garden Products, see Young, "State Intervention and Abuse of the Commons," 288.

69. Katherine Ellison, "Mexico Sheds Its Assets," *San Jose Mercury News*, October 22, 1989.

70. Alan Riding, "Bankers Cheer Mexico's Austerity Plan," *New York Times*, December 3, 1982.

71. Crewdson and Schodolski, "Price of Reform Cripples Mexico."

72. Penny Lernoux, "Rescue Missions Impossible: Lessons of the Mexican Bailout," *The Nation*, October 6, 1984.

73. Steven Zahniser and Zachary Crago, "NAFTA at 15: Building on Free Trade," Outlook Report No. WRS-09-03, March 2009.

74. Noam Chomsky, *Profit over People* (New York: Seven Stories Press, 1999).

75. Elisabeth Malkin, "Nafta's Promise, Unfulfilled," *New York Times*, March 23, 2009.

76. Timothy Wise, "Fields of Free Trade: Mexico's Small Farmers in a Global Economy," *Dollars & Sense*, December 2003.

77. Malkin, "Nafta's Promise."

78. Malkin, "Nafta's Promise."

79. Wise, "Fields of Free Trade."

80. George Dyer-Leal and Antonio Yúnez-Naude, "NAFTA and Conservation of Maize Diversity in Mexico," Commission for Environmental Cooperation of North America, 2003, www.cec.org/Page.asp?PageID=1180&ContentID=&Site NodeID=472.

81. Matilde Pérez, "En materia alimentaria para México, el TLCAN está reprobado: Oxfam." *La Jornada*, January 2, 2010, www.jornada.unam.mx/2010/01/02/index.php?section=politica&article=008n2pol.

82. Chomsky, *Profit over People*.

83. Dyer-Leal and Yúnez-Naude, "NAFTA and Conservation of Maize Diversity."

84. Olivier Pavón, "Afrontar 'con mucho corazón' apertura total del TLC, aconseja Alberto Cárdenas," *La Crónica de Hoy,* December 20, 2007, www.cronica.com.mx/nota.php?id_nota=338675.

85. Gilly, *The Mexican Revolution*, 337.

86. *Rural Poverty in Mexico,* vol. 4 of *Mexico: Income Generation and Social Protection for the Poor*, Report No. 32867MX (World Bank: Washington DC, 2005), 170. The CIA's World Factbook lists poverty rates as "18.2% using food-based definition of poverty; asset based poverty amounted to more than 47% (2006)."

87. Mark Smith, "Serial Murders a Source of Fear and Mystery/New Spate of Killings Baffle Police, Who Hold a Suspect," *Houston Chronicle*, March 31, 1996; Sam Dillon, "Rape and Murder Stalk Women in Northern Mexico," *New York Times*, April 18, 1998; Jodi Bizar, "9 Held in Juarez Slayings 6 Teen-Agers Among Serial Killing Suspects," *San Antonio Express-News,* May 7, 1998.

88. Charles Bowden, *Murder City: Ciudad Juárez and the Global Economy's New Killing Fields* (New York: Nation Books, 2010), xiii.

89. Bowden, *Murder City*, 104–105.

90. Jen Phillips, "The Cartels Next Door," *Mother Jones Magazine*, July/August 2009.

91. Warren Richey, "Drug Runners Shift Routes As U.S. Steps Up Pressure," *South Florida Sun-Sentinel,* November 24, 1989; Jole Williams, "U.S. Border's War on Drugs Shifts to Texas," *Denver Rocky Mountain News*, October 15, 1989; William Overend, "Adventures in the Drug Trade," *Los Angeles Times Magazine*, May 7, 1989.

92. "Columbia Drug Smugglers Using 'Mexican Pipeline,'" *San Francisco Chronicle*, January 1, 1988.

93. Astian Rotel, "Barons of a Bloody Turf War," *Los Angeles Times*, June 4, 1993.

94. James Brooke, "A Drug Lord Is Buried As a Folk Hero," *New York Times*, December 4, 1993; "Cali Cocaine Cartel Leaders Offer Surrender Deal," Agence France-Presse, December 17, 1993.

95. Ken Dermota, "Snow Business: Drugs and the Spirit of Capitalism," *World Policy Journal* 16, no. 4 (winter 1999–2000): 15–24: 15.

96. Anita Snow, "Mexican Drug Smugglers Get Sophisticated," *Contra Costa Times*, September 17, 1995.

97. Bureau for International Narcotics and Law Enforcement Affairs, "International Narcotics Control Strategy Report, 1996," US Department of State, www.state.gov/www/global/narcotics_law/1996_narc_report/index.html.

98. Jorge Chabat, "Mexico's War on Drugs: No Margin for Maneuver," *Annals of the American Academy of Political and Social Science* 582 (July 2002): 134–148: 136.

99. Tracey Eaton, "NAFTA Tied to Drug Traffic: U.S. Task Force Says Smugglers Exploit Rising Cross-Border Trade," *Dallas Morning News*, May 11, 1998.

100. Dermota, "Snow Business," 16.

101. Robert Collier, "Mexico's New Emperor of Narcotics," *San Francisco Chronicle*, February 26, 1996.

102. Nick Reding, *Methland: The Death and Life of an American Small Town* (New York: Bloomsbury Press, 2009).

103. Mark Fineman, "Vast Mexican Drug Empire Up for Grabs," *Los Angeles Times*, July 29, 1997.

104. Jorge G. Castañeda, "What's Spanish for Quagmire?" *Foreign Policy* 177 (January 1, 2010).

105. Quoted in "Mexicans Wince at U.S. Jab on Corruption, but Admit It's Accurate," EFE World News Service, June 15, 2005.

106. David Luhnow and Jose De Cordoba, "Mexico Detains Former Top Drug Cop," *Wall Street Journal*, November 22, 2008.

107. The sequence of statements is laid out by Jorge Castañeda, "The Danger Across the Border," *Newsweek* (International Edition), February 2, 2009. US Joint Forces Command, *The Joint Operating Environment 2008: Challenges and Implications for the Future Joint Force* (Suffolk, VA: US Joint Forces Command, Center for Joint Futures, December 2008), 36.

108. Jens Erik Gould, "Calderon Rejects 'Absurd' Reports on Mexico Drug War," Bloomberg.com, March 12, 2009, www.bloomberg.com/apps/news?pid=newsarchive &sid=axUjKcbAt82w.

109. Castañeda, "The Danger Across the Border."

110. "¿Qué quieren de nosotros?" *El Diario* (Ciudad Juarez), September 19, 2010.

Chapter 15

1. Oli Brown, *Migration and Climate Change* (Geneva: International Organization for Migration, 2008), 10.

2. Sam Knight, "Human Tsunami," *Financial Times*, June 19, 2009.

3. Andrew Ross, "Greenwashing Nativism," *The Nation*, July 29, 2010.

4. Melissa Del Bosque, "Droning in Dollars," *Texas Observer*, August 20, 2010.

5. Peter Andreas, "Redrawing the Line: Borders and Security in the Twenty-First Century," *International Security* 28, no. 2 (autumn 2003): 78–111: 88.

6. Giorgio Agamben, *State of Exception* (Chicago: University of Chicago Press, 2005), 2; Gopal Balakrishnan, *The Enemy: An Intellectual Portrait of Carl Schmitt* (Verso: London, 2000).

7. "Border Emergency," *Washington Post*, August 26, 2005.

8. "CBP Air and Marine Unit Gets New Helos for Border Security," *Aerospace Daily & Defense Report* 223, no. 23 (August 2, 2007).

9. "Securing America's Borders: CBP Fiscal Year 2009 in Review Fact Sheet," CBP.gov, November 24, 2009, www.cbp.gov/xp/cgov/newsroom/news_releases/archives/2009_news_releases/nov_09/11242009_5.xml.

10. "Stryker Soldiers Train in Southern New Mexico," *US Federal News*, November 15, 2005.

11. "Previously Secret Memos and Data Show Bush-Era Immigration Raids Were Law Enforcement Failure" (report by the Immigration Justice Clinic, Cardozo School of Law, New York, February 4, 2009).

12. "Raids on Workers: Destroying Our Rights," United Food and Commercial Workers International, 2009, www.ufcw.org/docUploads/UFCW ICE rpt FINAL 150B_061809_130632.pdf?CFID=10424600&CFTOKEN=46213002 (page 1).

13. "Raids on Workers," 5.

14. Margaret Ramirez, "'96 Immigration Law Causing Rise in Deportations," *Los Angeles Times*, September 22, 1998.

15. "Detained and Dismissed: Women's Struggles to Obtain Health Care in United States Immigration Detention," Human Rights Watch, March 17, 2009, www.hrw.org/en/reports/2009/03/16/detained-and-dismissed.

16. Dora Schriro, "Immigration Detention: Overview and Recommendations," Department of Homeland Security, Immigration and Customs Enforcement, October 6, 2009, www.ice.gov/doclib/about/offices/odpp/pdf/ice-detention-rpt.pdf; Nina Bernstein, "Report Critical of Scope of Immigration Detention," *New York Times*, October 6, 2009.

17. "Immigrants Face Lengthy Detentions but Have Few Rights Change of Policy," *Daily Herald*, March 22, 2009.

18. See "Treated As Criminals: Asylum-Seekers in the USA," chapter 5 of *USA: Rights for All*, Amnesty International, October 1998, www.amnesty.org/en/library/asset/AMR51/035/1998/en/fd3dc1e9-da98-11dd-80bc-797022e51902/amr5103 51998en.html.

19. William Fisher, "U.S.: Immigration Detention Abuses Continue," Inter Press Service, March 31, 2010.

20. Valeria Fernández, "U.S.: Detained Migrant Women Shackled During Childbirth," Inter Press Service, March 4, 2010.

21. Adam Nossiter, "Arkansas Woman, Left in Cell, Goes 4 Days with No Food or Water," *New York Times*, March 12, 2008.

22. Amy Goldstein and Dana Priest, "Some Detainees Drugged for Deportation," *Washington Post*, May 14, 2008.

23. Tom Barry, "A Death in Texas: Profits, Poverty, and Immigration Converge," *Boston Review* (November–December 2009).

24. Barry, "A Death in Texas."

25. "Locked Up Far Away: The Transfer of Immigrants to Remote Detention Centers in the United States," Human Rights Watch, December 2, 2009, www.hrw.org/en/node/86789.

26. Alexis de Tocqueville, *Democracy in America* (1835; New York: Harper Perennial, 1966), 237.

27. Kurt M. Campbell et al., *The Age of Consequences: The Foreign-Policy National Security Implications of Global Climate Change* (Washington DC: Center for Strategic and International Studies and the Center for New American Security, 2007), 85–86.

28. Campbell et al., *Age of Consequences*, 85–86; "Boyles Guest Brenda Walker Called Mexico 'One of the Most Despicable Countries on Earth'; Said 'Mexicans Are Good at . . . Establishing Smuggling Infrastructures' and 'Can Get Through . . .

WMDs,'" Colorado Media Matters, October 20, 2006, http://colorado.mediamatters .org/items/200610200003. A profile of Brenda Walker is available at www.adl.org/ immigration/blogosphere/Brenda_Walker.asp.

29. "Boyles' Guest Gheen Called Mexicans Who Contend Racism Is Driving U.S. Immigration Debate 'Brown Nazis,'" Colorado Media Matters, October 9, 2007, http://colorado.mediamatters.org/items/200710100001.

30. David Able, "Severin Suspended for Comments About Mexican Immigrants," *Boston,* May 1, 2009, www.boston.com/news/local/massachusetts/articles/2009/05/ 01/severin_suspended_for_comments_about_mexican_immigrants.

31. Able, "Severin"; "Savage: 'Burn the Mexican Flag!'" Media Matters for America, March 31, 2006, http://mediamatters.org/research/200603310008.

32. Madison Grant, *Passing of the Great Race, Or, the Racial Basis of European History* (New York: Charles Scribner's Sons, 1916). This book shaped the world-views of people like Theodore Roosevelt and William Randolph Hearst and helped justify American imperial expansion and the racially based immigration quotas of 1924.

33. "Boortz Suggested Superdome As Place to 'Store 11 Million Hispanics Just Waiting to Ship 'Em Back to Nicaragua, Colombia, Costa Rica, Mexico,'" March 29, 2006, Media Matters for America, http://mediamatters.org/research/200603290004.

34. "Boortz on Illegal Immigrants: 'Give 'Em All a Little Nuclear Waste and Let 'Em Take It On Down There to Mexico," Media Matters for America, June 22, 2007, http://mediamatters.org/mmtv/200706220005.

35. "CNN 'Conspiracy Theorist' Lou Dobbs Discredits His Network—One Wild Claim at a Time," July 23, 2009, http://mediamatters.org/mobile/research/2009 07230035.

36. Lou Dobbs, "Border Insecurity; Criminal Illegal Aliens; Deadly Imports; Illegal Alien Amnesty," CNN, April 14, 2005, http://edition.cnn.com/TRANSCRIPTS/ 0504/14/ldt.01.html.

37. Transcript of Beck available at "Beck Again Warned That If Muslims Don't 'Act Now' by 'Step[ping] to the Plate' to Condemn Terrorism, They 'Will Be Looking Through a Razor Wire Fence at the West,'" Media Matters for America, September 7, 2006, http://mediamatters.org/mmtv/200609070002.

38. From the May 1, 2006, broadcast of Westwood One's *The Radio Factor with Bill O'Reilly,* available at "O'Reilly Alleged Immigrant Protest 'Organizers' Have Hidden 'Hardcore Militant Agenda' to Take Back American Southwest," Media Matters for America, May 3, 2006, http://mediamatters.org/mmtv/200605030009.

39. Bill O'Reilly quoted in "Media Figures Attacked Mexican-Flag-Wavers, but Not Those Waving Irish, Italian, or Israeli Flags," April 3, 2006, Media Matters for America, http://mediamatters.org/research/200604030012.

40. Democracy Now, Headlines, May 11, 2010; Ken Silverstein, "Tea Party in Sonora," *Harper's* (July 2010).

41. Jonathan J. Cooper, "Ariz. Governor Signs Bill Banning Ethnic Studies," Associated Press, May 12, 2010.

42. Bill O'Reilly, "The Truth About Arizona and Illegal Aliens," FOX News, May 4, 2010, www.foxnews.com/story/0,2933,592129,00.html.

43. Paul Rubin, "One-on-One Time with a Pinal County Deputy—Whose Claim He Was Shot by a Drug Smuggler Is Full of Holes—Produces Startling Results," *New Times* (Phoenix), November 25, 2010.

44. Matthews said Republicans "have a right to fear" seeing a "majority Latino population" and challenged Goodman, "Do you live in a Mexican neighborhood?" March 31, 2006, http://mediamatters.org/research/200603310012.

45. In an NBC plug for Buchanan's anti-immigrant book, Matthews declared that "thanks to this show," the book would "probably" remain "number one on Amazon," August 25, 2006, http://mediamatters.org/research/200608250008.

46. Patrick J. Buchanan, *State of Emergency: The Third World Invasion and Conquest of America* (New York: Thomas Dunne Books, 2006), 1–2.

47. Buchanan, *State of Emergency*, 6, 12, 28.

48. Richard Hofstadter, "The Paranoid Style in American Politics," *Harper's Magazine*, November 1964, 77–86.

49. "Broad Approval for New Arizona Immigration Law: Democrats Divided, but Support Key Provisions," Pew Research Center for the People & the Press, May 12, 2010, http://people-press.org/report/613/arizona-immigration-law.

50. Jane Mayer, "Covert Operators," *New Yorker*, August 30, 2010; George Monbiot, "The Tea Party Movement: Deluded and Inspired by Billionaires," *Guardian*, October 25, 2010.

51. Ian Traynor, "Sweden Joins Europe-Wide Backlash Against Immigration," *Guardian*, September 24, 2010, www.guardian.co.uk/world/2010/sep/24/sweden-immigration-far-right-asylum.

52. Anthony Faiola, "Anti-Muslim Feelings Propel Right Wing," *Washington Post*, October 26, 2010.

53. Kate Connolly, "Gypsies Trapped Behind 'European Wall of Shame,'" *Guardian*, October 24, 1999.

54. Bill McKibben, *Earth: Making a Life on a Tough New Planet* (New York: Henry Holt & Co., 2010), 145–146.

Chapter 16

1. *Next Generation Nuclear Plant: A Report to Congress* (prepared by the US Department of Energy Office of Nuclear Energy, April 2010), 23, available at http://nuclear.energy.gov/genIV/neGenIV1.html.

2. Mark Hertsgaard, "Regreening Africa," *The Nation*, November 19, 2009.

3. One can find literature on this at the UN Development Program's Global Environmental Facility website at www.pnud-energia.org.bo.

4. For a great takedown, see Robert Skidelsky, *Keynes: The Return of the Master* (London: Allen Lane, 2009); Mark Weisbrot, "Brazil's Elections Will Matter for the Rest of the World," *Folha de Sao Paulo* (Brazil), October 8, 2010; Mark Weisbrot, "Who Will Allow Brazil to Reach Its Economic Potential?" *Folha de Sao Paulo* (Brazil), August 27, 2010.

5. Jia Lynn Yang, "Companies Pile Up Cash but Remain Hesitant to Add Jobs," *Washington Post*, July 15, 2010.

6. William Alden, "Wall Street Set for Best Two Years Ever, Thanks to Bailout," *Huffington Post*, December 13, 2010.

7. Aaron Lucchetti and Stephen Grocer, "On Street, Pay Vaults to Record," *Wall Street Journal*, February 2, 2011.

8. Matt Taibbi, "The Great American Bubble Machine," *Rolling Stone*, April 5, 2010.

9. See Index Mundi: www.indexmundi.com/commodities/?commodity=food-price-index&months=60.

10. Graphs are available at Index Mundi: www.indexmundi.com/commodities/?commodity=wheat.

11. Roxana Tiron, "Senate OKs Defense Bill, 68–29," *The Hill*, October 22, 2009; Robert Higgs, "The Trillion-Dollar Defense Budget Is Already Here," Independent Institute, March 15, 2007, www.independent.org/newsroom/article.asp?id=1941; Laicie Olson, "Growth in U.S. Defense Spending Since 2001," Center for Arms Control and Non-Proliferation, March 11, 2010, http://armscontrolcenter.org/policy/securityspending/articles/fy11_growth_since_2001 (accessed January 13, 2011).

12. "U.S. Individual Income Tax: Personal Exemptions and Lowest and Highest Bracket Tax Rates, and Tax Base for Regular Tax," Tax Years 1913–2008, Table 23, IRS.gov, www.irs.gov/taxstats/article/0,,id=175910,00.html. For more recent data, see "Revenues, Outlays, Deficits, Surpluses, and Debt Held by the Public, 1971 to 2010, in Billions of Dollars," *Budget and Economic Outlook: Historical Budget Data*, Congressional Budget Office, January 2011, Table E-1, 1.

13. "Dealing in Doubt: The Climate Denial Industry and Climate Science" (report by Greenpeace International, Amsterdam, March 24, 2010), 4; also see Chris Mooney, *The Republican War on Science* (New York: Basic Books, 2005).

14. "Exxon Still Aids Climate Skeptics," *The Australian*, July 20, 2010.

15. Jane Mayer, "Covert Operations: The Billionaire Brothers Who Are Waging a War Against Obama," *The New Yorker*, August 30, 2010; "Koch Industries: Secretly Funding the Climate Denial Machine" (report by Greenpeace USA, Washington, DC, March 30, 2010); "Toxic 100 Air Polluters," Political Economy Research Institute, March 2010, www.peri.umass.edu/toxic_index (accessed on January 1, 2010).

16. Christian Parenti, "Winning the War of Ideas," *In These Times*, October 2003; Kim Phillips-Fein, *Invisible Hands: The Making of the Conservative Movement from the New Deal to Reagan* (New York: W. W. Norton & Co., 2009).

17. "Fewer Americans See Solid Evidence of Global Warming Modest Support for 'Cap and Trade' Policy," Pew Research Center for the People and the Press, October 22, 2009, http://people-press.org/report/669/.

18. Andrew Malone, "My Life on the Run: The Police 'Spy' Lifts Lid on Eight Years As Eco-Warrior," *Daily Mail* (UK), January 17, 2011; Matthew Taylor and Paul Lewis, "Undercover Police Officer Mark Kennedy at Centre of International Row," *The Guardian* (UK), January 13, 2011. This outrageous abuse of police power took place under a Labour government purportedly committed to addressing climate change, and some of the intelligence gathered on radical grassroots activists went all the way to Prime Minister Tony Blair's desk.

19. Brian Tokar, *Toward Climate Justice: Perspectives on the Climate Crisis and Social Change* (Grenmarsvegen, Norway: Communalism Press, 2010), 13.

20. Suzanne Goldenberg, "Barack Obama's Key Climate Bill Hit by $45m PR Campaign," *The Guardian* (UK), May 12, 2009.

21. Robert S. Eshelman, "Cracking Big Coal," *The Nation*, May 3, 2010.

22. Henry Miller, *Tropic of Capricorn*, 293.

23. "Bolivia: Government to Announce Stimulus Package for SMEs," *El Deber*, September 2, 2009.

24. John Vidal and Jonathan Watts, "Copenhagen Closes with Weak Deal That Poor Threaten to Reject—Non-Binding Accord Limits Temperature Rises but Includes No Emissions Targets," *The Guardian* (UK), December 19, 2009.

25. Pablo Solon, "Why Bolivia Stood Alone in Opposing the Cancún Climate Agreement," *The Guardian* (UK), December 21, 2010.

26. Damian Carrington, "WikiLeaks Cables Reveal How US Manipulated Climate Accord," *The Guardian* (UK), December 3, 2010; also see the cable sent February 26, 2010, at 22: 41, "Secret Section 01 Of 03 STATE 018437," Guardian.co.uk, www.guardian.co.uk/world/us-embassy-cables-documents/251174?intcmp=239.

27. "Methane," Environmental Protection Agency, www.epa.gov/methane.

28. Jennifer Kho, "The Largest Cleantech VC: China," *GigaOM*, February 26, 2010; also see "Towards a Global Green Recovery: Recommendations for Immediate G20 Action" (report submitted to the G20 London Summit, April 2, 2009).

29. "EU Energy Chief Wants 1 Trillion Euro Network Revamp," Reuters, November 10, 2010.

30. Quoted in Christian Parenti, "The Case for EPA Action," *The Nation*, April 15, 2010.

31. On IBM, see Linda Weiss and Elizabeth Thurbon, "The Business of Buying American: Public Procurement As Trade Strategy in the USA," *Review of International Political Economy* 13, no. 5 (December 2006): 701–724: 704. For a view of the Indian government's role in building up a technology sector with its purchasing power, see Rajeeva Sinha, "Government Procurement and Technological Capability: Case of Indian Electrical Equipment Industry," *Economic and Political Weekly* 29, no. 48 (November 26, 1994): 142–147.

32. For discussion of leftist green theories of capitalism, see Robyn Eckersley, *Environmentalism and Political Theory: Toward an Ecocentric Approach* (Albany: State University of New York Press, 1992); Ted Benton, *Natural Relations: Ecology, Animal Rights and Social Justice* (London: Verso, 1993).

33. John Bellemy Foster, *Marx's Ecology: Materialism and Nature* (New York: Monthly Review Press, 2000).

34. Karl Marx, *Capital* (New York: Penguin Classics, 1976), 1: 637.

35. Mary Douglas, *Purity and Danger: An Analysis of Concepts of Pollution and Taboo* (New York: Routledge, 1966), 41.

36. Heather Rogers, *Gone Tomorrow: The Hidden Life of Garbage* (New York: New Press, 2006).

INDEX